OPPORTUNISM AND GOODWILL

Canadian Business Expansion in Colombia, 1867–1979

THEMES IN BUSINESS AND SOCIETY

Editor: Dimitry Anastakis

Themes in Business and Society explores new issues in Canadian and international business history. The series advances Canadian business history in a global context by publishing studies that examine firms, entrepreneurs, consumers, industries, the evolution of capitalism, business-government relations, the role of the state and regulation, and the changing business environment in national and international contexts. Supported by the L.R. Wilson/R.J. Currie Chair in Canadian Business History at the University of Toronto and the Rotman School of Management, Themes in Business and Society provides new perspectives on the central role and tremendous impact of business upon ordinary people, both in Canada and around the world.

Opportunism and Goodwill

Canadian Business Expansion
in Colombia, 1867–1979

STEFANO TIJERINA

UNIVERSITY OF TORONTO PRESS
Toronto Buffalo London

ISBN 978-1-4426-4686-5 (cloth)
ISBN 978-1-4426-6675-7 (EPUB)
ISBN 978-1-4426-6674-0 (PDF)

Themes in Business and Society

Library and Archives Canada Cataloguing in Publication

Title: Opportunism and goodwill : Canadian business
expansion in Colombia, 1867–1979 / Stefano Tijerina.
Names: Tijerina, Stefano, 1969– author.
Description: Series statement: Themes in business and society |
Includes bibliographical references and index.
Identifiers: Canadiana (print) 20200411098 |
Canadiana (ebook) 20200411195 |
ISBN 9781442646865 (hardcover) | ISBN 9781442666757 (EPUB) |
ISBN 9781442666740 (PDF)
Subjects: LCSH: Canada – Foreign economic relations –
Colombia. | LCSH: Colombia – Foreign economic relations – Canada.
Classification: LCC HF1480.15.C65 T55 2021 | DDC 337 .710861 – dc23

University of Toronto Press acknowledges the financial assistance to its
publishing program of the Canada Council for the Arts and the Ontario Arts
Council, an Ontario government agency.

Contents

Acknowledgments

This book is dedicated to Sandra Cáceres Tijerina, and Santiago Tijerina, my eternal backbone and support. I want to thank Ila, my mother, for showing me the importance of questioning the world around me. Scott See, thank you for believing in me and guiding me through the process of becoming a scholar of Canadian history. I also want to thank the University of Maine's Canadian-American Center and the Maine Business School for their financial support, as well as the Canadian Business History Association. Finally, I want to express my deepest gratitude to Len Husband and the team at the University of Toronto Press for making this dream possible.

OPPORTUNISM AND GOODWILL

Introduction

Canada's social, economic, political, and environmental impacts on the Western Hemisphere have been largely overlooked by historians and other social scientists. As a result, they have perpetuated a narrative of the relationships between North America and the emerging markets of the south that disproportionally focuses on the United States. By downplaying Canada's role in the historical development of the Western Hemisphere, they have fallen short in reconstructing the history that shaped the region. Canada, and more specifically Canadian businesses, played a critical role in the modern development of Caribbean and Latin American economies. This historical analysis of the relationship between Canada and Colombia shows that the agendas were spearheaded by Canada's private sector. From the early stages of nation-building to the late 1970s, before the era of neoliberalism, Canadian business interests were directly or indirectly involved in the development of Colombia's economy.

Contrary to other Latin American and Caribbean nations whose early nation-building experiences were affected by imperial paternalism, Colombia's trajectory was characterized by long-term internal political instability that deterred foreign business interests from entering the country. Numerous internal civil conflicts throughout the 1800s isolated the nation from the emerging international trade system that paved the way for the first era of globalization during the second half of the nineteenth century. The nation's untapped resources and markets made it a target for Canadian business interests that were looking for unexploited regions across the Western Hemisphere. Canada's involvement in the early modernization of Colombia's economy therefore merits an in-depth historical analysis, because its business sector filled in the vacuum left by Britain and the United States.

Since Confederation in 1867, Canada looked at Colombia and the rest of the region as alternative markets for its commodity exports and as potential suppliers of raw materials necessary for the modernization of the Canadian economy. Latin American and Caribbean nations, on the other hand, looked at Canada as a potential trade and political partner capable of reducing the region's dependency on imperial powers. It is perhaps a reason why regional actors have historically pressed Canada to assume a more active and independent role within hemispheric affairs.

In response, Canadian policymakers opted not to overwhelm their regional agenda with political and security issues, preferring instead to advance economic and trade-related agendas on behalf of their business sector. This strategy allowed Canada to differentiate itself from other industrialized nations interested in securing markets and resources for their own self-interest.

The way in which Canada conducted its strategy in the region helped it strengthen its international identity as a benevolent nation throughout the twentieth century. By emphasizing international trade over political and security issues, Canada was able to focus on regional economic development. This business-centred approach became the driving force behind its regional policy and the basis for construction of bilateral relations with countries such as Colombia.

Canada's penetration of the Colombian market relied on the ability of its private sector to fill the gaps left by Britain, the United States, and other Western economies. Sometimes working independently, and in other instances on behalf of foreign interests, Canadian businesses carved out niche markets that helped in the economic development of Colombia. Analysis of these temporal and spatial dimensions of history illustrates the opportunist spirit and adaptability of Canadian businesses, as they circumvented imperial interests throughout the early stages of Colombia's economic development.

The presence of Canadian business interests in Colombia was limited by spatial and temporal boundaries. The market gaps capitalized upon by Canadian businesses since the late 1800s were slowly filled by global business interests throughout the first half of the twentieth century, displacing them from their privileged market positions in the Colombian economy.

The potential advantages of the Colombian market had been identified in the late 1700s when, for the first time, informal trade via the Jamaican entrepôt connected the Canadian and Colombian economies. A shift in British trade interests in the Caribbean and a readjustment of British and American trade relations ended the dynamics of this initial connection.

Canadian businesses once again capitalized on their dominion status soon after Confederation. In many instances, mistaken as British citizens, Canadian business leaders, merchants, and investors working for British interests in the Caribbean surveyed other regional markets such as Colombia's in search of potential business opportunities. By the late 1800s Canadian banks and insurance companies operating in the Caribbean found their way into the Colombian market, marking the beginning of a new temporal and spatial historical dimension that extended into the early stages of the Second World War.

Canadian banks and insurance companies laid the foundation for other Canadian businesses to enter the Colombian market. Operating in this case as subsidiaries for British and American interests, Canadian subsidiaries such as Tropical Oil and Pato Gold Dredging represented the driving force behind the nascent Colombian gold and oil export industries.

After the Second World War Canadian businesses shifted strategies, taking advantage of their closer relationship with the United States, as British leverage dwindled. Nevertheless, rising American influence across the Western Hemisphere prevented Canadian businesses from capitalizing on regional business opportunities. During the 1950s and 1960s they mounted pressure on their own government, demanding development of federal institutions and programs that would catapult them back into the region. The establishment of diplomatic relations in the early 1950s and the 1953 Goodwill Trade Mission prepared them for a new strategy that ended the cycle of spatial and temporal boundaries.

Throughout the 1960s the Canadian government developed institutions and programs that supported initiatives of what international relations historian Emily Rosenberg referred to as the "promotional state."[1] Nevertheless, the revamped government-business partnership lacked a clear policy toward Colombia and the rest of the region. It was not clear how the Canadian promotional state would spread its brand across the Western Hemisphere. How could the Canadian government show the region that its "ideology of liberal developmentalism" was different from the American version?[2] The answer was to construct a promotional state supported by ideas of Canada as an anti-imperialist and benevolent nation—a "goodwill" nation that understood other emerging economies. The question then was how to link these ideas to Canadian businesses.

By the early 1970s, a clear-cut line policy for Colombia and the rest of the region surfaced under Prime Minister Pierre Elliott Trudeau, following the 1968 ministerial mission to Latin America that confirmed the importance of the region for Canada's own economic development interests.[3] Official Development Assistance (ODA) spearheaded the initiative throughout the 1970s, allowing the promotional state to advance

Canadian business interests across the region in the name of modernity, progress, and democracy.[4] ODA opened the doors for Canadian businesses in strategic markets such as Colombia's through infrastructure and other economic development projects. Nevertheless, by the end of the 1970s ODA had lost its strategic value to the emerging principles of neoliberalism promoted by the United States and Britain. The ideas to "curb the power of labour, deregulate industry, agriculture, and resource extraction, and liberate the powers of finance both internally and on the world state," adopted by countries like Colombia, became more attractive to Canadian businesses, marking a turning point in the bilateral relations between Canada and Colombia.[5]

This book centres on the ways and means by which Canadian capitalism expanded into the Colombian economy prior to the onset of the neoliberal era in 1979. The historical analysis of this bilateral relationship shows how Canada circumvented and managed imperial pressures in the region. It also sheds light on current debates on theories of empire, focusing on the role of Canada as a subordinate power and its functionality within the macro-expansion of global capitalism.

The first official contacts between Canada and Colombia during the late nineteenth century resulted from the penetration of Canadian banking and insurance companies interested in providing services to British and American multinational corporations in need of international financial services. This was followed by business cooperation between British and Canadian interests, as in the case of gold mining, where Canadian businesses served as subsidiaries for British mining companies interested in reducing risk and capitalizing on Canadian "know-how." Then, between the 1920s and 1940s, Canadian subsidiaries facilitated the takeover of Colombian oil production by Standard Oil of New Jersey. These dynamics, highlighted in parts one and two of this book, demonstrate that Canada's business initiatives in Colombia, during the first half of the twentieth century, played a subordinate role to British and American interests.

The way in which Canadian-Colombian relations were initially constructed confirms the views of internationalist John Holmes on Canada's economic development and foreign policy. Canadian businesses, in this case, were subordinate to the interests of the international system, since the security and survival of the nation depended on the long-term sustainability of the system, whose core was the imperial economies of Britain and the United States.[6]

From the perspective of liberal theorists, Canada's capitalist expansion into the Colombian market demonstrated that the state functioned as a subordinate because it permitted its business sector to serve the needs of the British and American empires.[7] Throughout its nation-building process, which culminated in Canada's Confederation, economic and political elites debated over their alignment with British imperial interests, but they never questioned the principles of capitalism. They were part of a Western capitalist class loyal to the classic economic principles of liberalism. For the sake of its own capitalist interests, Canada needed to develop its own internal markets and diversify its international trade around the notion of free trade, capitalizing on its dominion status and its increasing trade with the United States. The development of a nation state that allowed the private sector to use the power of the state to secure its economic interests resulted in a business culture that took advantage of its subordinate position to Britain and the United States. Canada's penetration of the Colombian market illustrates the historical development of a subordinate state, contributing not only to the theories of empire but to those of Canadian international relations as well.

The case of Canadian-Colombian relations under the Pierre Elliott Trudeau government also reveals the progression of Canada's own imperial objectives in Latin America and the Caribbean, confirming the thesis of contemporary Canadian internationalists such as Todd Gordon, Jeffery R. Webber, and Radhika Desai.[8] In search of greater autonomy, Trudeau's nationalist government created the institutions and programs that laid the foundation for Canada's promotional state, helping Canadian businesses penetrate markets like Colombia's through ODA, as illustrated in part three of this book.

Nevertheless, the expansion of Canadian capitalism into Latin America and the Caribbean during the 1970s confirmed once again Canada's role as a subordinate state, as Canadian businesses promoted free market policies and democracy, juxtaposing these initiatives against the model exported by the Soviet Union during the early stages of the Cold War. Through their initiatives in Colombia, Canadian companies defended the interests of the international system while at the same time backing the American Cold War policies for Latin America and the Caribbean.[9] They understood that their future "hinged on maximizing the benefits of the series of interdependent relationships that resulted from that order."[10]

The focus on the historical behaviour and interests of subordinate states like Canada contributes to an understanding of the dynamics between asymmetrical powers working for the expansion and preservation of capitalism within the international system, giving agency to Canada's role in the construction of market economies across the Western Hemisphere.[11] In the Colombian market, Canadian businesses and investors carved out niches of specialization, confirming Patrick

Lennox's structural specialization theory by developing key industrial and commercial sectors such as banking, insurance, oil, energy, paper, shipping, and mining.[12]

Theorists of empire reiterate that oligarchs, through their key political and economic structures, determined "where, with what instruments, and for what purposes" the imperial project was pursued.[13] They also remind us that those empires "evolve opportunistically and unpredictably," as new players enter the international system and technologies create new markets.[14] Subordinate states like Canada were not excluded from this process, for its business and political elite had imperial aspirations of their own that led them to form their own independent nation state, taking advantage of the geopolitical and market necessities of Britain and the United States.

Canada's colonial links to Britain provided its oligarchs with an opportunity to penetrate the Caribbean markets that were entry points to South American markets. Meanwhile its proximity and connectivity to the American market provided its business sector with an opportunity to expand international trade, secure foreign investment, and technological exchange that set it apart from the rest of the newly independent hemispheric nation states.

As this business and economic historical analysis shows, by the end of the nineteenth century, Canadian businesses were already taking advantage of their British links to enter that market, and by the turn of the twentieth century they were also profiting from their partnerships with American companies. Throughout the twentieth century they learned how to take advantage of this flexibility, focusing on an opportunist agenda that allowed them to fill the gaps left by the empires or making themselves useful to imperial interests.

Ultimately, this work focuses on moments when Canadian businesses were able to navigate the challenges imposed by imperial powers in Colombia. The sum of these junctions that brought together Canadian and Colombian interests represent the pillars of a bilateral relationship that has become increasingly complex.[15] I argue that Canada's business sector was the driving force behind the bilateral relationship, and that its investments and other business initiatives determined the modern economic development of both nations.

Analysis of the bilateral relation showed that the core of the relationship preceded the Pierre Elliott Trudeau era.[16] Archival research in Ottawa and Bogotá showed that contacts, although sporadic, dated back to the late 1700s. Since the early stages of nation-building, Canadian and Colombian bourgeois elites have pursued control of economic, political, and social power through management of the state and its institutions, and in both cases they were forced into peripheral roles in the international system, as their British and U.S. counterparts ensured that their own economic interests were not threatened by the aspirations and desires of Colombian and Canadian nation-builders. In pursuit of their own individual interests, Canadian and Colombian elites found common ground in the international market. Within the limitations delineated by the imperial powers and their dependence on commodity exports, they focused their attention on diversification of business and trade initiatives as key instruments of nation-building.[17] Within this strategy, Canada often set itself as an alternative trading partner that could counterbalance Colombia's dependency on other foreign markets.

International business and trade was the thread that tied the two countries together, the same thread that linked Canada to the Caribbean and the rest of Latin America. From the late 1700s, when the two regions began their informal exchange via the Jamaican entrepôt, to the Canada-Colombia Free Trade Agreement (2011), business leaders have used all the tools at their disposal to establish and preserve direct relationships, circumventing the obstacles and overcoming the pressures of other international powers. Through informal markets, private business relations, institutional development, legislation, diplomacy, and foreign policy, the two nations have pursued the preservation and expansion of market alternatives that reduce their dependency on imperial markets. Seldom has the initiative centred on a political or social agenda, but when it has, elites in both countries have made sure to tilt the agenda back to trade.

PART ONE

From Informality to Formality

1

The Jamaican Entrepôt

Soledad Acosta de Samper (1833–1913), the most prolific female Colombian writer of the nineteenth century, was a product of the internationalization of the global economic system that connected Canada and Colombia. Her mother, Carolina Kemble Rou, a Canadian-American, married Colombian historian, geographer, and patriot of independence Joaquín Acosta y Pérez de Guzmán. As in the case of Soledad Acosta's family, international trade became the linchpin of the two markets. Carolina, born in Kingston, Jamaica, spent most of her early years moving back and forth between the Caribbean and New York, where the family owned a lucrative cannon factory, and it was in New York that she married Pérez de Guzmán in 1832. Soledad Acosta was raised in the elite circles of Colombia's society, first studying in Bogotá's Colegio de la Merced, then moving to Halifax, Nova Scotia, where she continued her education "while living with her maternal grandmother," and finishing her formal education in Paris in 1850.[1] Like Soledad Acosta and her family, Canadian and Colombian commodities began to flow back and forth via the Jamaican entrepôt connecting North and South America. It was the endeavour of merchants, businessmen, smugglers, and consumers that set the tone of the bilateral relationship.

By the mid-1700s Halifax-registered schooners began to arrive at the port of Kingston, Jamaica, to sell their commodities for re-export and contraband, reaching other ports in the Caribbean and in other instances the northern ports of the Viceroyalty of New Granada.[2] In 1756, for example, a shipment of bricks, boards, and mackerel arrived in Kingston from Halifax, and in March 1765 the *Snow Joshua* schooner made its way into the Jamaican port with a cargo of 345 barrels of salted fish.[3] Portions of this merchandise found its way into the viceroyalty's ports via the informal market. By that point the ports of Cartagena, Santa Marta, Portobelo, Riohacha, Puerto Cabello, and Maracaibo were intertwined with the Jamaican entrepôt, shipping salt, mules, jackasses, horses, horned cattle, Nicaragua wood, fustic and mahogany, cotton, and cocoa for re-export in North America and Europe.[4] These ports traded in the Caribbean beyond the Spanish jurisdiction, importing European and North American commodities, dry goods, and provisions as demanded by local markets and the interior of the Spanish Empire.

Maritime goods were re-exported through Boston, Falmouth, Casco Bay, Portland, and Penobscot, reaching the viceroyalty's ports through Jamaica. Meanwhile contraband from these Spanish ports made its way back into eastern Canadian ports.

Re-exports made it difficult to track a commodity's port of origin, particularly when competing ports exported the same commodity, as with the Northeastern and Maritime ports that exported goods such as butter, flour, soap, oil, tar, shingles, lumber, staves, salted fish, mackerel, salmon, herring, spruce, oak, planks, candles, and even potatoes.[5] British Naval Office shipping records from the 1760s showed that indirect trade had been established between Halifax and the Vice Royalty of New Granada, thanks to the re-export of herring, shingles, and staves that had initially arrived in Kingston from ports such as Halifax.[6]

At the time, exports from the Maritimes were relabelled as commodities originating from present-day New England ports, in some cases, for lack of infrastructure or investment capital to ship directly to the Caribbean. In other instances, vessel owners were not interested in assuming the risks of shipping to the Caribbean and were content with regional markets such as Boston. Re-exports leaving Kingston were also relabelled and entered the French, Dutch, and Spanish Caribbean ports as British goods.

Exports originating in the Maritimes were part of the British North American network and were therefore considered British in origin. Commodities, like people, lost their identity behind the British flag. A barrel of salted cod from the Maritimes entering Cartagena via contraband was considered a British good and not a product of Halifax or Newfoundland. Any English-speaking merchant, a schooner's crew, and even a traveller in transit wandering the ports of the Caribbean was labelled as British, in spite of its place of birth. Carolina, Soledad Acosta de Samper's mother, was considered British, even though she was born in Jamaica and her parents were from Halifax and New York.[7]

British initiatives to inundate the Spanish colonies with licit and illicit trade indirectly connected the Maritimes to the northern South American markets. After the War of Jenkins' Ear (1739–48), it was evident that trade and not war would enhance Britain's initiatives in the Caribbean.[8]

British North America's resources and production systems would play significant roles in pushing this initiative forward.

By the late 1750s the northern ports of South America were more dependent on British trade than on interior regional trade controlled by the Spanish Crown. Jamaican traders had become chief suppliers of dry goods, commodities, merchandise, and contraband that found its way into interior markets of the Viceroyalties of New Granada and Perú. Farmers around Cartagena "ceased planting wheat because British flour sold so much more cheaply on the local market," and the same happened to numerous other commodities and goods once supplied through internal regional markets.[9]

Illicit trade between Jamaica and the northern ports of South America continued throughout the 1700s, expanding the trade of British, French, Dutch, and other European goods. Contraband entering these ports complemented the precarious Spanish import market; neither the prices nor quality of foreign goods could compare. Citizens of Cartagena and Portobelo operated between the licit and illicit world, while those in Santa Marta and Riohacha sustained themselves via illicit trade, in the absence of official Spanish institutional authority. Their economy functioned thanks to British and Dutch illicit trade, bringing these markets closer to the international trade system.

There was also an increasing presence of vessels from Halifax, Nova Scotia, and Saint John, New Brunswick, entering Kingston, particularly after 1776, following the American Revolution, which forced Britain to close Jamaican ports to American trade. The Maritime markets filled the licit and illicit market gap left by the Americans. Trade between the Maritimes and the northern ports of South America was enhanced as a result.

The British Free Ports Act of 1766 no longer covered the recently independent United States, allowing the Maritime ports to enhance their international trade with South America, via Jamaica, while protecting British interests in the Caribbean.[10] At about this time British manufacturers and merchants began to shift their interest from the West Indies to the whole Latin American and Caribbean region.[11] This greater scope of the market brought the Maritimes closer to the South American markets.

As a means to further restrict the American market, Britain issued the temporary 1783 Act followed by the 1788 Act, restricting commerce between the United States and the Caribbean.[12] These Acts did not restrict imports of sugar, rum, molasses, coffee, or pimento into the United States,[13] but they did restrict exports of timber, livestock, grain, flour, and bread from the United States, leaving them with the

option to import restricted goods only in British ships supplying the
Caribbean market.[14] Exports of meat and fish from the United States
were blocked, leaving supply in the hands of Canada, Nova Scotia, and
Newfoundland.[15]

Spain responded with its Bourbon Reforms, which led to the trade liberalization policies of 1778, 1789, and 1791.[16] These economic and political reforms were a direct response to the rising power of Britain and
France. Their objectives were to modernize Spain and generate interco-
lonial trade in the Americas, while strengthening Spain's control over
informal trade within its colonies. These regulatory initiatives extended
through the early 1800s, until the Bolivarian wars of independence.[17]

After independence the South American economies began a lengthy
integration into the international system. Britain, the United States, and
other European powers filled the vacuum left by the Spanish Empire.
British North America also capitalized on geopolitical changes across
South America and the Caribbean, by serving the needs of the British
Empire in the Americas. Nevertheless, its efforts were limited by British reforms that allowed their competitors, the Americans, to return to
the region.

The signing of the Treaty of Paris in 1783, which ended the American Revolutionary War and normalized relations between Britain and
the United States, allowed the Americans to strengthen trade relations
across the Western Hemisphere. Unregulated international trade across
the region allowed small competitors to target uncontested niche markets, avoiding regular trade convoys, and instead moving swiftly from
port to port "in pursuit of the last half-penny of profit."[18] The newly
independent ports of the Gran Colombia welcomed the unregulated
trade, as the region constructed a post-colonial economy.[19] Their connection with and dependence on the international trade system increased.

Merchants and traders from Britain, British North America, the
United States, France, and other parts of Europe strengthened their
business connections with the newly independent region, drawing
people, commodities, merchants, and markets closer together.[20] British North American trade remained dependent on re-exports and re-
imports from Jamaica, this time tailoring to the needs of Britain and the
United States.

British limitations on vessel dimensions and commodities diminished
access of the West Indies market to merchants from the United States,
forcing it to channel its trade strategy through British North America.[21]
This initiative marked the beginning of the interdependent relationship
between British North America and the New England region, pulling
both economies closer together.

Trade in the Caribbean that reached the Gran Colombia ports was regulated by an 1808 British law that authorized "the governors of the provinces of British North America, to open their ports for the importation of articles from the United States, for re-exportation to the West Indies."[22] British North America, once a point of re-export for West Indies goods destined for Europe, had now become an entrepôt between the United States and the West Indies. Meanwhile, the ports of New England slowly became re-exporting points for goods leaving the West Indies, further integrating the regional economy of northeastern North America.

The growing activity of British, American, and French merchants that followed the independence of Gran Colombia forced the Maritime ports back to their subservient role. Glasgow, London, Boston, and New York began to dominate trade in the Caribbean and South America, exploiting the Maritime ports for re-exports. A clear message had been sent to merchants and business leaders in British North America: their role within the international system was to be subordinate to British economic interests.

The revolutionary campaigns in South America and the War of 1812 led Britain to realize that its economic, political, and geopolitical interests benefited from increased commerce with the United States. After the war, the 1814 Treaty of Ghent moved both countries closer to the establishment of free trade.[23] Regulation of U.S. trade in the Caribbean had proven to be disadvantageous and it was, in part, thanks to the war, that London was "compelled to abandon" the protectionist policy.[24] The Caribbean and the newly independent nations of South America became a target of British free trade policy.

Britain's decision to allow U.S. business and trade to move freely across the Caribbean after 1815 reversed the groundbreaking achievements of British North American merchants and traders who had begun to carve out niche markets for themselves across the Caribbean. Decision-makers from Britain and the United States had agreed upon "the principles of free trade ... and reciprocal and friendly arrangements of negotiation," at the expense of Maritime colonial interests and those of the newly independent nations.[25]

As the West Indies markets were split between the two powers, it was decided that the Jamaican entrepôt would benefit British and U.S. business interests, leaving aside British North American businessmen and investors, who came face-to-face with the adversities of their subservient role. As a result, relations between the Maritime economies and the newly independent Gran Colombia continued to be informal and fragmented, and they remained the norm throughout the rest of the nineteenth century as all industrial powers contested for the unclaimed markets of the former Spanish Empire.

It was through British trade policy that British North America had been able to fill the gaps in the region, and it was through this same mechanism that its relation with the region came to an end. Central America became the target of the United States while South America became heavily influenced by British interests. Gran Colombia was the exception, its internal political conflicts and continuous civil wars making it unattractive and too risky for British investors. In 1831 Gran Colombia collapsed, splitting into three separate countries: Colombia, Venezuela, and Ecuador. An ideological struggle over nation-building continued throughout the nineteenth century, isolating and distancing Colombia from the international system as the first era of globalization unfolded, while Canadians took their first steps toward greater autonomy after Confederation.

2

Joining the International System

After independence in 1819, Colombia's economic development pattern was very dissimilar from that of most of its South American neighbours. It absorbed a large international debt through the London Stock Exchange in order to fund and sustain the wars of independence that stretched down the Andes all the way to Argentina, and it preserved a region-based economic development model inherited from the colonial times, isolating the republic's economy and delaying its incorporation into the international system. Industrialization, foreign investment, and social, cultural, economic, political, institutional, and infrastructural modernization was also hindered by conservative and liberal ideological struggles over economic development policy, leading to multiple civil wars throughout the nineteenth century that kept foreign investment away, even though U.S., Canadian, British, and other European investors were well aware that Colombia was a land "of untouched and unmeasured wealth."[1] Foreigners such as geographer Alexander von Humboldt provided first-hand accounts of the wealth of resources to be found there, but regionalism and isolationism kept it distant from foreign investors until the late 1800s. Regional rivalries over allocation of federal resources, its natural interconnectivity with international trading routes, a long history of contraband, and the penetration of classical liberal ideas eventually absorbed the Colombian coast into the orbit of the international system. Early international trade and foreign investment made its way into places like Colón, Barranquilla, Cartagena, and Santa Marta, slowly filtering into interior regions of the republic, in pursuit of highly valued commodities such as gold.

Nation-building followed a tangled and twisted path as the federalist idea of opening Colombia's market to the international system competed with preserving the regional economic and political power structures inherited from colonial times. The real debate was defining how and under what circumstances Colombia would join the international system. There was no turning back: independence and the 1825 Treaty of Amity, Commerce, and Navigation that followed linked the markets of Colombia and Britain.[2] Acting as the commercial and military power of the times, Britain not only recognized Colombia as a sovereign nation, it also established a contractual agreement that obliged each party to grant its "nationals a right of establishment and to engage in trade and commerce, as well as a right to the 'most complete protection and security,' under Most Favoured Nation treatment in the areas of trade, commerce, payment of taxes and duties on imports, and the administration of justice."[3]

In its early nation-building stages, Colombia became even more dependent on the international system after Simón Bolivar opted to borrow two million pounds from the London Stock Exchange in 1822 to finance the revolutionary campaigns, while facing opposition of parliamentary conservatives who repudiated the initiative, since they were against any policy that generated greater dependency on British credit.[4] In efforts to legitimize the revolution in the eyes of the international system, Bolivar strived to establish a centralist laissez-faire government in Bogotá with strong presidential powers. His efforts to establish a liberal model of economic development, as part of the nation-building process, was questioned by Francisco de Paula Santander and José Antonio Páez, who favoured a decentralized form of government and a protectionist, region-based approach.[5] Pro–free trade liberals with centralist tendencies challenged the anti-laissez-faire conservatives over political power and national economic policy, impeding establishment of a cohesive long-term economic development plan.

Nevertheless, pro and anti free traders welcomed foreign investment and business. The ideological dispute orbited around the degree of liberalism that should be incorporated into the nation-building process. Political rhetoric presented two conflicting ideologies, but in practice negotiations centred on what sectors of the economy to protect and which to internationalize – a process that was influenced by the push and pull of regional political and economic elites trying to protect their own self-interests. Tariff laws were relatively unaltered after independence. In the early 1820s, textiles continued to be protected by a 17.5 per cent import tariff, while "imports of cacao, coffee, indigo, sugar and honey were strictly prohibited."[6] Meanwhile strategic imports were exempt from tariffs, including scientific, medical, agricultural, and other technological instruments, as well as plants, seeds, books, maps, and printing presses.

Migration policies were established during this early period of nation-building in order to attract Europeans to Colombia. For example, migration policies welcomed navigational and manufacturing experts who would improve the navigational infrastructure of Colombia's rivers and lakes and would help develop a domestic cotton and wool textile industry.[7] Preferential treatment for foreigners had been put in place early on, together with protectionist policies that incentivized development of an internal market.

Legislation that gave preferential treatment to imports arriving in Colombian vessels was established in 1823, in order to develop and strengthen a domestic merchant fleet. Discriminatory policies were directed at vessels from Europe and the United States, but the main objective was to overcome dependency on West Indian intermediaries, and more specifically the Jamaican entrepôt.[8] Internationalists and protectionists envisioned an autonomous, prosperous, powerful, and influential Gran Colombia within the international system, with Ecuador as the agricultural and manufacturing region, Colombia as a mining region, and Venezuela as a producer and exporter of agricultural products.[9] The founding fathers stressed the strategic importance of the republic's geographical location, with access to two oceans and the potential to serve as a bridge between Europe and Asia.[10] They envisioned a role for the republic in the future expansion and development of commercial exchange between Britain and the United States; as Bolivar indicated, the republic was at the centre of the earth, "the heart of the universe."[11]

Efforts to establish an autonomous position in the Western Hemisphere were quickly curtailed by the British 1825 Treaty of Amity, Commerce, and Navigation, which forced changes in the implementation of tariffs on imports from Britain. Colombia continued to discriminate against other imports, particularly those from the United States, but was obliged to grant preferential treatment to British goods, even if they arrived in Colombia on dominion vessels.[12] British international trade policy prevented the republic from developing trade with Asia and forced it to compete against strategic partners such as Mexico and Argentina.

Throughout the 1820s, Santander, Bolivar, and other key political figures moved ambiguously between protectionist and free trade policies, as they struggled to identify the appropriate economic development formula that would protect the republic from British imperialism while securing an influential role for Gran Colombia within the Western Hemisphere. Nevertheless, British pressure to implement further free trade policies that reduced tariffs on imports and other restrictions forced Bolivar's administration to eliminate discriminatory norms in 1829. By that point British merchants had set up shop across Colombia's urban centres, inundating these markets with imports that slowly replaced local goods made by artisans and manufacturers. Protectionist sentiment escalated as consensus on economic development policy became unattainable. Minister of Finance and close advisor to Bolivar, José Rafael Revenga, criticized the liberal policy, emphasizing that the head start in industrialization, commercialization, legislation, and institutional development that benefitted the older nations of Europe and the United States made it even more imperative for Colombian authorities to control imports and foster the advancement of local industry.[13] From his perspective, some sectors of the national economy had already experienced irreversible consequences; foreign manufactured goods had replaced artisans and local producers, leaving no space for development of a national industry.[14] Colombia, said Revenga, was "exclusively agricultural; it will be a mining nation before it becomes a manufacturer; but it must tend to diminish its current dependency on foreigners."[15]

In 1829 the government implemented protectionist measures in favour of textile manufacturers of Quito, as well as other measures to protect agricultural production across Venezuela, as a means to avoid the break-up of the nation. These measures failed and by 1831 Colombia had lost a considerable part of its territory, as Venezuela and Ecuador declared their independence from Gran Colombia.[16] Bolivar's dreams had been truncated, leaving Colombia in dire economic straits, as the newly created nation inherited 50 per cent of the international debt incurred from the independence campaigns.[17]

Bolivar's initial loan from the London Stock Exchange had placed Colombia on the international system's map. Its payment default in 1826, the republic's break-up, the regional and isolationist tendencies, and the civil wars and political instability that followed rendered the nation unattractive to foreign lenders and investors.[18] The London Stock Exchange quickly recognized Venezuela and Ecuador by lending them money for their own nation-building, while denying new loans to Colombia. London was unwilling to take risks on Colombia's economic development and nation-building after the territorial dissolution, denying it the option of borrowing its way out of debt and isolating it from the international system.

In response to these circumstances, Colombian investors and large landowners opted to adopt the conservatives' region-based economic development model, investing in basic infrastructure that allowed interregional trade to flourish. Regional markets grew alongside British and other European manufacturing operations that had been established during the era of the Gran Colombia. The French-Colombian ironworks group Egea, Daste y Compañía continued to produce steel and iron in Boyacá and Cundinamarca, while development of navigational systems along the Magdalena River fell into the hands of British interests, together with the extraction of pearls on the Atlantic coast and gold at the Supía and Marmato mines.[19] With the exception of gold mining, foreign manufacturing operations capitalized on Colombia's regionalism, establishing monopolies that were welcomed by regional elites.

Meanwhile, British banks and investors were eagerly funding the economic development of other Latin American economies. By the 1840s and 1850s foreign investors were heavily committed in extractive projects across the hemisphere, including guano in Peru, copper and wheat in Chile, wool in Argentina, coffee and sugar in Brazil, sugar and tobacco in Cuba, and silver in Mexico.[20] The international market had recovered from the crash of 1825, and the British and other European powers were back to investing, trading, and lending across the region.

Between 1830 and 1850, Colombia remained at the margin of Latin America's economic boom triggered by foreign trade and an international loan frenzy that ended with the market crash of the 1870s. In the absence of strong international trade, Colombia's region-based economy continued to produce and commercialize goods and commodities for local consumption. With the exception of the Atlantic coast, the nation's economic development remained isolated from the international system.

This did not impede British merchandise from penetrating the internal market. Consumer desire for imported textiles, the adoption of European fashion, and a move away from locally based fibres, together with the Most Favoured Nation privileges, allowed British merchants to inundate urban markets with their luxury goods. By the 1830s, sectors from all social classes were demanding foreign textiles, as the lower prices of imports forced local textile production centres in Boyacá and Santander to compete against cheaper foreign imports.[21]

The inability to protect certain sectors of the economy from foreign imports, and the expansion of British influence in the economic, social, and political spheres, forced re-emergence of the debate over protectionism and free trade. The new republic was beginning to replicate patterns and tendencies that led to the earlier fragmentation of Gran Colombia.

Political instability, limited domestic capital, lack of regional political will, and the federal government's inability to produce excess revenues for development of national infrastructure impeded the economy from diversifying or expanding interregional trade. In 1839 another civil war left conservatives in power, forcing a return of protectionism and isolationism.[22] In 1843, two years after the end of the civil conflict, President Pedro Alcántara Herrán replaced the classic liberal-based 1820 Constitution, returning power to the central government and strengthening the region-based model. Fiscal, monetary, and other economic policies inherited from colonial times were also preserved as a means to strengthen the regional exchange, and social structures were also maintained for the same reason, including the hierarchical social system and the inclusion of the power of the Catholic church within matters of state.[23]

In political economy, the objective was to restrict and, in some cases, prohibit foreign trade by imposing high tariffs on both imports and exports, in order to accelerate domestic production, protect certain agricultural sectors, and strengthen small-scale manufacturing. The state promoted the idea of buying local, pushing autonomous regional economic development based on the abundance of natural resources that blessed the republic and the production capabilities that once existed in places such as Socorro, Tunja, Bogotá, and Pamplona.[24] According to protectionists, the nation's economic development had been truncated by the independence wars, the lack of investment capital, and permissive free trade policies. They argued that regulation of free trade would remedy the problem. There was a vague idea among policymakers that local autonomy was essential for cohesive and long-term economic development, and that before entering the international system a nation needed to implement protective measures that allowed it to develop competitive internal markets and industrial production systems, before enjoying the fruits of free trade.

These ideas were not incorporated into a bureaucratic body that could articulate the role of the state in the economic development of the nation.[25] Management of the state remained paternalistic and regionally dominated, denying the possibility of implementing a national economic development plan. Failure of the Colombian leadership to think in terms of the nation state ultimately led to the failure of protectionist policies.

High import tariffs of the 1840s stopped the entrance of foreign goods into the Atlantic ports, harming the regional economy by cutting its access to staples supplied by foreign markets. Colombia's interior markets were unable to supply coastal markets with goods, such as flour, that had traditionally been supplied by North America. Ports in the Panama region and across the Atlantic coast began to question the effectiveness of protectionist policies that did not take into account the impact on local economies. Caudillos and business leaders from the coast and interior regions that did not benefit from the protectionist policies began to push once again for a return to market liberalism.[26]

By the late 1840s competition for political and economic power escalated as liberal and conservative caudillos, elites, merchants, and other business leaders became anxious as they saw potential opportunities to capitalize from increasing foreign direct investment vanish at the expense of isolationist policies.[27] Elite circles became divided between those interested in preserving the protectionist model and those wanting to integrate the national economy into the international system.

Twenty-six years of protectionist policies had not guaranteed survival of the textile, shoe, furniture, apparel, beer, iron, copper, flour, gunpowder, saddles, grease, or crockery industries.[28] From the perspective of liberals, protectionism had moved the nation backward in time, while free trade policies had pushed countries like Brazil, Mexico, and Peru forward. A mixture of foreign direct investment and local capital had led the way for establishment of manufacturing industries, import of technology, and development of transportation infrastructure. None of these economic development initiatives had taken place in Colombia.

Internationalists fought their way back through questionable elections, establishing a long period of liberal control that lasted from 1849 to 1885. The administration of José Hilario López led the way to implementation of laissez-faire policies that would create the conditions necessary for the nation to once again borrow money from the international system, in order to reinvest in much-needed infrastructure that would facilitate international trade and accelerate the accumulation of capital. López decentralized public administration, abolished slavery, separated church and state, ended the state monopoly on tobacco, and ended the Resguardo system, freeing up the Indigenous communal lands, and setting off land reforms and land use patterns that resulted in the establishment of agro export industries.[29]

In economic development, the 1853 and 1858 constitutions guaranteed establishment of a federalist system that provided the political, institutional, and legal framework to support free trade policies. Import and export revenues began to expand national wealth and set the conditions for reinvestment in transportation infrastructure that allowed the nation to move away from the region-based model and instead tailor policies to the needs of the industrialized nations whose rapidly growing population, urban centres, and consumer demands created new market opportunities for Colombian producers of staples.

Foreign investment began to make its way into the country, while Colombian entrepreneurs experimented with the export of tobacco, cinchona bark, indigo, and coffee. At the same time, Colombia was playing catch-up with the Latin American boom of the times. Contrary to Bolivar's vision, the Latin American countries had become competitors by British design, as they marketed their natural resources to bidders from Britain, the United States, and other parts of Europe. The nation's broken terrain, deficient export infrastructure, ebbs and flows of international prices of commodities, precarious technology, and lack of foreign investment during the protectionist era made it difficult for investors to compete against other Latin American markets.

Colombia returned to the international system at a disadvantage, having yet to resolve political, social, economic, institutional, and infrastructural issues that crippled its path toward long-term economic development. Decentralization of public administration became an economic development constraint, as central funding was eliminated, leaving regional and local governments at their own mercy. The abolition of slavery and the elimination of the Resguardo created a source of cheap labour, while opening new land for speculation and creating a hike in food prices that had been kept low, thanks to the Indigenous communal system. Secular policies, on the other hand, led to the expulsion of Jesuits and the development of social and educational reforms. These, in turn, stimulated violent political opposition that created instability and generated investment risk.

Colombia was readmitted into the international system as a peripheral player, with a reduced territory, resources, and precarious national market. Soon after the liberals' return to power, in the 1850s, "the value of exports and imports grew much more rapidly than local production"; Colombia was well on its way to establishing an export commodity-based economy.[30] Elites, both conservative and liberal, were able to implement laissez-faire policies that served their interests as well as those of foreign investors. Their political and economic decisions established a new pattern of national economic development that affected land use, resource allocation, infrastructure development, social relations, labour relations, fiscal policy, trade, and foreign policy. Their decisions had an impact on how national wealth was generated, commercialized, and eventually redistributed.

Liberals became responsible for building market alliances and consolidating relationships with foreign financiers and investors willing to take risks in Colombia. As in the rest of Latin America, British capital initially monopolized investment opportunities and was responsible for initial infrastructure and extractive projects across the nation. It was the British presence in Colombia during the second half of the nineteenth century that opened doors to Canadian investment.

It was around this same time that Canada began to internationalize its own economy. The 1854 Reciprocity Agreement with the United

States began to pull the Canadian economy closer to its neighbour's market.[31] Canadian businesses and investors were now interconnected to the British Empire and American markets, offering preferential treatment and advantages to strengthen their international trade.

Dominion Status and the International System

After the U.S., Haitian, and Spanish American independence movements, British North America struggled to find its place within the international system. The international trade and commercial world carved out by Britain assigned it a peripheral role, limiting its participation in places like the West Indies and South America. Implementation of the 1814 Treaty of Ghent, which ended the War of 1812, limited British North America's manoeuvrability in the region even further, as the United Kingdom's recognition of American statehood, via the peace agreement, allowed the United States to compete for resources across the Western Hemisphere.

The United States contested the niche markets established by business leaders from British North America, changing, for example, the dynamic of the Jamaican entrepôt. The peace agreement enabled Americans to move trade freely across the Caribbean, turning them into key market competitors. It became evident to British North American stakeholders that the peace agreement never considered their business interests.

British and U.S. business leaders knew well that their British North American counterparts also wanted to capitalize on the profitable opportunities offered by the region's untapped resources. Navigational and free trade initiatives, and preferential treatment between Britain and the United States sent a clear message across the Western Hemisphere that there were now two powers in the region. British North American business leaders dealt with this reality as they tried to find ways to circumvent imperial interests in the region.

British implementation of the Importation Act of 1846, which set the tone for the expansion of global trade by eliminating tariffs on grain imports entering the British market, paved the way for similar tariff-reduction policies in British North America. The result was the 1854 Reciprocity Treaty with the United States, which brought the American and British North American markets closer together.

The initiative catapulted British North America into the international market and provided an exit route for U.S. exports. It also raised the possibility of British North America's annexation to the United States and the dire consequences that this could have for the British Empire. It also brought free traders and protectionists from Britain, the United

States, and British North America face-to-face with borderland economics and the region's future economic development.

Free trade imposed itself over protectionism, in the first era of globalization, guaranteeing a market for British North American fish, grain,
and lumber. The free trade agreement strengthened the North Atlantic
Triangle and set the tone for the dynamic of regional interdependence
that would unfold a century later. At the same time, it became a limita-
tion for British North American business leaders, who began to see their
role within the international system as defined by the parameters of
their relationship with Britain and the United States.

Their colonial status limited their manoeuvrability, keeping them
constrained to the trade, commercial, and business interests of Britain
and the United States. Many in the business sector were content with
supplying the two economic powers with cheap raw materials, as they
amassed individual fortunes. In general, business leaders and government authorities did not confront the situation, because it provided them
with the economic, social, and political stability necessary to preserve
their power and influence in local economic development. Nevertheless,
other businesses wanted the implementation of protectionist measures.

The 1858 Cayley-Galt Tariff implemented by local British North
American protectionists brought comfort to certain business sectors suffering from American and British competition.[32] The tariffs on
imported manufactured and partially manufactured goods stimulated
development of domestic manufacturing and generated local industrial development. The creation of local industrial production, together
with secure access to the American market for Canadian raw materials,
became the economic development model of the time.

By the 1860s, business leaders and local government authorities pursued a laissez-faire model that depended on a commodity export market tailored to the needs of the international system, and that heavily
relied on the American market. The bilateral free trade initiative did
not last long. The American Civil War interrupted the trade dynamic
and opened up a political space for increased protectionist rhetoric to
surface across both markets. Protectionists in Washington abrogated
the trade agreement and Reciprocity came to an end, forcing Canadian
producers of raw materials to seek new alternative markets after 1866.

British North America's response was Confederation in 1867. The
political, economic, and social reorganization allowed local political
and business elites to move a step further from British and American
dependency.[33] They began to centre their attention on other potential
global markets. This included key Latin American and Caribbean markets, such as Colombia.

3

Institutionalizing International Trade, 1867–1904

After Confederation, Canadian policymakers began to work hand-in-hand with local business leaders and investors to find ways in which they could reduce their dependence on Britain. It was a complicated task, considering that, in a dominion, Canadians had no influence over their foreign policy or even their own economic development strategy. This became even more evident after the Ministerial Trade Mission organized in 1866, which revealed their limitations in foreign trade. There was a desire for greater autonomy, knowing well that parts of the Latin American and Caribbean markets represented tremendous business opportunities that could result in greater access to raw materials and the expansion of their commodity export market. The conceptualization and establishment of the Department of Trade and Commerce in 1892 represented the initial step toward creation of a promotional state that would provide Canada's business sector with the support it needed to open markets overseas.

Nationalists shared the private sector's view that there was need to cast off colonial bonds and diversify their markets in order to "lessen the country's dependence on the two giants."[1] Free trade advocates also came to the consensus that Canada needed to diversify its export market, not only to avoid further dependency but also because it was the logical strategy for an economy willing to expose itself to the challenges and risks of the international system. As indicated by John Hamilton Gray, one of the Fathers of Confederation, "It would be impolitic in Canada, under any circumstances, even if separated from England, to tie her hands to one country, however good the market that country may offer. The more varied the channels of trade, the more diverse the nations with which she may have to deal, the more varied will be the development of her own powers, and the greater the stimulus to bring into existence latent, but unused sources of wealth."[2] Business leaders and policymakers were envisioning a prosperous and even influential and powerful Canada, just like Bolivar's vision for the Gran Colombia in its early nation-building stage.

The difference was that policymakers and business leaders had come to an agreement, under the parameters of Confederation, to push toward the same goal: capitalism, a free market, expansion of domestic industrialization, and diversification of markets for its commodity export-based economy. As in the United States, private actors began to work hand-in-hand with policymakers to design and influence federal economic development policy. Trade policy began to experience the intervention of "mercantile minds" interested in advancing liberal economic initiatives, making sure that economic development policy did not favour a particular nation at the expense of Canada's business sector.[3] Individual business leaders and the Canadian Manufacturers' Association had mounted greater pressure, indicating that the nation's manufacturing sector needed the support of government intervention in matters of international trade, since they were the only body that could facilitate that type of "business connections" across strategic markets.[4]

Business leaders were well aware that a promotional state and a strong navy were important tools for the advancement of free trade and Canadian values across the international system. In the absence of a navy and its limited autonomy in foreign affairs, Canada's business sector could rely only on the manoeuvrability awarded by Confederation to trade agents and commissioners. They, in fact, became the early face of the promotional state.

In order to better manoeuvre the international market, policymakers in Canada approved the creation of the Department of Trade and Commerce, which became operational in 1892.[5] It was the first institutional response to the private sector's needs for expanding export markets and the first entity with a global and non-colonial vision. The department was created with the political intention of "casting off colonial bonds" and "developing and maintaining everything connected with" Canada's domestic and international trade and commercial issues.[6] It became the official voice for Canada's early business initiatives in Asia, Australia, Europe, Latin America, and the Caribbean.

The department's initial mission was to reduce Canada's dependency on the British and American markets. By 1890, 43 per cent of Canada's exports went to the United States, 48 per cent to the United Kingdom, and only 9 per cent reached the rest of the international market system.[7] Meanwhile, 46 per cent of imports came from the United States, 38 per cent from the United Kingdom, and the other 16 per cent from the rest of the world.[8]

Protectionist policies had followed Canada's Confederation, including Canada's 1879 National Policy designed to reduce its dependency on British and American trade, but the initiative did not boost domestic industrial production or lessen the unbalanced trade relationship.[9] In 1892 tariffs were introduced by protectionist policymakers, but these measures were also not able to discourage this economic development tendency, and instead perpetuated the problem in the absence of a more diversified trading strategy.[10]

In response to the need to expand and diversify Canada's export market, the Department of Trade and Commerce began to recruit commercial agents, and placed them in strategic markets across the international system. Their mission was to thoroughly evaluate market conditions of the assigned region for opportunities for Canadian exports. Other tasks included gathering data and carrying out additional research on trade, domestic production and consumption, and the behaviour of trade relations with other competitive markets. Additionally, they were to report on the political and social conditions of their assigned region, looking for patterns of long-term stability or flares of instability that could affect future trade strategies. They were to serve as the linchpin between Canadian business leaders and regional political and economic stakeholders interested in developing or increasing future trade relations.

The West Indies became the initial target of the inexperienced Canadian promotional state. The first minister of trade and commerce, Mackenzie Bowell, targeted the region because of the historic colonial ties and the affinity between Canadian business leaders and local political and business authorities that dated back to the War of Jenkins' Ear. The first commercial agents "were all permanent residents of the West Indies engaged in business" across the region.[11] Although well connected in Trinidad, Jamaica, British Guiana, Antigua, Saint Kitts, and Barbados, their part-time status, lack of knowledge of the Canadian and provincial economies, and social and cultural disconnect with Canada generated less than favourable results, forcing Bowell back to the drawing board.

Bowell shifted to a more nationalist, professional, and committed representative, a person willing to set aside personal passions in exchange for the prosperity of the Canadian national economy. The candidate would be a Canadian native, hired full-time, and highly knowledgeable about the federal, provincial, and global markets.[12]

John Short Larke became the first Canadian trade commissioner under Bowell's new model. Assigned to Australia in 1894, he not only set the standard for future commissioners but also defined the role and peculiarities that would later characterize Canadian government officials working overseas. As the first full-time employee stationed overseas, Larke largely redefined his own job description and duties, establishing the routine of touring regions in search of markets for Canadian products, and incorporating market research and public relations as part of the daily tasks of trade commissioners.[13] He also took it upon himself to promote Canada's image abroad, turning the Department of Trade and Commerce into a promotional entity. Although in its infancy, Canada's promotional state, eagerly demanded by individual business leaders and the Canadian Manufacturers' Association, was well on its way to serve Canada's business sector, thanks, in part, to Larke's ability to market Canada's positive image abroad. Incrementally, the promotional state would become a key component of Canada's external affairs.

In Latin America, Bowell was unable to find a candidate who had the language and cultural skills to navigate the region's political, economic, social, and cultural diversity. Instead, he had to rely on Canadian businessmen who represented private interests in the region. In 1894 Bowell appointed Lewis E. Thompson, the representative of Watrous Engine Works of Branford in Chile, followed by Daniel M. Rennie, a Canadian business representative with connections in Argentina and Uruguay.[14]

As in the West Indies, the Latin American representatives failed to operate on behalf of the federal and provincial interests, and instead favoured their own personal or corporate interests. Their objective was to tour the neighbouring regions in search of opportunities for Canadian exports and promote the Canadian brand across the region. Instead, they remained centred on Chile, Argentina, and Uruguay, watching over the interests of Canadian companies in these strategic markets.

British, American, and other European interests were targeting the same markets as Canada. With the exception of Mexico, which was controlled predominantly by American business interests, Chile, Argentina, and Uruguay were the regional engines of modernization and industrial development. They were developing and accelerating domestic production, thanks to foreign investment in manufacture and infrastructure. Meanwhile, an increase in imports of finished and luxury goods revealed the emergence of a more diverse and sophisticated consumer society. British interests were heavily invested in railway construction as well as the meat and hide industry, while Americans were invested in copper and iron ore mining.

It was urgent for Canada to carve out its own market, knowing well that Britain and the United States had their eyes on these markets. There were also relatively untapped markets, such as Colombia's, but even it was beginning to feel the pressure from the imperial powers. By the late 1800s British and American interests were competing for control of regional markets. Moreover, Senate debates in Washington over the possibility of expanding free trade into Latin America made it even more imperative for Canada's business sector to act. The fact that the international system was focusing on the young Latin American and Caribbean markets meant that this region was open for business.

William D. Washburn, representative from Minnesota, emphasized in the April 1894 debates that the most "convenient and encouraging markets were those offered by the Latin American republics and colonies."[15] Washburn, pushing the free trade agenda, indicated that the region's fifty million plus market continued to overwhelmingly look to Europe for trade, importing close to five hundred million dollars from these markets while only importing one hundred million dollars from the U.S. economy.[16] He argued that a large part of these "imports could be furnished by American farmers and manufacturers at prices as low as those obtained in Europe."[17] Canada's business sector felt the same way: they could also replace European imports into the region.

This was the argument made by Canadian farmers and manufacturers. The problem was that they lacked the support of government institutions and did not have a clear-cut policy for the region. Faced with the dominion status of their country and unable to conduct their own foreign affairs, all they could rely on was the newly created Department of Trade and Commerce, which was crippled by its inability to find adequate personnel to represent the farmers' and manufacturers' interests in conquering the Latin American and Caribbean markets.

American business leaders did not have to face this problem. Merchants and manufacturers were determined "to obtain a share in the market which they had previously neglected," as a result of Washington's protectionist policies.[18] They were determined to challenge Britain's dominant position in the region and defend their own position against other competitors. Consular and diplomatic officers from the United States agreed with their countrymen, signalling that the best way to overcome the challenge of English capital, goods, subsidized steamship lines, and influence was by strengthening the outreach of their own promotional state in the region.[19] Washington was ready to ramp up support for goods stamped with the "Made in USA" label.[20] Government officials predicted that U.S. goods and services would eventually surpass foreign exports and slowly take control of the Latin American market if able to compete with lower prices.[21]

Canadian policymakers and business leaders were well aware of this reality, yet they were confident that they could capitalize where Britain had a strong influence or where anti-American sentiment prevailed. They also had the advantage that American policymakers did not see

Canadian merchants and manufacturers as a threat to their interests in Latin America and the Caribbean, because as Representative Washburn said, "The laws of nature and the laws of trade require Canada to come to the markets of the United States to purchase what she requires and to sell what she has to dispose of, and, in spite of the tremendous influences exercised by the officials and commercial organizations of England, in spite of the enormous amount of English capital invested in the Dominion, in spite of the restraint that is placed upon the people by the Government, and in spite of heavy duties they levy upon our products, nearly half of their trade is with us."[22]

Canadian policymakers and business leaders understood that they could capitalize on the arrogance of the American policymakers. They realized that this could become the Americans' Achilles heel. From their perspective, there were still numerous markets across Latin America and the Caribbean that remained untapped. Passenger lists in steamers and postal service statistics revealed to policymakers in Europe, England, Canada, and the United States that there was an increase in commercial travellers entering the region as well as more local buyers interested in purchasing and importing manufactured and luxury goods, and commodities.

By the late 1890s, the sporadic business ventures of Canadian merchants across Latin America and the Caribbean were followed by more organized business initiatives. Canadian business leaders overcame the limited capability of their Department of Trade and Commerce by relying more on British government bonds, direct investment, and joint British and Canadian capital investments that allowed them to expand their influence across the region more effectively.[23] In 1896 the Manufacturers Life Insurance Company of Canada began operations in Kingston, Jamaica, slowly extending its coverage across the West Indies, and reaching Colombia's Caribbean coast in 1899.[24] Other Canadian financial, mining, and oil companies followed the insurance company's footsteps between 1905 and 1918, strengthening the presence of Canadian businesses across the region.

Early Efforts in Colombia

Business expansion was paralleled by mounting pressure from Canadian business representatives and the Canadian Manufacturers' Association that demanded the presence of an official trade commissioner in Colombia, as competition escalated there. British, American, French, and German diplomatic and consular representatives had been laying the groundwork since the 1880s, when Colombia's economy began to transition from tobacco to coffee exports, giving birth to its late-blooming modernization stage.[25] British and U.S. investors controlled railway transportation that connected the Atlantic and Pacific Oceans through Panama, at a time when Panama was still part of Colombia's territory. Steamship lines were split between the four industrial powers, while British merchants, who additionally controlled gold-mining operations and other infrastructure projects, monopolized the country's internal markets.

U.S. merchants and manufacturers challenged the Canadian and British initiatives in Colombia. They had narrowed in on the Colombian market, targeting Colombia's cotton and hemp import markets as a means to build leverage there.[26] Its greatest worry was the British monopoly of the domestic Colombian market as well as the anti-American sentiment that had spread across the hemisphere as a result of the Mexican-American War. These concerns diminished in 1899 when the American-owned United Fruit Company entered the Colombian market, taking advantage of the liberal economic policies introduced by President Manuel Antonio Sanclemente's government that welcomed the expansion and diversification of foreign investment.

Canada's Manufacturers Life Insurance Company and the American banana exporter would experience first-hand the challenges and benefits of doing business in Colombia. Initially they faced the negative impact that the War of a Thousand Days had on the country's domestic market, but a few years later benefitted from the subsidies, tax exemptions, and other foreign investment incentives designed by President Rafael Reyes's government in order to "jump start the national economy."[27]

The market aperture would be short-lived for the United States, as President Theodore Roosevelt's Canal Zone–motivated intervention, on behalf of Panama's independence in 1903, generated an anti-American sentiment across Colombia that temporarily closed the doors on other American companies interested in entering the market. For Canadian businesses, it represented a unique opportunity to fill the gaps left by the Americans.

Canada's Department of Trade and Commerce responded to the incident, under pressure from Canadian merchants and manufacturers interested in capitalizing on the anti-American sentiment that resulted from Roosevelt's gunboat diplomacy.[28] In 1904, just months after the Panama incident, the Department of Trade and Commerce named A.E. Beckwith as the commercial agent for Colombia and A.W. Donly as Canada's representative in Mexico.[29] Beckwith's appointment showed the government's willingness to facilitate opportunities for Canadian

businesses in Colombia. The Canadian promotional state had found in
America's muscular diplomacy an opportunity to offer the region a different and more friendly alternative of foreign investment.

Beckwith was initially stationed in the port of Cartagena from where
most of the international commerce flowed, and eventually ended his
ten-year term in Medellín, working on behalf of Canadian gold-mining
operations. His work was crucial in consolidating the links between
British and Canadian investors attracted by the Antioquia gold rush of
the early 1900s.[30]

The initial effort of commercial agents such as Beckwith did not generate greater cohesion across the Latin American and Caribbean markets. Their locally centred efforts kept them distant from the advances
by other Canadian agents across the hemisphere. For example, the
efforts of Trade Commissioner Rivington Poussette in Argentina and
E.H.S. Flood in the British West Indies did not complement Beckwith's
work in Colombia. Canada lacked a cohesive regional policy or strategy, revealing the weakness of the early Canadian promotional state.

In the absence of the autonomy to advance its own foreign affairs,
improvisation and opportunism characterized Canada's early initiatives in the region. A year before Beckwith's death, news of a possible
trade mission across South America headed by Rivington Poussette
generated great expectations among Canadian merchants and manufacturers operating in Colombia.[31] Poussette left Buenos Aires, Argentina, in February 1913 with plans to study possible market expansion
opportunities in Chile, Peru, Ecuador, Bolivia, Venezuela, Colombia,
and Panama.[32] Unfortunately for Beckwith, Poussette disembarked in
the Colombian Pacific port of Buenaventura and travelled directly to
Bogotá. Beckwith never had an opportunity to meet his colleague stationed in Argentina, and was unable to strengthen the case for Canadian-Colombian relations back in Ottawa. Poussette visited Bogotá,
seeking political contacts and overlooking the potential markets of
the Atlantic coast and the Antioquia region, where Beckwith was well
connected.

The experience revealed the lack of coordination and efficiency of
the newly created Department of Trade and Commerce. Poussette left
Colombia without seeing first-hand the gold-mining operations of the
British-Canadian joint venture, Oroville Dredging, on the headwaters
of the Nechí River, as well as the thriving Cartagena market where
Manufacturers Life Insurance was operating. Poussette left with a less
than favourable image of Colombia, remembering the scars of a "tax-
ing and unusual journey" that included a severe malaria attack as he
crossed the Andes.[33]

For the most part, Canadian merchants and manufacturers had to navigate the Latin American markets on their own, in the absence of direct government representation, forcing them to compete from a disadvantageous position against British, U.S., and other European interests.[34] Nevertheless, the initial efforts of the Department of Trade and Commerce represented a starting point from which to build upon. In the absence of a fully autonomous government, Canada's private sector began to mould Trade and Commerce to its liking, tweaking it here and there in order to find an edge over its international competitors.

Three strategies were designed to overcome its disadvantages, including the enhancement of communications between exporters/ importers and the representatives from the Department of Trade and Commerce, the need to move away from the cookie-cutter approach used by the United States in the region, and an enhancement of the language skills of trade commissioners and commercial agents in order to tailor their approach to each Latin American and Caribbean market. Commercial agents and trade commissioners were required to keep a well-stocked inventory of catalogues, price lists, discount rates, detailed information on Canadian importers and exporters, and other market-related information that would benefit and effectively market Canadian products abroad.[35] Highly familiarized with the ways in which English merchants and manufacturers carried out their business in the Americas and across the world, Canadian manufacturers were encouraged to tailor their products to the needs and demands of the local markets and avoid the U.S. approach of disregarding local cultural uniqueness. For example, Canadian manufacturers needed to "study and cater to the demands of the Colombian trade," just like their British counterparts often did.[36] Besides tailoring products to the specific market, business leaders and trade representatives needed to speak the local language if they wanted to advance trade relationships and differentiate themselves from the Americans. It was evident across the business community that "ignorance" of the local language made "usual business methods impossible," building "a barrier bigger than the tariff."[37]

In theory, the strategy seemed effective, but in practice it was limited by personnel capacity, budget allocation, and the mere inability to navigate the international system under a dominion status. By 1914 the Department of Trade and Commerce had expanded its presence throughout the Americas, establishing trade commission offices in Mexico, British West Indies, Bermuda, British Guiana, Cuba, Argentina, and Brazil, in addition to commercial agencies in Jamaica, Trinidad and Tobago, Bahamas, Colombia, and Venezuela.[38] Canada, the only other industrialized nation in the Western Hemisphere, was gearing up to fight for its share of the Latin American and Caribbean markets.

Canada's presence in the region resonated against U.S. thirst for the expansion of influence in the region and received "little encouragement" from Great Britain, which wanted to keep tight control over the expansion of "more neighborly relations between the outlying portions" of the Empire.[39] British influence continued to expand across the region during the early twentieth century. Meanwhile, the United States pushed forward with their Monroe Doctrine, expanding and maintaining diplomatic and consular presence even in places across the Western Hemisphere where they had no commercial relation, all for the sake of promoting their commercial interests across the region.[40] The United States had indicated, soon after its Civil War, that the trade of the world was to be contested and more evenly divided between them and Great Britain.[41] They claimed, by the turn of the nineteenth century, that "not much more than a foothold" had been gained in places like Latin America.[42]

Latin American nations also wanted to expand their "foothold" in the region, racing to conquer markets such as Canada's for their own commodity export economies. By the early twentieth century most of the regional actors had established consular presence in Canada, the United States, and across Europe. Cuba, Mexico, Dominican Republic, Guatemala, Honduras, Panama, Argentina, Brazil, Colombia, Chile, Ecuador, Paraguay, Peru, Uruguay, and Venezuela had consular presence across the provinces.[43] These were signs that there was great interest to expand trade with Canada and develop a partnership to counterbalance their dependency on the United States and Britain.

As the twentieth century unfolded, regional actors began to demand a greater hemispheric role for Canada. Nevertheless, its dominion status and Washington's increasing influence in the region limited its outreach in the region. Instead, Canadian business leaders, with the help of the Department of Trade and Commerce, hand-picked their partnerships across the Western Hemisphere, weighing their options against British and U.S. influence, while providing the region with a third alternative. Such was the case of Colombia, where British presence was not as robust, when compared to other South American and Caribbean markets, and where the anti-American sentiment was vibrant.

Colombia's consular presence and other diplomatic initiatives remained unanswered, even though the Canadian Manufacturers' Association continued to press for a more active promotional state.

Bilateral relations continued to be moulded by mutual business interests in the absence of diplomatic exchange and a clear bilateral policy. Private Canadian initiatives came to represent the way through which Canada expanded its presence in markets such as Colombia. The strategy was reduced to filling the gaps left by British and American interests, capitalizing on the region's accelerated growth of the early 1900s.

PART TWO

A Foothold in the Region

4

Colombia and the Emerging Latin American Market, 1904–1910

By the early 1900s Canada was in direct competition with the industrial powers of the time over control of emerging markets across Latin America and the Caribbean. Although the United Kingdom continued to dominate trade across the Western Hemisphere, the United States surged as a powerful challenger, particularly after the Spanish-American War and their takeover of the Panama Canal Zone. Meanwhile, Canada's government-business partnership was coming to terms with the realization that the United Kingdom was invested in the region only to protect its self-interests and not Canada's and that the United States had gained enough military, political, and economic power to challenge Britain's hegemony. Nevertheless, control over the region's resources and markets was unsettled, and the stakes were extremely high, considering that this was the most dynamic regional market, within the emerging markets of the time. Between 1910 and 1929, total imports had increased 123.2 per cent while exports had risen 125.7 per cent.[1]

Knowing well that they could not compete head-to-head against British or U.S. interests, Canadian investors opted to continue with their strategy of filling in the gaps. They narrowed in on markets where they could take advantage of their close relationship with British authorities and business partnerships, as in Brazil and Argentina, and in other instances they focused on untapped markets or those where there was vibrant anti-U.S. sentiment, as in Colombia.

Colombia was transitioning from another wave of protectionism and violence that culminated with the War of a Thousand Days and the territorial loss of Panama in 1903. The costs of numerous civil wars throughout the nineteenth century had left the national economy in shambles, and its experiment with tobacco exports had failed to produce sustained economic growth. Colombia had not achieved the levels of growth of other regional economies such as Brazil, Peru, Argentina,

Chile, Cuba, and Mexico, unable to define a clear-cut economic development policy after almost one hundred years of independence.

Internal war, protectionist regionalism, a weak government, a primitive system of financial intermediaries, limited internal capital and foreign investment, lack of industrial capacity, and antiquated infrastructure resulted in latent economic development.[2] This changed with the expansion of coffee exports, which replaced the tobacco experiment, marking a shift in the nation's economic development pattern. Colombia's private sector initiatives, mostly centred in the Antioquia region, set the tone for accelerated economic growth spearheaded by local coffee entrepreneurs.

The shift from tobacco to coffee benefitted from an increasing demand for coffee in the international market as well as the steady increase in the international price of the commodity.[3] Coffee production continued to expand throughout the early 1900s, ultimately becoming Colombia's top commodity export.

President Rafael Reyes (1904–9) used coffee exports to modernize and stabilize the nation's economy. His post-war reconstruction program centred on the expansion of coffee exports, the attraction of foreign investment through tax and tariff incentives, heavy investment in modernization of the nation's infrastructure, and promotion of domestic industrial production. He incorporated laissez-faire policies that generated the healthy political, economic, and fiscal climate necessary to attract foreign investment and accelerate local production.

Reyes was convinced that national economic development depended on the import of foreign capital, industrial goods, and technology necessary for the development of local industrial production and eventual export industries.[4] Together with the country's business elite, he accepted the nation's fate as determined by the international system; Colombia, like Canada and the rest of the Latin American and Caribbean economies, was going to develop economically via a staples-dependent export economy. He was therefore willing to defend the interests of local entrepreneurs who wanted to develop local export industries and was willing to support the expansion of monopolies in economic sectors that favoured foreign corporations and open Colombia's economy to foreign interests.

He envisioned an active role for Colombia within the international system, competing head-to-head with other regional economies. In efforts to project internal stability and compete effectively against other regional economies interested in attracting foreign investment, Reyes professionalized the nation's military force to enhance national security, developed government bureaucracies and institutions to manage the state's resources and policies, devalued the peso, eliminated taxes on exports and imports, and increased borrowing from the international system.[5] Consular offices were expanded to key strategic parts of the world, fiscal efficiency was generated thanks to more effective public administration, and new institutional development and policy modernization generated trust within the international market. In 1905 the Central Bank was created, that same year the Reyes administration negotiated new credits in London without the reduction of old capital and interest, taking the necessary steps to strengthen the nation's reputation as a trustworthy borrower within the international system.[6]

The international loan was then used to develop and expand the national infrastructure, in efforts to facilitate international trade. His economic development plan included expansion of the railway system, modernization of the navigational system of the Magdalena River, and development of port infrastructure, in both the Pacific and Atlantic coasts. By 1909 the Antioquia railway had been expanded, together with the Sabana line, and the Honda-Dorada, Bogotá-Zipaquirá, Tolima, Cauca, Buenaventura, Amagá, and Santa Marta lines.[7] Other short branches were built to give port access to commodities destined for the international market, including United Fruit Company banana exports. Reyes also invested in development of road infrastructure in response to the introduction of motor vehicles, envisioning the automobile as a possible solution to Colombia's systemic problem of extraordinarily high transportation costs.[8] Colombia's road infrastructure was limited to primitive native and colonial road networks for horse and mule that dominated interregional trade as a result of isolationist economic development policies of the early republic. Reyes wanted to redesign the national road infrastructure so that it looked outward into the international system, facilitating international trade and reducing transportation costs.

President Reyes opened the nation to the international system, reversing all that had been done by protectionists such as Rafael Núñez. Reyes believed that economic progress would result in greater liberty, and that this could be achieved only by integrating Colombia into the international system and accepting a peripheral role within its power structures. During his administration, he tried to reverse the anti-U.S. sentiment, convinced that "Colombia's future economic development depended on the normalization of relations with the United States," since they were the new power to contend with and the largest importer of Colombian coffee.[9]

His administration introduced business-friendly fiscal policies to encourage the presence of foreign investors. In efforts to compete against other regional economies for the attraction of foreign investment, taxes and tariffs were lowered. Decree 832 of 1907 established export tax exemptions for coffee, tobacco, rubber, and cotton, and Law 9 of 1908 awarded the United Fruit Company an initial eight-year export tax exemption.[10]

Under his administration subsidies and fiscal investment incentive policies were implemented to accelerate domestic industrial production. Pro-business policies were designed to attract foreign and domestic investors willing to develop a domestic industrial sector that could alleviate the nation's dependency on foreign imports of goods and services. Tariffs were increased on certain strategic imports in order to protect local infant industries, and tax reliefs were implemented to attract foreign and domestic investors willing to assume the risks of start-up companies. His policies set the foundation for the emergence of a national textile industry centred in Medellín, and the start-up of industrial production of paper, glass, acid, food, china, agricultural and mining machinery, soft drinks, beer, cigarettes, tobacco, candles, matches, mills, cement, chocolate, and other food products.[11]

Nevertheless, the engine behind the expansion of trade and capital necessary for reinvestment into local industries came from increasing coffee exports. The development of infrastructure and the expansion of the bureaucracy, for example, were funded by increasing coffee exports. These were also responsible for the expansion of the textile industry, the emergence of a working class, and the rising demand for industrial products. Between 1900 and 1910 coffee exports increased 55 per cent, from 387,207 to 707,020 sixty-kilo sacks, reflecting the positive transformation of the Colombian economy.[12]

Coffee exports and the policies introduced by Reyes changed the international system's perception of the country. Foreign investment increased, contributing to the development of local industry and strengthening the newly adopted export-based model of economic development. Colombian elites, foreign-born immigrants, and foreign-owned corporations fostered industrial development as well as banking, commerce, retail trade, plantation agriculture, and small business entrepreneurship.[13]

A decade of exceptional economic growth followed. Export growth reached over 11 per cent per annum between 1910 and 1919.[14] Close to one hundred years of political and social instability was replaced by a long period of relative peace that projected the nation internationally as "serious, democratic, and pacifist."[15] Political power was shared between liberals and conservatives at all levels of government, as the bureaucratic and institutional structures were expanded and professionalized in order to manage and preserve the bipartisan import and export interests of local elites and foreign investors. Constitutional reforms of 1910 enhanced the liberal economic development model, while the continuation of tariff relief assured greater foreign investment.

Colombia's economy began to be noticed by foreign investors. The export expansion experienced between 1910 and 1928 quickly turned the country into an important player within the hemispheric market, particularly because of the continuous expansion of coffee exports and the diversification of national production, including oil exports in the 1920s. The radical changes experienced during such a short time transformed the nation politically, culturally, socially, economically, and environmentally.

Social order, political stability, an emerging domestic consumer market, and the bipartisan advancement of free market policies during the first two decades of the twentieth century generated confidence within the international system, unleashing an international race for control of the nation's untapped resources and markets. Canadian, U.S., British, and other European capital entered the market during this period, contributing to the expansion of the national economy while releasing the forces of capitalism that left national economic growth in the hands of a small elite and foreign interests.

Emerging Latin American Markets

By 1910 the sporadic business ventures of Canadian merchants and business leaders across Latin America and the Caribbean were followed by more organized business initiatives and investment strategies designed to capitalize on the region's modernization and transition to industrialization. British, U.S., and other European powers were also aggressively pursuing the same objective. Throughout the next thirty years, they contested for the region's resources, industrial production, and emerging consumer markets. Canada capitalized on its dominion status and its close relationship to the United States in order to leverage on British and American business presence in the region as its entry strategy into the regional market.

Canada's private sector and policymakers recognized that the size of their domestic market constrained capitalist expansionism, and that their access to the region's raw materials and natural resources was conditioned by their relations with Britain and their dependency on the shipping infrastructure of the United States.[16] Politically, Canada was forced to defend the interests of Britain, but it was economically compelled to play the U.S. card.[17] Faced with this dilemma, Canadian business leaders, merchants, and entrepreneurs launched their way into the region, trying to identify their best options based on their limitations. British firms and investors monopolized markets in Argentina, Brazil, and the West Indies, while U.S. presence was strong in Mexico, Central America, and parts of the Caribbean. Germans and the French were also active across the region, including in Colombia. Although limited in their capabilities, Canadian business leaders recognized that there were many untapped subregions as well as numerous internal markets to develop.

The infant stages of infrastructure development, industrial production, and market development made Latin America and the Caribbean a highly desirable regional market. Lewis Nixon, U.S. delegate at the fourth Pan-American Conference in Buenos Aires (1910), reported that the resources across the region remained "quite untouched" and that South America, in particular, would become "the theatre of the world's most active exploitation" of resources.[18] He also pointed out that the Europeans had secured "commercial sovereignty" and erected "a wall of prejudice" between the United States and their regional neighbours.[19] It was evident from the sentiment of the times that the powers of the West would dispute control over the untapped resources and markets.

It was no secret that Argentina, Brazil, Cuba, and Mexico dominated the region's international trade and attracted the most foreign investment. By 1910 Argentina had consolidated its position as the leading Latin American market, controlling 31 per cent of the region's total foreign trade, thanks to British direct investment and its active participation on the London Stock Exchange.[20] Its urban centres were comparable to the largest cities in the United States and Canada. Buenos Aires had even earned the reputation as the "Paris of South America" for its architecture, sophisticated urban planning, modern infrastructure and modern comforts such the opera house, its electric tram system, public docks, and other modern public spaces.[21]

Foreign and local private sector investment in Argentina had resulted in accelerated industrialization and infrastructure development. This, together with meat exports, ultimately led to unprecedented economic growth during the first two decades of the twentieth century.[22] The same was true for Brazil and rubber, Cuba and sugar, and México and oil.[23] In other instances, internal political instability, regional conflicts over economic development policy, depletion of resources such as guano in Peru, and lack of export infrastructure impeded other regional players from competing during the early stages of the expansion of international trade in the region. Colombia, a latecomer to the international scene as a result of its long-lasting internal political instability, was one of those cases.

Colombia's total foreign trade in 1910 represented only 1.5 per cent of the region's total trade.[24] It was a peripheral player within the region and mostly disregarded by foreign investors. Yet it was rich in natural resources, blessed with a strategic geographical location, and topographical and climatic advantages for the production of food.

The entrance of foreign investment into the Colombian market was in its infancy. Canada's Manufacturers Life Insurance Company had just began operations in the country's Atlantic coast, the United Fruit Company was only ten years into its banana operations in Santa Marta, Germans continued to buy most of the nation's tobacco production and controlled beer-brewing operations in several urban centres, British, U.S. and French investors were in a race for the control of gold-mining operations, while U.S. and British companies competed for development of the nation's urban and regional transportation markets. American companies such as J.G. Brill Company of Philadelphia controlled urban tramway lines through companies such as Bogotá City Railway. This firm developed the first electric tramway lines in Bogotá in 1908, expanding its lines across the urban centre, and developed a similar system in Medellín.[25]

Even though Colombia was rich in natural resources, its backward infrastructure, political instability, and complex geography deterred many foreigners from investing. As clearly synthesized by the chief engineer of Mata Mines in Colombia, P.E. Fuller, it took "concentrated capital to operate" mining and any other business endeavour in Colombia, particularly in the impenetrable jungles where most of the natural resources were buried.[26] Foreigners depicted Colombia as an untamed beast, a place in the wild, tropically unpleasant, and "primitive."[27]

Fuller's experience in the gold-mining zone of Antioquia draws a clear picture of the Colombia of the times. He said that everybody mining for gold in the Antioquia region was a placer miner, even the Americans, using the technology of the "days of the '49" gold rush.[28] The jungle, rain, and isolation drove people mad; foreigners, said Fuller, were "compelled to take a vacation of six weeks every ten months" to keep their sanity.[29] The terrain and geography was so challenging that it took personnel and equipment days of navigation down the Magdalena River, followed by days of mule-back riding and narrow-gauge railroad travel before reaching the mine.[30] But even though it was rugged and primitive, he was always willing to return to the region because he was convinced, as his company was, that the Antioquia region would eventually "rival both California and the Klondike in the production of gold."[31]

Canadian investors, seeing it as an untapped market with minimal foreign presence, began to slowly narrow in on the Colombian market, carefully navigating around British and U.S. interests, in efforts to secure their own access to markets and resources.

It was then that Canadian financial entities jumped at the opportunity that opened a door into the Colombian market. The country, as stated by the president of Sun Life Assurance Company of Canada, came to represent "a virgin field for life insurance" and other financial services.[32] The Royal Bank of Canada, Sun Life Assurance Company, and Manufacturers Life Insurance Company capitalized on the opportunity to expand Canadian businesses abroad by linking their services to the initial growth of coffee and banana exports and the accelerated presence of gold-mining interests that followed. The Colombian Caribbean ports of Cartagena and Barranquilla became the focus of Canadian financial entities in the early 1900s.

As in colonial times, the Atlantic coast became the bridge to the international system. Coffee, tobacco, gold, and banana exports left through these ports in exchange for foreign imports of luxury goods, machinery, technology, human capital, and investment capital that fuelled Colombia's modernization. Jamaica, the entrepôt that once connected the Maritimes and the ports of Spanish Main, now served as Manufacturers Life Insurance's bridge between the West Indies and the Colombian market.

Colombia's Atlantic coast became the core of economic and infrastructural development, making it the nation's international business hub. It was the perfect place for Canadian financial entities to advance their Colombian strategy. As the nation's economy continued to steadily grow, so did the business relations of Canadian financial entities. Colombia's exports jumped from US$17.6 million in 1910 to US$76.6 million in 1919, while imports increased from US$17.3 million to US$46.0 million, a growth of 351 per cent in total trade.[33] Nevertheless, Colombia's contribution to Latin America's total international trade continued to lag behind, with 2.0 per cent of the region's total trade.[34]

Executives from Canadian financial entities operating in Colombia were well aware of Colombia's market potential. It was no secret among international investors that the nation's untapped resources represented a bright future for any business venture. As long as they could hold onto their position in that market, they would be ready to serve the financial needs of all transnational actors entering the untapped market.

Colombian policymakers, business elites, and foreign investors welcomed the presence of Canadian financial entities. They spearheaded modernization of the nation's financial system and provided international finance and banking services that had been limited. Canadian financial institutions such as Manufacturers, the Royal Bank, and Sun Life Assurance became trusted intermediaries between Colombia, Canada, and the international system.

Canadian financial entities were tied directly to Colombia's economic growth of the early 1900s, facilitating international trade, providing services such as currency exchange, offering banknotes and other financial instruments, and servicing local economic development projects. They managed foreign and domestic capital, helped foreign companies repatriate profits, and assisted Colombian investors who wished to move their money overseas.

The Interwar Years

During the interwar years, industrialized nations were particularly attracted to the Latin American and Caribbean markets for their vastly untapped natural resources and their emerging consumer market. While the U.S. private sector navigated its way into the region thanks to Washington's implementation of a mixed bag of Big Stick and Good Neighbour policies, European powers pushed their way through diplomacy and free trade policies, leaving Canada with very few options to manoeuvre in the region.[35] Canadian businesses were eager to diversify their export markets in order to reduce their dependency on a weak European market that was slowly recovering from the First World War. Nevertheless, they were limited by Canada's dominion status, which favoured British over Canadian interests. Therefore, those interested in expanding business across the Western Hemisphere pressed the Canadian government to strengthen the capabilities of the promotional state. Ultimately, they demanded greater support and representation overseas, particularly after the 1926 Balfour Declaration, which gave Canada and other dominions control over their own foreign policy.[36]

Canada's private sector had embarked on its own fact-finding mission in 1921, in the absence of a robust promotional state. Headed by the Canadian Manufacturers' Association (CMA), a delegation of Canadian exporters travelled across the West Indies and South America to identify potential business opportunities and exchange ideas with Canadian businesses in the region. Upon their return, business delegates emphasized that the West Indian and South American markets were worth developing and that the government should step up its efforts to help Canada "establish business connections."[37] By doing so, said the business delegates, "Canada was assured a hearty response on the part of the Southern people."[38]

Canadian business representatives assessing the southern markets identified the need for greater government presence, making their claim through local media, at business conferences, and by lobbying policy-makers in Ottawa. Speaking to manufacturers, wholesalers, and others responsible for handling imports from South America, business representative E.C. Austin took advantage of the CMA's meeting in Montreal to shed light on the need to expand trade with Colombia and Venezuela, indicating that these two countries were beginning "a remarkable period of expansion."[39] The mission had convinced exporters of a need to diversify their Latin American strategy and move beyond the Argentine and Brazilian markets.[40] Colombia was a good option because the Royal Bank of Canada was well positioned there and could help other Canadian companies get their foot in the door.

The president of the Royal Bank of Canada, Sir Herbert Holt, also pushed for Canada's business expansion into the Colombian market. In a 1925 company report, Holt stressed that there were "few storehouses of untouched and unmeasured wealth to compare with the resources that remain[ed] to be developed in the Republic of Colombia."[41] Having assumed control of a considerable part of Colombia's personal banking sector by 1925, Holt escalated the demand for the presence of Canadian government officials in strategic foreign markets such as Colombia's, in an effort to protect its market share from other foreign interests. After his 1925 Latin American tour, he publicly declared that Canadian trade commissioners were "hampered and handicapped" by limited government support resulting from Canada's dominion status.[42] Business leaders such as Holt mounted pressure on the liberal administration of Prime Minister William Mackenzie King to step up its efforts in the region.

In 1927, a year after the Balfour Declaration, an official trade mission to Latin America was organized under the leadership of Canada's minister to Washington, Vincent Massey, and deputy minister of trade and commerce, F.C.T. O'Hara.[43] Although exploratory, the mission represented a symbolic step toward development of an independent foreign policy for the region.

The delegation was scheduled to visit Mexico, Brazil, Argentina, Chile, Bolivia, Peru, Ecuador, Venezuela, and Colombia. The build-up for the mission highlighted the potential for Canadian business and stressed the importance of greater independence in foreign affairs. Massey's push for expansion of the external affairs agenda into Latin American received pushback from conservatives that eventually blocked the initiative.[44] Internal debates over the focus and direction of the nation's external affairs forced a parliamentary debate, and the mission was eventually cancelled.

Nevertheless, the Canadian Chamber of Commerce and the CMA continued to push their Latin American agenda. Advocates for expansion of the trade commissioner service, under the parameters of the Balfour Declaration, stressed that the trade "handicaps" needed to be resolved so that Canada's business sector could be at par with all other nations "that were in a battle for world trade."[45] Canada, they argued, could not even compete against nations that were marginal players in the global market system because at least they had complete representation abroad, including diplomats and consular offices.[46] They made a strong case for establishment of consular, diplomatic, and trade commissioner services across Latin America and the Caribbean, as part of a strategy to favour Canadian business interests in the region. The CMA, for example, emphasized that the Canadian government needed to start looking after its own interests abroad, now that Britain was pushing its own trade agenda in regions such as Latin America and against Canadian interests; it was time "for a strong national policy," one "designed to strengthen Canadian trade and prestige abroad."[47]

The autonomy granted by the British Parliament to the Canadian government left these Canadian businesses to their own devices, in the absence of a strong promotional state. In Colombia they had no official government representative to negotiate on their behalf or market Canadian brands. In the absence of representation, Canadian businesses interested in expanding into the Colombian market found themselves relying solely on the Canadian subsidiaries and financial entities that had established a base in Colombia. Together, they reinforced the demand for establishment of diplomatic and official trade relations across Latin America and the Caribbean.

In the early 1930s, for example, business representative E.C. Austin wrote to the *Manitoba Free Press* from Barranquilla, Colombia, demanding the expansion of trade commissioner service across Central and South America, since it was "impossible for a Canadian trade commissioner stationed in the West Indies to properly look after" such an immense territory.[48] He joined the voices of the CMA, the Royal Bank of Canada, Tropical Oil, Andian National Corporation, and other Canadian businesses interested in expanding the presence of trade commissioners in the region.[49] Austin urged his government not only to re-evaluate its policy on Central and South America, but also to assign commissioners who were well versed in Spanish. Bilingualism, said Austin, was "indispensable for good business relations," since it guaranteed effective communications with governments, chambers of commerce, and other trade organizations across the region.[50] He complained that while the United States and Britain had official government representatives in

Colombia who served as brokers for their respective business interests, the Canadian government had not assigned a single trade representative there, even though Colombia had consular presence in Canada. Bilingual agents well-versed in the culture and customs of the region would give Canadians leverage over the control maintained by British and U.S. authorities.[51]

Members of the CMA were aware that the southern republics were eager to establish strong trade relations with Canada. This was old news within the Ottawa circles, yet the federal government was not responding accordingly. Political and business actors were well aware of the increasing presence of Latin American consular offices in Canada that emerged throughout the interwar years. It was clear that the region was eager to incorporate Canada into the dynamics of hemispheric trade in efforts to fight off its dependency on the U.S. market, but the Mackenzie King administration was too distracted with the constitutional crisis that erupted in 1926, also known as the King–Lord Byng Affair. The Canadian government was busy dealing with domestic nation-building while its business sector was pushing for expansion of its export markets.

Ottawa was not prepared to play the role of the promotional state, because it lacked human capital and the financial resources. By the late 1920s, it was evident that the penetration of the Latin American and Caribbean markets would continue to depend exclusively on the initiatives of Canada's private sector.

In Colombia, Canadian companies and subsidiaries such as the Royal Bank of Canada, the Manufacturers Life Insurance Company, Sun Life Assurance Company, Pato Consolidated Gold Dredging, Tropical Oil, and the Andian National Corporation had positioned themselves within Colombia's mining, oil, financial, and insurance sectors. Tropical Oil had spearheaded development of oil exports in Colombia, while the Andian National Corporation had developed the pipeline infrastructure to make these exports possible. The Royal Bank of Canada had established branch operations across the nation's emerging urban centres, and Sun Life Assurance had become the leading insurance house in the nation. Nevertheless, they struggled to keep afloat during the increasingly competitive interwar period. The 1920s were favourable for Canadian investors but by the early 1930s the trend shifted. Canadian investors struggled to compete against British, German, French, Italian, and U.S. investors who had more capital and were backed by their respective federal governments.

Under such disadvantages, Canadian firms continued to mount pressure on their government. Besides an increasing presence of Spanish- and

Portuguese-speaking trade commissioners, Canadian exporters identified the establishment of direct steamship service, an increasing effort to market the Canadian brand through printed propaganda, and implementation of initiatives to attract young Latin Americans to study in and learn about Canada as key components of an initial Latin American policy.[52] They argued that the presence of Canadian trade commissioners would reduce dependency on British representatives and guarantee negotiations that would favour Canadian interests. Direct steamship service, argued business leaders, would overcome their dependency on American vessels and guarantee that products exported to Central and South America remained labelled as "Made in Canada" and not "Made in USA."[53] Meanwhile the absorption of Latin American students into Canadian universities strengthened the "Canada" brand across the region, since a student educated in Canada would become, "on return to his own country," a first-class promoter of Canadian "goodwill."[54]

These plans were halted by the Great Depression of 1929. None of these issues were addressed during the 1930s, even though the Statute of Westminster (1931) freed the nation to exercise sovereignty over its foreign policy. Local issues prevailed, redirecting the focus of policymakers to provincial relations and the recovery of the domestic economy. Nevertheless, the private sector continued to demand a more active role from its government while pursuing its own independent initiatives across the region.

Canadian companies that carved themselves a niche market across Latin America and the Caribbean during the first four decades of the twentieth century paved the way for new Canadian businesses after the Second World War. These pioneering companies marked an important chapter in Canadian–Latin American and Canadian-Colombian relations, providing alternative market opportunities. Their strategy across the Western Hemisphere created a precedent for understanding how a subordinate state could compete against imperial powers for control of markets and natural resources in the Global South. Such was the case of Canadian banking, insurance, gold mining, and oil extraction in Colombia.

5

Internationalizing Banking and Insurance, 1886–1939

Canadian financial institutions such as Sun Life Assurance Company of Canada, the Manufacturers Life Insurance Company, and the Royal Bank of Canada began to offer their services in Colombia between the late 1890s and the early 1900s. At the time, these companies capitalized on Canada's unregulated financial system, which gave them an advantage over their British and American counterparts. Insurance companies were first-movers in the Colombian market, focusing on its relatively untapped market. Meanwhile banks took advantage of restrictive British and U.S. banking policies and regulations that gave them an "edge over potential rivals" across the Western Hemisphere.[1] Development of these markets provided a solution to Canada's limited domestic market, offering them an opportunity to expand business internationally while building the nation domestically.

During the late 1800s, Canadian financial institutions moved aggressively into the Caribbean market "in order to finance trade with the United States" and tailor to the insurance needs of foreigners operating in the region.[2] The industry's inclusion of Colombia's Caribbean region, as part of its broader Caribbean market, eventually linked the whole hemisphere to Canadian banking and insurance. Upon their arrival in Colombia in the late 1890s, the Manufacturers Life Insurance Company and Sun Life Assurance Company found an antiquated market controlled by a few locally owned businesses such as Compañía Colombiana de Seguros.[3] Meanwhile the Royal Bank of Canada found stronger competition on its arrival in 1920 but was able to make its presence felt as a result of its close relationship with Canadian subsidiaries such as Tropical Oil and the Andian National Corporation.[4]

In both cases, the Colombian market represented a solution to the limitations of the Canadian domestic market.[5] The expansion of Canadian financial institutions across the Western Hemisphere affected the nature of the industry; they became "pioneers," combining domestic retail operations with international branch banking, international trade finance, and insurance services.[6] Their ability to offer domestic and international products made them unique within the industry. Moreover, their products were hard to imitate because they were backed by loose regulatory structures that were unavailable to their competitors.

The Canadian financial institutions that arrived in Colombia between the late 1800s and early 1900s were fully owned by Canadian capital and enjoyed full support of the Canadian government. This allowed Canadian banking and insurance institutions to act independently of Britain and United States. The government's decision not to regulate or control banking and insurance legislation throughout this period allowed these pioneering businesses to preserve their edge over their international competitors. Inaction, in this case, had been the government's way of supporting business expansion overseas.

By the mid-nineteenth century it had been decided among British banking-industry leaders that joint-stock banks would refrain from involvement in foreign business in order to mitigate risk.[7] This forced British banks operating in Latin America to depend on networks of corresponding banks, thus decentralizing power, reducing their decision-making capabilities and their leverage over profit margins. For the United States, the dual regulatory system in itself generated business constraints, but it was the National Bank Act of 1864 that blocked any possibilities for American banks to carry out operations overseas.[8]

Canada opposed the British idea of separating domestic and international operations as a means to reduce risk, as well as the American protectionist approach.[9] Canadian bankers, with the support of their government, were willing to assume the risks of international banking in order to push the national economy forward.

Their international expansion had two objectives: to establish operations overseas to facilitate trade between Canada and the region, assuming a future expansion of Canadian business and investment, and to serve as provider of financial services for U.S. and British interests in the region. Unable to negotiate bills of exchange with their domestic banks, U.S. corporations had to rely on Canadian banks to carry out their international transactions. In Colombia, institutions such as the Royal Bank of Canada became intermediaries for transnational business interests. Corporations such the United Fruit Company became dependent on the Royal Bank for their international transactions. Its service provided foreign clients with much more efficient and cost-effective means of doing business, since every operation was handled through a "single banking network."[10]

Canadian banks were well positioned, at least until the United States deregulated banking through the Federal Reserve Act of 1913. Prior to that, institutions such as the Royal Bank had the power to negotiate the best bills of exchange deal for clients, thanks to its extensive single banking network, which minimized its use and dependence on corresponding banks.[11] They internalized the process of negotiating bills and foreign currency transfers through their own branch networks, which was a particularly convenient service for foreign clients. This was particularly advantageous for American businesses because the Royal Bank had "agencies in New York and other major U.S. cities."[12] Canadian institutions were experienced in dealing "in foreign exchange and financing foreign trade," and more important, their services were "a necessary part of U.S. commerce."[13]

It is therefore no surprise that in the early twentieth century Canadian financial entities responded to the international market's demand for financial services by branching out into emerging markets across Latin America and the Caribbean. In Colombia, for example, they responded to the demands of foreign and domestic interests that welcomed its diversified services. Companies such as the Manufacturers Life Insurance Company and the Royal Bank turned the Colombian market into the entry point to the South American market, thanks to their foreign exchange and financial foreign trade services.[14]

Insurance

Canadian insurance companies were highly competitive within the international system as well, offering unique products and marketing themselves as leaders in product and service development. The Manufacturers Life Insurance Company began to sell policies in Colombia in the late 1890s, followed by the Montreal-based Sun Life Assurance in 1905.[15] The Toronto- and Montreal-based companies centred their business in Cartagena and Barranquilla, taking advantage of the dynamic economy of these two Atlantic port cities. Elites from this region had a more outward view and a "readiness to accept new ideas," marking a clear difference between their liberal ideals and the conservative and isolationist views of the interior parts of Colombia.[16] Local business leaders and policymakers had historically pursued the region's incorporation into the international system, and by the late 1800s they had set out to attract foreign business into the region as part of their regional economic development strategy. The United Fruit Company, for example, was attracted by cheap access to land and labour in the Magdalena region, Cartagena's shipping infrastructure, and Barranquilla's business facilities. British and U.S. mining companies used the main coastal ports to ship gold, while foreign merchants managed their import-export businesses from cities such as Barranquilla. The Atlantic coast was a cosmopolitan region, an epicentre for Colombia's international trade and commerce. From the strategic point of view of international insurance business, it was the perfect place to launch operations.

In 1901 the head office of Manufacturers Life Insurance Company issued a press release stating the company was absorbing Temperance and General Life Insurance, in order to become a stronger player in the international market.[17] Mergers like this became the industry's solution to a deficient small regional agency model, leading to the emergence of nationwide institutions such as Manufacturers Life Insurance.

Their expansion into the Caribbean became feasible thanks to a stronger U.S. military presence in the region that indirectly provided security to a broader international market. The establishment of branches in countries like Jamaica and Colombia was therefore placed "under the umbrella of U.S. imperialism," reinforcing the idea of Canada as a subordinate state that was willing to take advantage of the rapid regional growth in trade and commerce in exchange for greater dependency on the United States.[18]

The Manufacturers Life Insurance Company, like the Royal Bank of Canada, looked overseas to make up for its limited domestic market. In order to become more profitable and reinvest in Canada's economic development, the company needed to underwrite more policies. The Canadian government became a facilitator, preserving lax industry regulations that allowed Canadian companies to be competitive in the international insurance market. Manufacturers Life Insurance executives explained that Canadian insurance laws were advantageous, enabling it "to get foreign business at less cost than its competitors."[19] Buyouts, or what the company called "concentration and amalgamation of financial and other interests," was its objective overseas. The company explained that this was the way in which it would compete effectively in the global market.[20]

Canadian insurance companies willing to expand overseas benefited from pro-business federal policies. For instance the government set aside a reserve to ensure that policyholders were paid, providing guarantees that no other international competitor could offer.[21] They approved a three million dollar reserve "for the protection of policyholders," which was unheard of in the industry. With this advantage, insurance companies such as Manufacturers launched themselves with confidence into the West Indies and Colombian markets.[22]

Commonwealth Caribbean markets were the first to be targeted by Manufacturers Life Insurance Company. By 1896, the company had established a branch office in Kingston, Jamaica, under the management of Ivanhoe Gadpaille, while South American operations were assigned to William E. Young.[23] The Colombian market was initially tapped by Young, who tailored Manufacturers business to the needs of educated elites who understood the benefits of the financial product. He also sought high-level executives and professionals from Canada, Europe, and the United States who resided in Colombia and were interested in protecting their family assets from the dangers of the rugged, wild, and untamed tropics.

Manufacturers, like all other foreign financial institutions operating throughout the Americas, understood that business success could be achieved only if regional elites were targeted, since the masses (the popular class) did not represent a profitable market as it did in Canada. Concepts tailored to the U.S. and Canadian markets such as savings and retirement planning were introduced to Colombia's elites. Basic financial planning was introduced by manufacturers, marketing ideas such as "It is not what you earn but what you save that counts," or "How easy it is to save by means of Life Insurance."[24]

Upon its arrival, the Canadian company found it challenging to compete against several local and foreign-owned insurance companies, particularly because they had physical offices in Colombia and did not rely on the regional representative model for business expansion. The competitors' long-standing acquaintance with coastal elites also gave them an edge over Manufacturers. Nevertheless, as a government-backed product, Manufacturers had an advantage over its competitors and slowly took over a share of the local insurance market. Canadian insurance companies also benefited from the anti-U.S. sentiment of the early 1900s as well as Britain's declining influence in the region after the First World War.

Another Canadian insurance company that entered the Colombian market at around the same time was Sun Life Assurance Company. The beginning of its operations in the Colombian Caribbean were established through the company's Western Department in 1905. They were part of a market expansion strategy across Latin America that resulted from the success of the Northern and Central British West Indies operation.[25]

Sun Life Assurance capitalized on the anti-U.S. sentiment that kept American insurance companies out of Colombia, as well as on the highly regulated British insurance market. The Canadian insurance company also benefited from the 1906 state legislation in the United States that limited the amount of new business "which New York–based life insurance companies could write," forcing U.S. companies such as Equitable

Life Assurance Society and New York Life Insurance Company to abandon their Caribbean and South American operations.[26]

Sun Life entered the Colombian Caribbean market offering an "unconditional policy," a product that trumped the efforts of all other competitors in the market.[27] In essence, the product made life insurance products accessible to anyone without restrictions, including the selectivity of risk.[28] By the time it entered the Latin American market, Sun Life "had an individuality and a character which distinguished it from all rivals; in respect to the terms of the contracts it offered it was indeed in a class of itself."[29]

Cartagena and Barranquilla represented prospective high-volume, low-cost markets in a "new and almost non-competitive field" where other domestic and foreign competitors had to assume greater risks.[30] Nevertheless, these were unfamiliar territories for Canadian businessmen. The dangers that stereotypically characterized the tropics at the time provided Sun Life executives with an opportunity to adapt insurance products to the challenges of the market. Although preserving the "unconditional policy," the company established premium tables for the tropical region based on available mortality statistics and other contingencies.[31] All tropical markets, including Colombia's, were considered a special class in and of itself.[32]

Colombia's unregulated financial market allowed Sun Life Assurance to define the costs and the characteristics of the products offered to locals, based on the firm's own interpretation of the risks of doing business in Colombia, a country that, as an American traveller put it, "was indeed weird and wild."[33] Risks had to be measured differently in a country where, for example, the child of a foreign oil worker "was swallowed by an alligator," where the jungles were infested with "snakes, tigers, monkeys and insects," and where lepers and victims of smallpox "walked the streets of inland cities without restriction."[34]

The unregulated market allowed Sun Life to protect its foreign operations from the high risks of international investment. The Canadian company mandated that foreign business be self-supporting and not financed or supported by domestic premiums; therefore, business risks were assumed by each Latin American office, tailoring policies to the particular needs and perils of each case.[35]

Sun Life also benefited from the failed attempts of several U.S. insurance companies. In 1922, American-owned Equitable Life Assurance Society reinsured its Colombian policies with Sun Life, and in 1923 New York Life Insurance Company followed suit.[36] By 1927 Sun Life Assurance had expanded its operations to include a broad share of the international market.[37] Its foreign markets were so important that the president recognized that Canada's market share of total profits was less than 10 per cent and concluded that although profits were "being earned by Canadian brains and Canadian enterprise," foreign premiums were the driving force behind the company's success.[38]

Sun Life took advantage of Colombia's 1920s "dance of the millions."[39] It generated business from the inflow of capital that stemmed from Washington's 1921 reparation payment to Colombia for the loss of Panama and the increasing flow of U.S. private investment into the Colombian economy.[40] Colombia was open for business, and Canadian financial institutions were well placed to capitalize on the nation's economic boom of the interwar period.

The presence of U.S. companies and Canadian subsidiaries such as Tropical Oil and Andian National Corporation turned the Colombian Caribbean into an attractive insurance market. Cartagena and Barranquilla became important business hubs for Sun Life Assurance. Cartagena, the historic port city, became a desired destination for Canadian winter cruises that sailed the Caribbean. The city's tourist industry became an important market for foreign companies such as Sun Life; it offered a concentrated core of traditional wealth, an emerging merchant class, and a strong presence of foreigners that tailored to the needs of a growing tourist industry.[41]

By 1930 three foreign-owned companies controlled close to 54 per cent of Colombia's insurance market: Sun Life's policies represented half of this share, and the rest was split between Manufacturers Life and New Orleans–based Pan American Life Insurance Company.[42] By then, the Colombian life insurance market was, for the most part, underwritten by Canadian companies.

The success was short-lived, as the Great Depression forced President Enrique Olaya Herrera to implement a series of nationalist policies that conflicted with the interests of foreign companies operating in Colombia. Protectionist policies such "as placing the oil industry under government regulation" sent a negative message to Canadian insurance companies that quickly re-evaluated their strategy in Colombia.[43] Additionally, the fine-tuning of risk evaluation that resulted from the outcomes of the First World War led Sun Life and Manufacturers to revise their position in the Western Hemisphere. In the 1930s, for example, Sun Life Assurance of Canada opened no new offices in the region and instead closed thirteen. "It withdrew from underwriting insurance in Chile, Colombia, El Salvador, Dutch Guiana (Surinam), French Guiana, Honduras, Mexico, Nicaragua, and Peru," leaving the market open for U.S. and local insurance companies.[44]

This did not impede the company from growing its insurance business elsewhere. President T.B. Macaulay reported shareholder gains "of more than $36,000,000 in assets" for 1931, highlighting the possibility of expanding business to the recovering North American market.[45] Canadian insurance companies had changed their strategy, retracting from Latin America and concentrating on the Canadian and American middle class.

Latin America was no longer an attractive market as a result of the rise of protectionism across the region. In Colombia, nationalist policies threatened foreign business interests, and the possibility of social unrest and political instability increased risk for insurance companies. After the 1930s Colombia had become politically unstable once again, as the internal debates over sovereignty, protectionism, and nationalism escalated.

Almost thirty years passed before Sun Life and other insurance institutions reconsidered returning to the Colombian market. The political pact between conservatives and liberals, known as the Frente Nacional (1958–74), served as a means to regain the confidence of foreign investors in the Colombian market.[46] Similar trajectories were experienced by Canadian banks that entered the Colombian market in the early 1900s.

Banking

Canadian banks could penetrate the Latin American and Caribbean markets for two main reasons: the support they received from their federal government, and the banking leaders' knowledge about the changing dynamics of geopolitical power in the region. The Canadian government was "instrumental in creating a protected market, in which banks could develop competitive strengths," providing a "cornerstone for international growth strategies."[47] Meanwhile, industry leaders such as former Royal Bank president Sir Herbert Holt were instrumental in helping Canadian institutions navigate the murky waters of the struggle for imperial power in the Western Hemisphere. The bank aggressively entered the Colombian market in 1920 with the objective of carrying out branch banking operations across the country, and was able to remain competitive for the next forty years. In the 1960s, Royal Bank began to experiment with investment banking through consortium banking strategies, following the footsteps of the Bank of London and Montreal, that entered the Colombian market with mixed banking products in the late 1950s.[48]

In the early twentieth century, institutions such as the Royal Bank received Ottawa's approval to expand beyond its national borders, unleashing international banking operations that "boomed in the 1920s, assisted directly and indirectly by provincial and federal governments that were eager to facilitate the country's expansion."[49] The efforts of the Royal Bank of Canada, Bank of Nova Scotia, and Bank of Montreal contributed to Canada's rapid economic development of the 1920s, aided by increased federal powers that orchestrated economic production and a centralized banking policy in Ottawa.[50]

Ottawa implemented flexible and more progressive banking governance to ensure that banking contributed to economic development and nation-building. Policymakers established a stable industry that encouraged the inward flow of capital, therefore choosing "chartered banks as the dominant financial institution in Canada."[51] Contrary to other industries, banking became a Canadian-controlled industry designed to facilitate provincial and international trade; its infrastructure was intended to assist government financing.[52]

In the absence of diplomatic or consular presence in the region, Canadian policymakers and business leaders envisioned banks operating as intermediaries between Canadian interests and local Latin American and Caribbean markets. It was not such a far-fetched idea: the British institutions operated in this fashion and the U.S. banking industry was slowly moving in the same direction. At the 1915 Pan-American Financial Conference in Washington, U.S. delegates revealed their interest in tapping the financial markets of peripheral nations such as Colombia, where there was no real foreign banking presence.[53] Chairman of the Ethelburga Syndicate, Otto H. Fuerth, recommended to U.S. delegates at the conference that, when the time came, their banking institutions should not act only as bankers, but also "as commercial agents and as reporting centers on credit, financial and other conditions."[54]

Canadian banks moved into the region with this idea in mind. By 1916, one year after the Pan-American Financial Conference, the Royal Bank of Canada had opened branch operations in Cuba, Costa Rica, the Dominican Republic, and Venezuela.[55] That year Holt visited Cuba, Puerto Rico, Santo Domingo, Costa Rica, and the British West Indies to familiarize himself "with local conditions and to meet ... leading customers."[56] He also visited Venezuela, where the bank had recently opened its first branch, and stopped in Colombia to discuss with local authorities and the British government the possibilities of opening branch offices there as well.[57] Soon after, at the bank's annual meeting, he reported to shareholders that "he was gratified to receive from Viscount Grey, the late [British] Foreign Secretary, his approval of the establishment of branches" in Colombia.[58]

By the end of the First World War, the Royal Bank of Canada was well positioned across the Western Hemisphere. The bank profited from Holt's understanding of the region; not only was he familiar with the geopolitical realities and the business culture, he also understood the importance of taking advantage of the opportunity for Canadian banks to compete shoulder-to-shoulder with U.S., British, and other European counterparts.

The war had forced Latin American and Caribbean economies to diversify their pool of foreign investors, bringing them closer to Canada. It provided a chance for Canadians to displace European banks from the region and, according to Holt, it had revealed to Canadians their "economic power" and the possibilities of expanding their presence in the Americas.[59] Royal Bank's success stimulated other Canadian businesses to take on more risk across the region.

By 1920, when the bank first began operations in Colombia, it provided services including personal and intermediary banking with Canada, Europe, and the United States, through its vast branch network.[60] This was crucial, because most European-owned banks operating in Colombia had left as a result of the war, while American banks were deterred not only by their own federal regulatory structures but also by the anti-American sentiment generated by the U.S. Senate's inability to approve a reparation payment to Colombia for U.S. involvement in the separation of Panama.[61]

The Royal Bank of Canada filled the gap left by foreign competitors and satisfied the demand of local and foreign businesses for intermediary banking services. U.S. companies became dependent on its services throughout the interwar years in the absence of their own national branch networks. The U.S. Department of Commerce's 1915 report *Banking Opportunities in South America* pointed out this deficiency and indicated that West Virginia's Continental Banking and Trust Company had intentions of establishing "a branch at Santa Marta" to accommodate the needs of the United Fruit Company, together with the Mercantile Bank of the Americas, which planned to aggressively extend branch operations across Colombia, Venezuela, Ecuador, Peru, and Central America.[62] The snail's pace at which American banks reacted to the Department of Commerce's initiative provided Royal Bank with a chance to control the Colombian market throughout the 1920s. It took almost a decade before any of these initiatives solidified.

Nevertheless, Herbert Holt became concerned with the September 1922 announcement that the U.S.-owned Bank of Central and South America had taken over all branch operations of Mercantile Bank of the Americas in Central and South America.[63] This meant that National Bank of

Nicaragua, Banco Mercantil de Costa Rica, Banco Mercantil Americano del Peru, Banco Mercantil Americano de Caracas, and Banco Mercantil Americano de Colombia were now controlled by U.S. interests.[64] With British banks out of the picture, all seemed to indicate that the Royal Bank would go head-to-head with U.S. financial and banking interests in Colombia. American businesses believed that U.S. banks rather than Canadian institutions should serve their needs, but Holt believed that Canadian financial institutions should service Canadian subsidiaries.

Holt, who had a particular affinity for Venezuela and Colombia, never gave up the fight for the control of these newly developed markets. He demanded greater government support in order to help the company hold its position in Colombia. There was much to be gained for the Canadian economy and its manufacturing sector, if only they could preserve their influence in the Colombian economy. The 1925 bank report indicated that there were "few storehouses of untouched and unmeasured wealth to compare with the resources that remain to be developed in the Republic of Colombia."[65] This, speculated Holt, was a strategic market for Canadian business interests.

Colombia was a diamond in the rough and many Colombians were not aware of it. The 1925 report highlighted that the nation's international debt of close to twenty-two million dollars was not a significant figure and that the banking industry was sound, thanks to the establishment "of the central reserve bank modelled after the Federal Reserve system."[66] Rapid economic development, said the report, had not been achieved because of the limited development of land transportation and other infrastructure facilities.[67] Developing these sectors would catapult the Colombian market into the international market system and Canada would be well positioned to take advantage of this transition, as a first-mover.

There were signs that the country's economic development program was moving in the right direction. The report indicated that German development of the commercial hydroplane industry represented a step forward, but that a railroad system was needed in order to unify the country's economy.[68] Royal Bank could capitalize on this opportunity by financing the project, but for now it was content with servicing the needs of the United Fruit Company, the German-owned Sociedad Colombo-Alemana de Transportes Aéreos (SCADTA), and other foreign interests.

Herbert Holt insisted on defending the company's interests in Colombia. In efforts to control what he referred to as "the vast stretches about which little is known and the possibilities of which have been only vaguely suggested," the Royal Bank went a step further and absorbed an American bank that had recently entered the Colombian market.[69] In February 1925 the bank "purchased all of the shares of the Bank of Central and South America," thereby expanding its outreach in Colombia and Latin America.[70] The Bank of Central and South America, which had been in the market for only three years, found itself in financial trouble and unable to successfully carry out business in Latin America. Holt relished the opportunity to establish greater distance between the United States and the Royal Bank in the region by buying American interests in Colombia. He incorporated the branches of the Bank of Central and South America into his branch network, solidifying its position in the Colombian market.[71]

The Canadian institution had, by that point, been singled out as "one of the largest competitors of American banks doing business in Latin America."[72] It became even more evident after Holt's decision to absorb seventeen additional branches in the region.[73] In 1927 the bank once again registered record growth. Holt's report to the board of directors indicated that it represented "the most successful year in the history of the bank."[74] Like the president of Sun Life Assurance, Holt credited a large part of the growth to its operations in Latin America and the Caribbean.[75]

The Royal Bank of Canada continued to dominate international banking operations in Colombia throughout the interwar years, strengthening Canadian-Colombian relations. Its operations became more interconnected with the Colombian economy as the bank began to service the needs of Canadian gold-mining and oil-extraction subsidiaries. Ultimately, the bank would manage all international financial operations linked to oil and gold mining in Colombia.

The bank's success was interrupted by the outbreak of the Second World War. The industry's reorientation toward a war economy and the presence of German U-boats in the Caribbean forced the bank to re-evaluate its strategy in Colombia and the rest of the region. Although it did not close its branch operation, it did retract from further expansion, allowing banks from the United States to challenge the Royal Bank's position in several strategic markets.

After the war, the Royal Bank began to reclaim its position in the Latin American and Caribbean markets, but it found stiff competition from U.S. institutions that had inundated the market throughout the war. The inflow of American capital after the Second World War, Washington's vigilance over its emerging sphere of influence, a return to a locally controlled domestic financial market, and a decreasing presence of Canadian businesses diminished the bank's ability to retake the market.[76] Americans had capitalized on Canada's reorientation toward a war economy.

Professor Edwin Walter Kemmerer's mission to Colombia in 1923, at the request of the Pedro Nel Ospina's administration, had marked the beginning of the U.S. takeover of Colombia's financial markets.[77] Implementation of his economic development policies had sent a clear message to foreign competitors, such as the Royal Bank, that eventually they would have to adapt to new market realities that centred international lending in Wall Street and placed the region's economic development in the hands of American interests.

Kemmerer's second mission in 1930 accommodated Colombia's budget, tax, banking, customs, and public credits systems to the needs of the American banking system.[78] In 1931 President Olaya Herrera announced that an American banking group headed by the National City Bank of New York, the First National Bank of Boston, and the Continental of Illinois was providing loans for Colombia's regional economic development.[79] In 1936 the Bank of London and South America announced the takeover of the Anglo South American Bank, giving it a stronger presence in Colombia and other parts of Latin America.[80] By the late 1940s, American banks were well positioned in Colombia and across the Americas.

After the war, the Colombian economy "expanded so rapidly" that it outstripped its banking capacity to keep pace with its financial requirements.[81] Colombian bankers and government officials turned to the United States for venture capital and other investment possibilities. U.S. banks and post-war multilateral lending agencies such as the International Bank for Reconstruction and Development (IBRD) became driving forces behind the nation's economic development, leaving behind a once close and interdependent relationship with the Royal Bank of Canada. The bank's operations in Colombia declined as U.S. interests took over. In 1948 the bank closed its branch operations in Cali, followed by other branches that were taken over by Colombia's Banco de Bogotá.[82]

Canadian financial institutions left their mark on the Colombian, Latin American, and Caribbean markets. Although their presence declined after the Second World War, they left solid foundations on which other Canadian companies built their entry strategies into the Colombian market. The financial institutions strengthened the organizational capabilities of Canadian oil subsidiaries and mining operations. They also made it possible for other Canadian businesses to effectively navigate Colombia's legal and political system. Nevertheless, it became clear that, because Canada was a subordinate state, Canadian businesses had to strategize around windows of opportunity provided by the market in order to act as first-movers, filling market gaps before American businesses reacted. Such was the case of Canadian oil subsidiaries operating in Colombia during the first half of the twentieth century.

6

Tropical Oil and the Andian National
Corporation, 1918–1945

Nineteen-thirteen was a very active year for foreign diplomats and foreign private sector representatives visiting Colombia. Rafael Reyes's (1904–9) free market reforms were attracting foreign investment and so was the nation's political, economic, and social stability. That year Canadian Trade Commissioner Rivington Poussette travelled to Bogotá in search of trade opportunities for Canadian products. At around the same time, American envoys also visited the Colombian capital to scrutinize oil concession negotiations between the British firm Pearson and Son and the Colombian government. Canadian business interests were looking for market gaps to fill, while the British and Americans were beginning their dispute over control of Colombia's oil.

The rumour of the presence of high-quality oil in Colombia during the early twentieth century attracted foreign investors, who knew well that it was an unclaimed resource. Foreign engineers and other members of expedition companies venturing into the "oil jungles of Colombia" described a surreal world where "oil, nearly as fine as gasoline," was seen flowing effortlessly from the ground.[1]

Canadian, British, and U.S. private interests were eager to get their hands on this fine oil. The Mexican Revolution and the nationalization of oil that followed had destabilized the flow of international oil, causing a crude oil shortage in the global economy, as more and more nations shifted toward an oil-based economy. There was increasing demand in Latin America and the Caribbean, the U.S. government and domestic producers were playing with the idea of regulating production, and Canadian companies such as Imperial Oil had not tapped enough domestic oil to supply their own domestic market. British, Dutch, U.S., and Canadian interests had therefore looked south for relief, finding in Colombia, Venezuela, and Peru potential solutions to the scarcity problem.[2]

Capitalizing on the anti-American sentiment of the time, British interests mobilized their promotional state in Colombia in order to secure the De Mares concession for themselves.[3] The American promotional state, on the other hand, used as leverage the reparation payment to Colombia from the 1903 Panamanian independence incidents as a means to negotiate a deal on behalf of Standard Oil of New Jersey, but Colombian nationalists made it difficult for the American company to enter the Colombian market. Eventually, the American company opted to strategically rely on the Canadian "goodwill," using a Canadian subsidiary, Tropical Oil, as a means to overcome the negative propaganda and secure the concession, even though the British offer was initially favoured.[4]

British investor Weetman Pearson positioned himself in the Colombian market in 1913 after President Carlos Restrepo's (1910–14) administration and the Colombian Congress passed pro–free market legislation that established that the "owner of surface land was also the owner of its subsoil."[5] Ownership of resources found in foreign subsoil became very attractive to international investors, particularly for those who had invested in Mexican oil extraction and now found themselves under threat of nationalization of oil resources as a result of the Mexican Revolution.

Weetman Pearson was also aware that local efforts to extract oil had failed for lack of capital, "know-how," and access to technology, and that the Colombian government was desperate to tap the resource in order to generate revenues to fund national economic development. He organized a team to negotiate the rights to oil concessions with the Colombian government, confident that Colombia's interest would counterbalance nationalist initiatives in Mexico.

Pearson and Son sent Lord Alexander Murray of Elibank and Martin Robin to Colombia to negotiate a deal with the Colombian government and secure the De Mares concession. Meanwhile explorations headed by U.S. and Canadian engineers continued along the Magdalena basin, challenging British interests in the region.

Standard Oil of New Jersey was determined to control development of oil extraction in Colombia and other parts of South America. The company was facing crude oil supply shortage as a result of a dissolution decree imposed on them by the U.S. government for violation of the Sherman Act of 1911, which prevented them from developing an oil monopoly. The company was forced to restructure its organization and give up some of its crude oil sources, leaving them with no other option but to seek alternative supply sources in the international market. Left with a substantial refining capacity and a shortage of crude oil reserves, the company ventured south, taking advantage of the experience and technological "know-how" of its Canadian subsidiary, Imperial Oil Company.[6] On the other hand, the Canadian subsidiary was eager to find oil for its own domestic market after failing to find significant reserves in its own territory.

Standard Oil of New Jersey responded to Pearson and Son's initiatives and to the aggressive regional initiatives of its Dutch competitor, Shell, through Imperial Oil's international exploration initiatives via their subsidiary, International Petroleum (IP), which by then was surveying vast acreages in Peru and Colombia. Meanwhile Pittsburgh-based Transcontinental Oil Company was moving aggressively as well, purchasing close to 900,000 acres of potential oil fields in Colombia.[7]

The world's conversion into an oil-based market turned the region into contested territory throughout the interwar period. The legal and political struggle over Colombia's oil revealed Britain's decaying influence across the region, as Pearson and Son struggled to close a deal with the Colombian government.[8]

In desperation, the British reached out to former president Rafael Reyes, offering him monetary compensation, in hopes that he could intervene on the company's behalf, but the effort backfired. Instead, one of Reyes's sons approached Chester Thompson, Standard Oil of New Jersey's representative, and recommended the creation of "a Canadian company (to avoid anti-American feelings) and submit an oil contract to the Colombian government."[9]

A second British offer resulted in a deal that made it all the way to Colombia's Congress. U.S. Ambassador Leland Harrison "reported to the U.S. Department of State that the contract did not represent a threat," but Standard did not share the same view and sent its own negotiators to block congressional approval.[10] After numerous attacks by the United States to denigrate the British firm in local media, and after launching legal challenges within the Colombian judicial system, the Colombian Supreme Court declared the contract legal on 25 June 1913 and returned it to Congress for approval.[11]

In July, the contract passed the first congressional hearing.[12] Although Congress members were sceptical about the decision, members of the commission appointed to study the oil concession concluded that "the project merited approval because of the jobs that would be created and the boost it would give the economy."[13] Even the nationalists, who initially disagreed with the idea of awarding more national territory and resources to foreign corporations, joined the consensus that the nation would be better off placing oil extraction and infrastructure development in the hands of the highest private bidder, in hopes that the power struggle between British and American interests would result in a better deal for Colombia.[14]

President Woodrow Wilson's administration was not willing to let Pearson and Son outperform the American company at the negotiating table. The British tried to use the anti-American card to their advantage, but the American government-business partnership responded by reminding Colombia about the principles of the Monroe Doctrine and the importance of protecting the Pan American Union. Wilson declared "he would oppose any attempt by foreign companies to control the economies and policies of poor countries eager to garner capital for modernization."[15]

The efforts of the American government-business partnership prevented British interests from moving closer to an oil deal, setting a precedent for what would unfold during the interwar years in Colombia and across the Americas. They used Colombia as the launching ground for a hemispheric anti-European campaign, while at the same time securing foreign oil, through a Canadian subsidiary, for their own self-interest.

The issue of reparation payments for the loss of Panama eventually became the key negotiating point for oil concessions and the reason why Pearson and Son failed to take over the oil concession. President Wilson recognized that they needed to settle the reparation payment with Colombia over Panama's independence, particularly if they wanted to keep European business interests away from its sphere of influence and win the hearts and minds of Colombians.

President Restrepo's administration was eager to lobby Washington for a favourable reparation payment and used Pearson and Son's initiative to pressure Washington. The Wilson administration responded by tying the reparation payment to an impending cancelation of the Pearson and Son contract.[16] By the end of September, U.S. Secretary of State Bryan sent a strong message to Restrepo stressing that "the U.S. Government was not indifferent to the proposed concession to Pearson," that, in principle, the United States disagreed with concessions to European governments, and that they hoped that British interference did not delay their oil negotiations.[17]

On 24 November 1913, Pearson and Son withdrew the contract, blaming the U.S. government and saying they were "used as pawns in Panama negotiations."[18] They claimed that they had been accused unfairly of being a monopolistic venture and a threat to the Monroe Doctrine.[19] The door was left wide open for Standard Oil to carry out its initiatives in Colombia, via the Canadian subsidiary, Tropical Oil. According to the British, the Americans had conquered their "newest Latin American aspirations."[20] Nevertheless, it was a victory whose celebration had to wait, for the First World War soon engulfed the world. The American company was forced to stall its initiatives in Colombia until after the war.

During the early stages of the interwar period, U.S. speculators George Crawford, Joseph Trees, and Michael Benedum established the Tropical Oil Company of Oklahoma, with their eyes set on "the oil scented land" of Barrancabermeja, Colombia.[21] Desperate to extract Colombian oil and put the British-U.S. scandal behind, José Vicente Concha's administration (1914–18) awarded Canada's Tropical Oil Company the De Mares concession in 1918.[22]

After overcoming the challenges of the humid tropical terrain of the Barrancabermeja region, Tropical Oil reported its first considerable oil discovery.[23] This encouraged the Vicente Concha administration to develop a comprehensive petroleum law that was initially tainted with nationalism. The policy, inspired by the Mexican Revolution, included increased taxation, higher royalties, a thirty-year limit on concessions, and a provision that declared "the subsoil the property of the state for both public and private lands."[24]

Standard, which was eager to return to negotiations with the Colombian government, disliked the nationalist policy and once again leaned on its government in order to bring back the issue of reparation payments as a means to force a change in policy. The American government-business partnership took advantage of the change of government and pressured the Marco Fidel Suárez administration (1918–21) to change the policy that they had inherited from the previous administration, once again using the reparation payment as leverage.

In 1920, the pro-American Suárez decided in favour of Standard and overturned Vicente Concha's nationalist oil policy. That year the Colombian Supreme Court declared the nationalist legislation unconstitutional, and one year later the U.S. Congress approved the US$25 million reparation payment to Colombia. A chapter in Colombia-U.S. relations had been closed and a new chapter had started, one that included Canadian oil subsidiaries in Colombia.

La Troco

During the winter of 1919 negotiations were concluded between Tropical and Standard Oil executives, awarding control of the De Mares concession to the Canadian subsidiary. Standard executives agreed that Imperial Oil's subsidiary, International Petroleum Company (IPC), would take over Tropical Oil, leaving the richest of all oilfields in Colombia in the hands of Canadians.[25] After the confrontation between British and U.S. interests, Canadians ended up carrying out the exploration, development, transportation, and expansion of Colombia's oil industry. Tropical Oil took over extraction, while Andian National Corporation Limited, another Canadian affiliate of Imperial Oil, took over pipeline construction projects that connected the Barrancabermeja oilfield to the exporting facilities in Cartagena.

"La Troco," as Tropical Oil was locally referred to, was allowed some decision-making autonomy that allowed it to build a direct oil link between Canada and Colombia throughout the interwar years. Canada's transition to an oil-based economy would be initially fuelled by Colombian and Peruvian oil.

Imperial Oil was the largest integrated oil company in Canada, and at the same time it represented a "symbol of foreign domination of Canada's economy."[26] The Canadian side of Imperial "was little more than a legally distinct entity … controlled by Standard Oil," but in South America it functioned as an integrated organization "with expanded refining capacity … an enlarged capital base" and a growing supply of crude oil.[27]

Tropical Oil assumed a relatively independent role as a subsidiary, thanks to the efforts of Walter Teagle, who engineered an active role for the company in Colombia and for IPC in South America. Imperial's operations in Peru, Colombia, and Venezuela became essential for Standard's overall supply of crude oil, particularly after failed attempts in the 1920s to produce oil in Canada. Standard initially supplied Canada's demand for oil through its Canadian subsidiaries in South America. Canada became an important market for Standard's oil as well as for fiscal interests.

Imperial represented a tax haven for Standard's operations in Latin America. By operating under IPC, the American company enjoyed the "safety of a legally external domicile with physical proximity to 26 Broadway."[28] Teagle's operation also "proved to be a handy surrogate, enabling Jersey Standard to circumvent anti-American sentiments in Colombia," and allowing the oil operation to hide behind the Canadian "goodwill."[29]

Under Teagle, Imperial Oil served not only the interests of Standard Oil of New Jersey but those of Canada as well. This was evident in his management of the Colombia, Peru, and Venezuela operations. He advocated for Canadian local autonomy in domestic operations and marketing.[30] He intervened in favour of Imperial, defending Canadian markets and operations from other Standard New Jersey units, and he enlarged Canada's refining capacity by channelling more of the South American oil his way. Imperial's operations in Colombia facilitated the expansion of bilateral trade, redirecting more of the Barrancabermeja oil to Canada for refinement and distribution.

The bilateral exchange continued to expand throughout the interwar years. By 1938, Colombia represented "the largest Latin American supplier of Canada's imports … eighth among all sources of imports."[31] Throughout the 1930s, petroleum accounted for more than half the total imports from both Colombia and Latin America. By the time the Second World War started, 60 per cent of Canadian imports from Latin America were oil related, most coming from the operations of La Troco in Colombia.[32]

The success of the De Mares concession resulted in greater Colombian petroleum exports to North America. Between 1938 and 1944, imports from Colombia entering the Canadian market topped the list of Latin American imports, thanks to increasing demand for both oil and coffee.[33] Canada's development of an oil-based economy became dependent on Latin American oil.

Imperial's failure to produce sufficient oil inside Canadian territory during the early 1920s forced it to concentrate its efforts on its operations in Peru, Colombia, and later Venezuela. In 1923, C.O. Stillman, president of Imperial Oil, said that he "had not given up hope of developing a large oil field in Canada" but that for now, the company's operations in South America counterbalanced "the absence of success in Canada."[34] Peru, Colombia, and Venezuela had the comparative advantage.

La Troco's operation helped Canada's oil-driven economic engine take off during the interwar years. In part, Colombian oil fuelled Canada's economic development; its "oilfields proved to be more productive than the Canadian ones," plus the Colombian government was more open to the expansion of oil investments "than the government of Canada."[35]

There were high expectations in Colombia and the international oil market because of the quality and amount of deposits available for extraction. By 1921, when exports first began, the Barrancabermeja operation was "considered the most prolific in the world."[36] Experts in the field even predicted then that South America, and particularly Colombia, would eventually become the key source of supply to the North American market.[37]

It is no wonder why Standard Oil of New Jersey had secured operations in South America. Under the leadership of Walter Teagle, its Canadian subsidiary became an important player in the international oil market, as the South American operations proved to be the real deal, and it was under the leadership of G. Harrison Smith that Colombia's operation became a key component of the company's vertical integration strategy.[38]

Throughout the 1920s Imperial's president, G. Harrison Smith, opted to increase its presence in Colombia because he believed it was a pivotal market for regional expansionism. In 1922 Tropical Oil had been able to refine an average of only 600 barrels per day, but production quickly picked up, reaching an average of 2,600 barrels per day in 1932.[39] A quadruple increase in production more than convinced Smith and his bosses at Standard Oil that the Barrancabermeja operation was a key business priority.

Smith's reliance on the Colombian operation paid off, and soon his reputation led some in the Canadian media to refer to him as the "uncrowned oil king of Latin America."[40] Imperial's operations in Colombia and Peru represented "Canadian courage … ability and … patriotism," turning Smith into the miracle worker who turned an impoverished nation into a "major oil producer."[41] Canada's "good-will" became ingrained in Smith's success.

Tropical Oil capitalized on weak regulatory legislation and a high demand for export revenues. It took advantage of the business climate of the time, in order to develop both exports and internal markets. By 1923 La Troco had established a strong extraction operation, an export market, and a domestic market with "sales agencies in the principal cities" for the distribution of refinery products.[42] Thanks to Imperial's subsidiary, the Colombian economy was well on its way to becoming not only an oil exporter but an oil-based economy as well.

In 1923, 13,339,627 barrels of South American oil entered the Canadian market.[43] Unrefined oil left the South American ports, was then refined by Imperial Oil in Canadian territory, and eventually distributed to the Canadian consumers. Thirty per cent of that total corresponded to La Troco's production in Colombia.[44] By 1924, oil exports from Barrancabermeja reached 425,000 barrels and experienced a tremendous jump after completion of the pipeline, reaching 13,674,478 barrels in 1927.[45] La Troco was well on its way to monopolizing Colombia's oil production. In 1930, oil exports reached 19,113,106 barrels, from which 99 percent belonged to La Troco.[46]

Completion of the Barrancabermeja-Cartagena pipeline infrastructure in 1926 took the Colombian operation to another level. The Andian National Corporation, another Imperial Oil subsidiary, became another key stakeholder in the development of Colombia's oil industry, leaving a mark in the country's Atlantic region through the construction and development of hundreds of miles of pipeline, as well as a company town in Cartagena.[47]

The Andian National Corporation began construction of the 500-mile pipeline in 1925, following the path of the Magdalena River to its mouth in the Caribbean.[48] As part of Imperial's vertical integration, Andian National became responsible for unleashing the true capabilities of the De Mares concession, whose more than twenty wells had been "completed and capped for lack of transportation facilities."[49] Andian's completion of the infrastructure in 1926 opened the gates for expansion of Colombia's oil export industry. That same year, production jumped more than 290 per cent.[50] The vertical production chain had been completed, beginning in Barrancabermeja, passing through Cartagena, exported to Canadian refineries, and ultimately reaching the Canadian consumer. Oil extraction and exports had consolidated the Canadian-Colombian connection.

The expansion of the export market paralleled the increase in domestic sales. Construction of road infrastructure accompanied growth of the automobile market and other gasoline-based transportation industries that boosted domestic sales. Local sales increased 65 per cent by 1926, a clear indicator that Colombia's society was quickly moving toward an oil-based economy. The Colombian operation was so successful that by 1927 it had surpassed production levels of IPC's operation in Peru.[51]

Andian National Corporation was forced to develop new infrastructure to increase its transportation capacity, as production at Barrancabermeja increased in response to increasing international demand, particularly Canada's. By then it was clear to investors that the Barrancabermeja complex and the Andian National pipeline were the top priority of Imperial's operations in Latin America. Colombia would remain the key South American market throughout the interwar years. The rising industry generated pride as well as distrust among Colombians.

Colombian nationalists, labour organizers, workers, socialists, and communists wanted to see the increase in oil exports reflected in the improvement of social conditions for Colombians. They argued that Colombians were not getting a fair deal from the benefits of the oil boom; Tropical Oil's success was not trickling down. A series of labour strikes that extended from 1927 into the late 1940s revealed popular discontent against La Troco.[52] The decision of President Miguel Abadía Mendez (1926–30) to use the national police and the country's military force against its own people confirmed the leftist argument that the government was willing to go to any length to protect the interests of the American company. To Canadian engineers, executives, and others working in Colombia, it revealed the benefits of being under the U.S. imperialist umbrella. The domestic impact of La Troco symbolized Canada's role as a subordinate power and its functionality within the macro-expansion of global capitalism.

The lack of accountability of foreign companies such as La Troco became a key item on the agenda of Colombia's political Left. This gave rise to the nationalist administration of Alfonso López Pumarejo (1934–8), which pushed for revision of the oil royalty policy set back in the 1920s. Among other things, he demanded a greater share of revenues for the Colombian economy. The 10:90 per cent ratio that favoured the Canadian subsidiary was not a good deal for Colombians, considering that nations like Mexico were capitalizing on 100 per cent of their oil revenues. The nationalist initiative and the beginning of the Second World War eventually shifted the direction of Canadian-Colombian relations.

By 1938 Canada was a significant market for Colombia's oil exports, and Colombia had become the top Latin American exporter to Canada.[53] Throughout the 1930s, petroleum accounted for more than half of total imports from Latin America, and Colombia topped the Latin American supply market, eclipsing IPC's operations in Venezuela and Peru. By the beginning of the Second World War, Canada increased its demand for oil, improving Colombia's market share even more. This pattern changed as the Second World War progressed and the Caribbean became a target of German U-boats.

Domestic negotiations over royalties, efforts to expand the infrastructure, and other business initiatives were truncated by the war. Colombia's accelerated growth during the interwar period slowed as the United States and Canada began to develop their own war economies, eventually pulling their investments from Colombia and other markets across South and Central America. Meanwhile the Caribbean became a strategic military zone, as German intelligence began to target the North's oil supply routes.

The presence of German U-boats in the Caribbean forced the Canadian subsidiary to re-evaluate its oil supply lines. Imperial Oil tankers became the target of U-boats, and in February 1942 the "U-109 torpedoed and sank the SS *Montrolite*," which was en route from Venezuela to Halifax, followed by the sinking of the SS *Victolite* bound for Venezuela, and the SS *Calgarolite* bound for Cartagena.[54] By 1942, the Royal Canadian Navy chose to provide escort only to oil convoys leaving the Commonwealth Caribbean and Venezuela. Canada decreased its dependence on the Colombian oil operation. The U-boats destabilized oil supply routes in the Caribbean and altered the trade relation between Colombia and Canada.[55] From that point forward, Colombia's oil was redirected to the U.S. consumer market.

The result was devastating for the Colombian economy: "Exports of crude from Colombia to Canada fell from 12.6 million barrels in 1941 to 1.5 million in 1942 while imports from Venezuela tripled from 3.2 million barrels in 1940 to 9.4 million in 1942."[56] Colombia's total oil production decreased from 34,553,000 in 1941 to 10,590,000 in 1942, as a result of decreasing Canadian demand.[57] The decreasing oil trade relation between Colombia and Canada reduced Imperial Oil's influence over the Barrancabermeja complex, and it damaged the once important trade relations between the two nations.

This transformation opened the door for a more direct relationship between Standard Oil of New Jersey and Colombia. The United States filled the gap left by the Canadians, and soon "Colombian output was accelerated to supplement petroleum supplies to the Pacific theatre."[58] The historical spatial dimension of Canadian-Colombian oil relations had come to an end.

By 1944, Colombia's oil production had recovered to 22,647,000 barrels and the economy had been injected with U.S. foreign capital worth US$20 million destined for development and expansion of the petroleum industry.[59] U.S. foreign direct investment had rejuvenated Colombia's oil industry, and by 1946 petroleum had become the second-largest national export after coffee.

The United States emerged from the war as "the main and unchallenged foreign investor in the region."[60] After the war it surfaced as the world's superpower, relegating Britain, Germany, France, Italy, the Netherlands, and Canada to a peripheral role in Latin America and the Caribbean. Imperial's influence in Colombia as a subsidiary had been reduced to ashes as Canada's oil imports from Barrancabermeja became insignificant.

The De Mares contract came to an end shortly after the end of the war. In 1951, oil production, infrastructure, and equipment went back to the Colombian government, under the newly created Empresa Colombiana de Petróleos. Nevertheless, the United States continued to rely on the Canadian subsidiary for tax purposes. Although the infrastructure and equipment was transferred to the Colombian national company, the actual operation of the fields and refinery were leased to IPC's "newly established subsidiary, International Petroleum of Colombia, Limited."[61] A new ten-year agreement signed by the administration of President Laureano Gómez's (1950–3), under the recommendation of World Bank's economist and Canadian native Lauchlin Currie, allowed IPC to continue with oil extraction and refining while Esso-Colombia, the newly created Colombian-U.S. company, took over distribution and marketing of oil derivatives across the Colombian market.

The transfer of ownership of the Barrancabermeja operation was the first time "that an oil complex, developed by a foreign company, had been returned to the nation in virtue of the contract's expiration" without violent consequences.[62] In exchange, Standard secured the rights to oil reserves while at the same time developing the domestic market. IPC was no longer pioneering Canadian-Colombian relations, and instead was developing Colombia's domestic oil consumer market.

The temporal and spatial dimension of oil extraction that brought together Canadian and Colombian interests was paralleled by the gold extraction industry. Canadian gold-mining subsidiaries working on behalf of British interests were also pivotal in enhancing Canadian-Colombian relations during the first half of the twentieth century. As in oil extraction, their window of opportunity to expand their presence in the Colombian market was short but effective, paving the way for other Canadian business interests. These experiences helped Canadian businesses build a case for a more robust and effective promotional state that would defend the interests of Canadian businesses abroad.

7

Canadian Gold Dredging Operations, 1909–1962

During the later stages of the Regeneration period in Colombia, free market advocates knocked on the doors of the industrial world in efforts to attract foreign investment and establish an import-export market, while at the same time discrediting nationalist protectionist policies.[1] Such was the case of a former resident of Colombia who in 1898 published in the editorial pages of the *New York Times* a petition for investors from the United States to pay closer attention to the Colombian market. He questioned how U.S. investors could pass on such a grand opportunity—a country with "immense natural resources ... eight times the size of the New England States," of which three-fourths were "virgin, untouched, uninhabited even."[2] No other nation in the region was blessed with a similar wealth of natural resources in the Western Hemisphere, said the Colombian expatriate.[3] He went on to affirm that "as a mining country," Colombia had no comparison, rich in "iron, copper, lead, emeralds, amethysts, rubies, rock-crystal, marble, porphyry, jasper, jet, salt, coal, sulphur, lime, gypsum," gold, and silver.[4] Of all the untapped resources that the nation had to offer the global market, it was gold that ended up attracting foreigners, and it was not the United States that developed this industry, but the British and Canadians. The relatively untapped gold mines of the Antioquia region brought together U.S., British, Canadian, and Colombian interests after Pato Mines Colombia Ltd. began operations in 1909.

Gold had been extracted from the Antioquia, Cauca, Cundinamarca, and Tolima regions since pre-colonial times, and it continued to be exploited by Spaniards throughout three centuries of colonial rule. After independence, foreigners were attracted by Colombia's gold rush of the 1860s, but they were deterred by violent clashes between liberals and conservatives. The second gold rush followed implementation of laissez-faire policies under the Rafael Reyes administration (1904–9).

The arrival of French, German, U.S., British, and Canadian interests was accompanied by innovative dredging technology for the industrial extraction of gold. In Antioquia, their highly capitalized operations displaced the local Antioqueño elites that monopolized the sands and gravels of the Cauca, Nechí, Pato, and Ponce Rivers, leaving gold extraction and exports in the hands of foreign interests.[5]

In the late 1800s, British capital powered the competition, leaving them in control of gold-mining operations in Colombia until the eve of the Second World War. Canadian investors, engineers, and entrepreneurs were directly linked to British operations in the Antioquia region, and remained linked to the region even after U.S. companies took over extraction in the 1950s.

Canadian native Harry Stuart Derby, a well-known figure in international mining circles of the early 1900s, was the pioneer behind development of the Nechí River gold-mining operation.[6] British capital helped him establish Pato Mines Colombia Ltd., the company that took over the concession of 40,000 acres along the river back in 1909.[7]

Derby and his British investors beat the French and U.S. speculators who had been competing for the Nechí concession since the late 1890s. In 1901 "a party of 100 men, including civil engineers, mechanists, mining experts, essayists, and guides" left Chicago in a quest for gold appropriations, taking advantage of their close connection to Inland Steel Company and Block-Pollak Iron Company, which had taken over the nearby concession of Zaragoza, two hundred miles south of the Nechí River, in the region of Antioquia.[8] As in the case of oil extraction, British and Canadian business interests capitalized on the anti-American sentiment of the time.

British, Canadian, and U.S. engineers, mechanics, and carpenters, together with local labour, finished construction of the dredge operation in 1912, but the project was eventually halted as a result of the First World War. In 1920 mining activity was reignited. Pato Mines and its sister company, Nechi Mines Ltd., the two Oroville Dredging Limited subsidiaries, became "the only large placer mines found to be profitable" in the region.[9]

Pato's experience in Colombia confirmed the benefits of utilizing subsidiary companies as an international business strategy, and it unmasked the interconnectivity that initially existed among U.S., British, and Canadian investors, entrepreneurs, professionals, and highly skilled workers such as welders and carpenters. This triangular relation resulted in a transnational cooperation that included capital and management, as well as technological and scientific "know-how."

Development of a gold-extraction industry in Colombia revealed how cooperation among the North Atlantic Triangle members pulled resources from stakeholders to break down the business venture into smaller parts "as a means of reducing risks ... and 'spreading bets.'"[10] This explains why control over the concessions of the Zaragoza, Cauca, Nechí, Pato, and Ponce regions changed continuously throughout the first half of the twentieth century, and particularly throughout the interwar years when U.S. capital challenged British business interests in this and many other industries.

Triangular Dynamics

After one year of operations, in 1910, British-owned Consolidated Gold Fields of London acquired Pato Mines Colombia. The British company placed management of the Nechí River operation in the hands of its Canadian subsidiary, Pato Consolidated Gold Dredging.[11] As in the case of oil extraction, Canadian gold-mining subsidiaries serving the interests of British business interests carved a niche in the Colombian market.

Pato Consolidated, with headquarters in Vancouver, managed the Colombian operation for the next six years. A direct link between the two nations had been established, thanks to the business advantages offered by the provincial fiscal legislation that made it an attractive place to establish subsidiaries. British Columbia, Quebec, and Ontario would eventually compete against each other to attract British and U.S. businesses, offering fiscal and economic incentives in order to advance the economic development of their respective regions.

Oroville Dredging Limited continued expansion in Colombia via the establishment of multiple subsidiaries. By the early 1930s, Nechí Concern Development Limited, Nechí Mines Limited, and Asnazú Gold Dredging Limited joined Pato Consolidated in the Antioquia region, making them the dominant mining group in Colombia.[12] On the other hand, subsidiaries with headquarters in Canada such as Pato Consolidated Gold Dredging provided British shareholders with the opportunity to capitalize on tax loopholes that allowed them to avoid paying taxes on dividends.[13]

Canadian laws allowed British shareholders to reduce their taxes on revenues, as income taxes in Britain increased steadily with implementation of welfare policies. British investors had no need to register the Canadian subsidiary in their own country, particularly since most of the subsidiary's capital was privately owned through individuals and other investment firms.[14] This was crucial to British investors, since Oroville Dredging began to pay back dividends to its shareholders four years after they began operation in the Antioquia

region. Business was so good that in 1914 Frederick W. Baker, chairman of
Oroville, reported to the board that the company was in a position to pay
its shareholders "regular dividends at the rate of 10 per cent," and that he
expected this rate to increase to "30 per cent per annum" by 1916.[15]

Oroville continued to expand its operation in Colombia throughout
the 1930s as the price of gold increased in the international market.[16]
The move also came in response to Colombian efforts to stimulate economic development through advancement of the gold-mining industry. Nevertheless, efforts to modernize the mining industry and expand
road infrastructure never gained momentum because the British-Canadian operations were unwilling to invest in such economic development projects. The old dredging techniques continued to be the norm,
as neither the Colombian government nor the private sector was willing
to take risks on infrastructure development. The failure of Oroville's
U.S. subsidiary, Colombian Corporation of Delaware, at the Constan-
cia mine in Anorí, and the government's million-dollar fiasco resulting
from construction of the Dos Bocas and Anorí road that led to nowhere,
convinced government and foreign investors that they should continue
conducting business as usual.

The interwar years saw the emergence of a U.S. challenge on British
interests across the Western Hemisphere. In Colombia, the strong position held by the British-Canadian gold operation slowly deteriorated.
U.S. investors took over the position of British investors in many of
Oroville's subsidiaries, out-powering them by the eve of the Second
World War. This forced Canadian investors to strategically change their
support for U.S. interests. The shift of Canadian investors from British
to American mining interests revealed Canada's flexibility to adapt to
geopolitical changes within the international system. It also showed the
marketability of Canadian mining "know-how," initially supplying the
British and then the Americans with technology and human capital at
their demand.

U.S. investors and policymakers had their eyes on Colombia's gold,
but British interests stood on their way. The 1921 reparation payment
to Colombia that tilted the oil concessions in favour of Standard Oil
of New Jersey also helped American gold-extraction interests position
themselves in the Colombian market. President Franklin D. Roosevelt's
Good Neighbor policies had renewed the faith in the U.S. goodwill,
convincing policymakers such as President Enrique Olaya Herrera
(1930–4) on the mutual political and economic advantages of moving
away from their dependency on Europe.[17]

In 1934, President Alfonso López Pumarejo (1934–8) promised "to
end the right of 'privileged companies' to exploit the natural resources

of Colombia."[18] He was talking directly to the British-Canadian operation, and other foreign interests that had capitalized from the anti-U.S.
sentiment that had forced investors to miss out on valuable extractive
business opportunities. López Pumarejo emphasized that his administration would remove the exploitation of national resources "from the
hands of the few privileged companies," opening Colombia's market
"to the world at large."[19]

By this point U.S., British, Canadian, German, French, and other
European investors had recognized that Colombia's "natural wealth"
was more attractive than that of "any other country in South America."[20] Because Canada could not manage its international affairs independently as a result of its dominion status, Canadian investors took
a step back while they watched U.S. investors incrementally take over
control of gold-mining operations in Colombia, waiting for a favourable opportunity to counter-respond. By 1930 American influence could
be felt. Oroville then controlled only 36 per cent of both Pato Mines and
Pato Consolidated.[21] The increase in American foreign direct investment did not fully repel Canadian investors. The increase in the global
demand for gold opened a window of opportunity for Canadian investors. Vancouver-based Placer Development Incorporated stepped up,
challenging Oroville's position in Colombia.

In 1932 Placer Development took over Pato Consolidated, forcing
Oroville to share control over the Nechí River operation. Placer Development also split control over other subsidiaries, including Nechí
Consolidated Gold Dredging.[22] The company was a much more global
and modern operation than Oroville; it represented the typical mining operation of the modern era with a very diverse corporate direc-
torate that included Canadians, Americans, British, and Australians.[23]
The conglomerate controlled mining operations and held options in the
United States, Canada, Colombia, South Africa, Australia, New Guinea,
and New Zealand.[24] It controlled, for example, international companies
such as Canadian Exploration Limited, Bululo Gold Dredging, and Cor-
onet Oil Company in Texas.[25]

By the eve of the Second World War the remaining British control
over Pato Mines Colombia (stock, equipment, and infrastructure)
was sold to Placer Development, giving it full control over the Nechí
operation.[26] In 1939, the Montreal-based firm Minera Timmins Ochali
Company took over the El Limón Mine, expanding Canada's control over another area of the Antioquia region.[27] By the early 1940s
Canadian mining companies had filled the gap left by the British in
Colombia. Control over gold was left in the hands of U.S. and Canadian interests.

Throughout the Second World War, the Montreal- and Vancouver-based companies monopolized extraction along the pre-eminent gold-mining belt of northeastern Antioquia. The Canadian connection facilitated operations in the region, sharing equipment, engineers, and crucial "know-how." After the war the cooperative business strategy came to a halt, as the United States emerged as the global superpower.

Placer Development Incorporated became one of the only Canadian companies in Colombia to overcome the pressure of U.S. investors in the region. By the 1950s the Canadian company had become a power-house in global mining, controlling diverse mining interests including gold, zinc, emeralds, platinum, oil, and tungsten ore.[28] Mining opera-tions were no longer linked to nationalist interests, as in the case of Oro-ville, and instead were connected to the interests of top shareholders and directors in search of personal reward. Individual investor interests replaced national interests.

The transnational nature of individual investors prevented the com-pany from channelling profits to Canada's own national economic development. The gold extracted from Colombia and the Canadian company's revenues flowed globally and not back to Canada, as in the case of oil. Canada's mining success benefitted the global market and not the Canadian market, illustrating its subordinate role within the dynamics of the international gold industry.

The End of the Cycle

As in oil, the end of the Second World War marked the end of the tem-poral and spatial dimension of Canadian gold mining in Colombia. The rise of the United States as a global power was manifested in its increasing presence across strategic sectors of the Colombian economy. In the absence of a strong promotional state, Canadian gold-mining companies attempted to stop the American surge, but at the end failed to stop American companies from taking control of the Colombian gold-extraction industry.

In an effort to protect its operations from the aggressive expansion of U.S.-owned South American Gold and Platinum, Placer Development decided to join their two operations in Antioquia into one single subsid-iary. In 1953 Placer announced the merger of Nechí Consolidated and Pato Consolidated Gold Dredging.[29] Placer executives increased their operational risk in Colombia, but temporarily secured control over the resource.

This did not deter American companies from accelerating their pen-etration into the Colombian gold market. South American Gold and

Platinum began to build its Colombian operation back in 1919 but became interested in expanding its operations in Antioquia only after British influence declined in the 1930s, and by 1937 it began extraction in the Telembí River. A more aggressive strategy followed President Gustavo Rojas Pinilla's (1953–7) decision to deregulate the sale of gold in the international market after 1953.[30] Market deregulation and lax subsoil concession policies that favoured foreign interests continued to attract more foreign investors in the 1950s.

In 1954 the board of directors of South American Gold and Platinum opted to change the company's upper management for the Latin American operations, hiring a "new top team" of American executives with transnational experience, including President Lewis B. Harder and Vice President Robert C. Stanley Jr., both of whom had vast experience in Canadian mining companies operating across the Western Hemisphere.[31] That same year the company took over 1.2 million shares of Pato Consolidated Gold Dredging, giving it one-third control over the Canadian operation.[32] This gave the U.S. company "the right to name three of the six directors," setting the stage for a slow takeover.[33] By 1956 South American Gold and Platinum controlled 35 per cent of Pato's interests, and by the 1960s its control over the Canadian operation had reached unprecedented levels.

During the late 1950s South American Gold and Platinum continued to expand its mining operations across South America, thanks to mergers and the creation of new subsidiaries. In 1956 it took over a third of the last considerable British operation in Colombia, Frontino Gold Mines.[34] By the early 1960s the U.S. corporation had, for the most part, displaced British and Canadian interests from the key hemispheric mining regions. Through its network of subsidiaries, South American Gold and Platinum was able to secure strong positions in countries such as Bolivia, Ecuador, Paraguay, and Colombia.

In 1962, the company finalized its takeover of Pato Consolidated Gold Dredging, securing 62 per cent ownership.[35] Then in 1963 the company's stockholders approved the merger of South American Gold and its subsidiary, International Mining Corporation, leaving control of global mining operations under International Mining.[36] By that point the American company controlled nearly 25,000 acres of river bottomland across the Antioquia region.[37]

The deep pockets of U.S. mining corporations such as South American Gold and Platinum and International Mining transformed the power structures of mining across the Western Hemisphere. Harder and Stanley Jr. found more effective use for the US$6 million surplus capital from their Colombia operation, moving away from traditional cash and bond management, and instead utilizing the funds to expand and diversify mining operations across Latin America.

Reading the geopolitical realities of the time and responding to regional threats to capitalism and democracy, South American Gold and Platinum increased its foreign direct investment. Harder emphasized that he responded to the region's rapid economic development and demographic growth and predicted an "acceleration of trade between North and South America in view of the huge barrier created by the Iron Curtain countries."[38]

Harder's ability to align the company's interests with Washington's Cold War agenda revealed the clear difference between his management vision and that of his company's Canadian counterparts. On the eve of the Cold War it was evident that the success of its international business strategy would depend on a more intimate government-business partnership. International Mining Corporation was prepared for this new business approach but not Canadian businesses.

Canadian gold-mining companies operating in Colombia suffered from the absence of a strong promotional state that protected and supported their business interests. As a result, they failed to hold their position in the Colombian market. Moreover, the company was a victim of an overly diversified pool of directors that succumbed to the interests of the international market and not Canadian interests.

Contrary to Canadian mining companies, the American mining industry received full support from its government, constructing an effective government-business partnership in order to secure resources across the Western Hemisphere. Truman's Point Four Program, President Kennedy's Alliance for Progress, and the security and economic development initiatives behind the hemispheric Cold War policies all paved the way for American companies to control key resources across the region, including gold in Colombia. The strong presence of U.S. interests prevented Canadian companies from capitalizing on the region's emerging business opportunities that surfaced during the early stages of the Cold War. From the U.S. perspective, this aggressive initiative was not only "important economically but also vital for the defense of the Western Hemisphere."[39]

Colombia's economic development and security also became more dependent on foreign direct investment; the success of foreign corporations operating in Colombia became an integral part of the country's national security policy.[40] This pro-business stance increasingly attracted transnational investors, but U.S. influence in Colombian politics gave them an advantage over their competitors. Gold extraction in the 1950s and early 1960s illustrated this point.

Under British and Canadian management, gold had been exploited in the absence of policy or economic development initiatives that added value to gold, platinum, or any other mining resource. Companies such as Placer Development were more than content to pay taxes and other export fees necessary to move the resource and profits out of Colombia and into the international market, but they were never interested in fomenting nation building; nevertheless, the Cold War led American companies to play this role in Colombia.

In the early stages of the Cold War the alignment of American business and U.S. government objectives allowed them to effectively advance nation and market building in Latin America and the Caribbean. In Colombia, the U.S. government-business partnership shared the view that the South American nation was "a dynamic economy" that was "beginning to boom"; it was a country with a highly productive labour force, rising industrialization, and a growing consumer society with rising purchasing power potential.[41] It was the reason why Americans used Colombia as a nation-building experiment, targeting it with external aid policies, using multilateral institutions such as the World Bank to advance a market-driven economic development model, promoting free trade principles through its private sector while deterring the expansion of communism by arming the Colombian military.

In the absence of a cohesive government-business partnership, Canadian businesses opted to serve the needs of the U.S. anti-Communist agenda, promoting capitalism through their own independent business endeavours across the Western Hemisphere, while pressuring their own government to establish a stronger promotional state.

During the early stages of the Cold War, Canadian companies became ambassadors of the Canadian subordinate state, advancing the interests of the international market system through their own international business initiatives. Ultimately, a more cohesive government-business partnership was consolidated in the late 1960s under the Pierre Elliott Trudeau administration, allowing the Canadian government to align its objectives to those of its private sector. The partnership's success was limited, nevertheless, for by the early 1970s Canadian businesses were once again competitive in markets like Colombia.

PART THREE

The Early Promotional State

8

Limitations under the Cold War

Aside from budgetary and human capital constraints, the creation of a promotional state to help Canadian businesses penetrate the Latin American and Caribbean markets was a complicated task because of a lack of "political will." After the Statute of Westminster of 1931 that allowed Canada to take a crucial step toward foreign policy independence, legislative efforts to expand the nation's international role came short. It was not until the 1940s and 1950s that Canada incrementally expanded its official relations across the world through diplomatic and trade initiatives. Initially, Canada's foreign affairs centred on building a closer relationship with the United States and greater independence from Great Britain. Additionally, it was eager to show the world its rejection of colonial rule, while at the same time defending the principles of the North Atlantic Treaty Organization (NATO) and the U.S. global security initiatives against communism. Multilateralism also became an important part of Canada's foreign affairs strategy, identifying it as a means to reduce its dependence on the United States. What the strategy lacked, initially, was a clear policy on the emerging markets of the world, particularly those across Latin America and the Caribbean.

The events that took place during the Ninth Pan-American Conference of 1948 in Bogotá, Colombia, forced the Canadian government to take a closer look at its Latin American and Caribbean relations. It set the tone for what would become Canada's promotional state for the region, as the United States used its rising power in order to leverage its private sector interests across the Western Hemisphere. The Ninth Pan-American Conference was used as the launching ground for American hemispheric Cold War economic and security policies.

While Canada opted not to participate at the hemispheric conference in response to the anti-British agenda introduced by some delegates, Colombia saw the conference as an opportunity to project an image of stability and progress to the international community, marketing the nation to foreign investors. Americans, on the other hand, arrived to sell their anti-communist and market-driven economic development program to the regional delegates. Unfortunately, plans were derailed soon after the conference's inauguration. The assassination of Colombia's liberal party leader Jorge Eliécer Gaitán on 9 April 1948, while the conference was in session, changed the course of Colombian history as well as that of the Western Hemisphere.[1]

His death unleashed Colombia's civil war known as La Violencia. It also set the stage for the development of the Organization of American States (OAS), the unanimous approval of a hemispheric anti-communist agenda, and the marketability of Truman's Point Four program. The violent incidents that followed the assassination marked the beginning of the Cold War in the Americas, a period in which nationalism confronted liberalism, and unleashed the forces of transnational capitalism across the region.

U.S. Secretary of State George C. Marshall capitalized on Gaitán's death, building a case against communism and economic nationalism, and in favour of a market-driven economic development model for the region. Weeks after the violent protests against Gaitán's assassination, known as *El Bogotazo,* the creation of the OAS was collectively approved, with the exception of Canada, which opted not to accept full membership, in one of the last demonstrations of loyalty to Britain.[2]

In Canada's political sphere, the long debate oscillated between those who thought that the overpowering influence of the United States over the OAS resulted in a machinery that "was less than ideal" for Canada, and those who thought that it was a window of opportunity to strengthen the country's promotional state. Those in favour of joining the OAS believed that joining "would open up new trade opportunities with various countries of Latin America."[3] Aligning with the U.S. hemispheric initiative was good for certain Canadian businesses dependent on the international market, but there were also public, political, and economic sectors that opposed the expansion of American imperialism in the region, accusing the Americans of monopolizing the Latin American and Caribbean markets.

Canadian businesses that shared the American vision implicitly supported General Marshall's initiative, particularly those that had been doing business in Colombia, such as financial institutions, gold mining, and oil subsidiaries. They recognized the importance of fighting nationalism and protectionism in places like Colombia, and therefore favoured the open market policies advanced by the United States. Therefore many Canadian business sectors welcomed the assassination of Gaitán.

Jorge Eliécer Gaitán was well known among foreign business circles operating in Colombia, particularly after his 1929 comments during the debate over the banana plantation massacre that took place at the installations of the United Fruit Company in Santa Marta.[4] He was seen as a nationalist and a populist who supported leftist ideologies, an instigator of the masses and the working class, and a supporter of protectionist ideas.

During the first half of the twentieth century, Jorge Eliécer Gaitán emerged as the only political leader able to democratically challenge the status quo established by the ruling elites since the era of independence. He publicly criticized the role of multinational corporations in the nation's economic development as well as his government's decision to protect the interests of foreign investors over its own citizens.[5] He had questioned the dynamics of labour relations imposed by foreign interests and their control over the nation's natural resources, centring his attacks on foreign companies such as La Troco.[6] His arguments were pertinent at a time when foreign investment was aggressively expanding into Colombia and the rest of the region. They resonated in places such as Cuba, Guatemala, and Chile where the Left was beginning to ask the same questions.

The Canadian Response to El Bogotazo

By the beginning of the Cold War it was clear to North American industrial powers that the economic, political, and social stability of the Latin American and Caribbean nations was crucial for the containment of communism across the hemisphere. The growing criticism of democracy and capitalism represented the greatest threats to their geopolitical and economic long-term plans, considering that the Canadian economy was slowly becoming an integral part of the U.S. industrial machine.

A preliminary report from the U.S. Office of Financial and Development Policy, in preparation for the conference in Bogotá, confirmed that Latin America was of "economic and strategic importance" and that much would be gained from development of the Latin American and Caribbean economies.[7] The region was key to the capitalist expansionist plans of Canada and the United States. It provided multinational corporations access to raw materials, had potential industrial growth capacity, and represented a potentially profitable consumer market ready for growth and development. The American and Canadian governments agreed with their respective private sector that this was a strategic region, and therefore communism and nationalism were unacceptable nation-building models.

The strengthening of democracy and the free market in the Americas needed to be protected at any cost. Both governments saw the Soviet Union as the greatest threat to hemispheric economic, political, and social stability. With this in mind, the United States arrived in Bogotá, in early April, with the intention of convincing the other hemispheric nations that its vision should also be their nation-building priority. From the U.S. perspective, its government-business partnership would work collaboratively to enforce the economic and security policies, while the Canadians played a secondary role as promoters of democracy across the region.[8]

Canadians in power shared this view, but they believed that the best way to advance democracy in the region was through social reform and self-determination within each country.[9] This position distinguished Canada from the United States throughout the Cold War. Nevertheless, its limited power and influence in the region made it difficult to advance this agenda, particularly in the absence of a strong promotional state. Its inability to influence the U.S. foreign policy toward Latin America during the early stages of the Cold War led it to abstain from active participation in the region's geopolitical dynamics. That explained why Canada did not send an official delegation to the conference in Bogotá.

Washington's economic development program for Latin America and the Caribbean required that all regional members open their economies to private investment and commit to "self-help, cooperation, and internal stabilization measures."[10] Contrary to the Marshall Plan, it imposed limitations and reduced national autonomy over economic decisions. Moreover, Washington tied economic aid and foreign investment to unconditional support for U.S. anti-communist policy.[11] Selling this plan at the conference in Bogotá was crucial for President Truman's administration, but there was no hemispheric consensus on the initiative; Canada's absence spoke to the lack of cohesiveness of the policy.

Leftist organizers and student activists from all corners of Latin America and the Caribbean had arrived in Bogotá to protest against the plan that was to be delivered by Secretary of State George Marshall. They seemed to share Gaitán's position that "while the U.S. gave Europe the Lucrative Marshall Plan," all Latin America could expect was U.S. opposition to popular movements that went against the new hemispheric plan.[12]

George Marshall also faced opposition from delegates representing Uruguay and Argentina. They had expressed concerns about Washington's military power at the Rio summit of 1947 where the Inter-American Treaty of Reciprocal Assistance was signed. The initial stages of the hemispheric mutual defence treaty against aggression had left many unresolved issues that were supposed to be clarified at the Bogotá conference. The government of Argentina led the opposition against a treaty that, for the first time, requested "joint armed action to keep peace in the western hemisphere."[13] Opponents wanted the hemispheric members, particularly the United States, to recognize Argentina's "claims, and those of other republics, against European powers possessing colonies of 'de facto possessions' in the Western Hemisphere," particularly British presence in Belize and the Falkland Islands.[14]

Guatemala's delegation, on the other hand, had called "for an end of colonial regimes in America and said that final action taken should be 'more than a hope' of settling the problem."[15] The unanimous claim for autonomy and opposition to European holdings in the hemisphere pushed Washington into a corner, and Canada all the more so because of its historical allegiance to Britain. If the United States wanted the support of the hemispheric members, it needed to fully comply with the principles of the Monroe Doctrine, which the William Lyon Mackenzie King's government was not willing to support. The debate over British colonial presence in the region also explained why Canada refused to send a delegation to Bogotá.

Canada did not have a clear hemispheric policy. Canadian international businesses wanted a clear-cut line policy as well as a promotional state that supported their initiatives in the region, but politicians were split between support for the North Atlantic Treaty and greater economic integration with the United States.[16] It was clear that they were interested in enhancing and diversifying their trade relations with the region, but they were not willing to sign off on the Truman initiative or fully support the anti-British proposition backed by the Inter-American system. This Catch-22 prevented Canada's business sector from capitalizing on these emerging markets.

Canada's position on hemispheric issues was "one of detached interest."[17] A spokesperson from External Affairs further explained that Canada had never "been officially invited to join the Pan-American Union" and had not received an invitation "'either public or private,' to attend the Bogotá conference."[18] Canada's strategy was to watch the developments closely from the sidelines, calibrating the developments in Bogotá before committing to any policy that would result from the conference.

Some sectors of the Canadian media lamented the nation's absence from the hemispheric conference, considering that for the first time, the twenty-one members were going to "make use of the United Nations charter" that promoted the organization of regional systems within the broader international body.[19] As Canada's *Lethbridge Herald* indicated, it was, after all, "the biggest event in its 400-year history."[20] For those Canadians concerned with the overpowering control imposed by Washington on the Pan-American Union, the idea of linking the regional organization to the multilateral norms of the United Nations represented a more autonomous venue for Ottawa to become involved with hemispheric issues. This was exactly what Washington did not want, and therefore did not encourage Canada to participate. For many in Washington, Canadian membership meant a vote for British interests within their post-war construction of an inter-American system.

The United States did not oppose a Canadian role within their hemispheric policy. They wanted Canada to contribute financially to a Latin American reconstruction plan, in addition to promoting democratic and capitalist values across the region via Canadian businesses. While Secretary of State Marshall marketed aspects of this reconstruction plan in Bogotá, U.S. and Canadian officials held parallel talks back in Washington, in efforts to define the financial aspects of the European reconstruction plan. It was envisioned that part of the allocation of reconstruction funds would be recycled back into the Western Hemisphere in the form of commodity purchases destined for Europe. It was at around that time that Canada's director general of the Economic and Research Branch, Department of Reconstruction and Supply, Alex Skelton, met with his counterparts in Washington and drafted details for the "allocation of nearly $900,000,000 worth of goods for Britain and Europe to be bought with U.S. dollars in Canada in the 1948–1949 fiscal year."[21]

Based on Washington's plan, the Marshall Plan for the reconstruction of Europe represented a "total of $21,000,000,000 worth of Western Hemisphere supplies to be bought for Britain and Europe, of which $17,000,000,000 would be bought in the U.S. and $4,000,000,000 from other Western Hemisphere nations."[22] This meant that the United States would benefit from 81 per cent of the sales to Europe, leaving the other 19 per cent to the rest of its hemispheric partners, including Canada, which was assigned 23 per cent of the remaining share.[23] The allocation of this small portion was a topic that some Latin American nations wanted to discuss in Bogotá, and something that the Canadians had to content themselves with if they wanted access to the regional markets under the new hemispheric design.

The economic development program, similar in theory to the European Recovery Program (ERP), was presented in Bogotá at the time of the conference. This Marshall Plan for Latin America and the Caribbean was inferior to the European plan. Preparatory material from the U.S. Office of Financial and Development policy showed that the hemispheric economic development plan was limited in scope; it stated that the amount of assistance that could be "effectively utilized for development purposes in Latin America" was "quite small in contrast to that being planned for European recovery."[24] The Truman administration had no interest in strengthening the Latin American and Caribbean economies to the extent that they had envisioned for Europe. The interest was purely utilitarian, centring on the region's resources and not on their long-term economic development. The Canadian government accepted the deal and was willing to move forward with the initiative, because the deal was potentially beneficial for Canada's business sector. While the idea was being sold in Bogotá, Ottawa was setting up an inter-departmental committee and a Cabinet to supervise the allocation of the 23 per cent of the procurement assigned to it under Washington's plan.[25]

On 8 April 1948, one day before Gaitán's assassination, President Truman addressed the U.S. Congress, requesting an increase of US$500 million in lending authority for the Export-Import Bank. The *New York Times* reported that the United States recognized that the economic development of Latin American countries depended on foreign financing, and that the "United States, by reason of its close relations with these countries and its strong economic position," was going to be the principal lender and the main source "for equipment, materials and technology."[26] Confirming U.S. lending policies, Truman told Congress that, in exchange, Latin American nations were expected to take the necessary actions in order to "attract private investment capital and mobilize their investment resources."[27] In other words they were expected to comply with the new policy of containment in order to preserve a good business climate. Truman noted that the economic development of Latin America, the expansion of production, increased trade activity, and rising standards of living were strategically important for the United States and that, collectively, these represented compelling reasons to invest in the economic development of the region.[28]

U.S. and Canadian business sectors interested in leveraging on the new hemispheric policy welcomed the initiative. Such was not the case among the Latin American delegates present in Bogotá. At the request of Secretary Marshall, the conference's secretary general read President Truman's message, and to his surprise, the message was not well received: "Delegates sat quietly while the statement was read. They did not applaud when it was finished. There was absolute silence, not even the rustle of paper."[29] U.S. delegates were "stunned by the Latin American reaction," and so were other observers who said that "they never had seen anything like it – there was not even a polite diplomatic applause."[30] Latin American delegates had delivered a diplomatic blow.

They made it clear that they were not in Bogotá to sign off on the U.S. initiative, and that instead they wanted to discuss the possibilities of creating a plan that truly benefitted the region. The pendulum was swinging in favour of the Latin American and Caribbean delegates, but the momentum was cut short.

The next day Gaitán was assassinated as the conference in Bogotá was in session. Violent street protests were unleashed and the city became engulfed in El Bogotazo.[31] Secretary Marshall, Colombian elites, and international and local mainstream media took advantage of the chaos to construct an anti-communist propaganda campaign that would eventually convince the Latin American and Caribbean delegates that the U.S. agenda was the best alternative for the hemisphere.

Negotiators of the reconstruction plan continued back in the United States while blood was being spilled in the streets of Bogotá. The day Gaitán was killed, William McChesney Martin Jr., president of the Export-Import Bank, told those attending the negotiations that the United States understood that private capital had to "play the major role in the economic development of Latin America," and therefore the bank was willing to step up its efforts in the region by supplying capital as well as "stimulating and facilitating private investment."[32] The bank's representative was speaking on behalf of foreign direct investors and multinational corporations interested in capitalizing on the new economic development plan for Latin America and the Caribbean.

Canadians did not need to be present in Bogotá; their strategic interest was back in the United States, where negotiations over the reconstruction plan for the hemisphere were taking place. Approval of the deal that would benefit foreign direct investors and multinational corporations was an indirect victory for Canada and represented a first step toward consolidation of a Canadian promotion state.

The vision of the Export-Import Bank and Truman's Point Four Program indicated that economic development of the Western Hemisphere was going to be spearheaded by the private sector. Foreign Direct Investment and other international business strategies would pave the way, as long as the threat of communism was contained. Canada would comply with the containment initiative, as long as its private sector could compete in these emerging markets.

Canada's private sector continued to pressure its government in order to develop a strong promotional state that would allow it to compete with the U.S. government-business partnership. The policies of the Point Four Program and the Export-Import Bank were favourable only if backed by a strong promotion state. While the United States and the European nations offered their business sectors support and representation, Canada had minimal diplomatic presence in the region and lacked a clear long-term policy.

The Canadian government was persuaded to incrementally develop an effective promotional state that would allow Canadian corporations and investors to compete against other foreign interests in Latin America and the Caribbean. Steps were taken to increase its diplomatic presence in the region. Meanwhile trade delegations were launched in order to build bridges between Canada and the rest of the region.

In the 1950s and 1960s Canada continued to grapple with its bipolarity, slowly moving away from British ties and strengthening its interdependence with the United States, while navigating its way into self-determination in the region. By then, Canada's refusal to occupy the twenty-second seat at the OAS was no longer the result of geopolitical pressures but part of a strategy to communicate to regional members that it had an independent voice within hemispheric matters, in spite of the fact that it was more dependent on the U.S. economy than ever before.

The Canadian government used this symbolic independent position as a diplomatic tool to construct its own identity in the region, while complying with its role of promoting democracy. Its advocacy for social reform and self-determination as pillars of democracy would allow Canada to dissociate itself from American hard-line Cold War policies. This would eventually evolve into the perception of the "goodwill" nation, a recognition that would be shared by many in the region during the later parts of the century, and a diplomatic tool that would become an asset for Canadian businesses and investors opening markets overseas.

In addition to strengthening its diplomatic and consular presence in the region, Canada's promotional state relied on multilateral work and financial support via the United Nations and other multilateral agencies such as the World Bank. This approach was followed in the 1960s by allocation of Official Development Assistance (ODA) through multilateral agencies.

The establishment of diplomatic relations with Colombia in 1953 represented a significant step toward development of a promotional state that worked on behalf of Canadian businesses and investors interested in doing business in Colombia. Negotiations revealed the eagerness of the Mariano Ospina Pérez (1946–50) and the Laureano Gómez (1950–53) administrations to strengthen the relationship between the two countries in order to leverage U.S. influence while also providing Colombian exporters with new market alternatives. They also revealed the internal conflicts within the Canadian government over the definition of a Latin American and Caribbean policy. For the United States, they represented an opportunity to strengthen its Cold War policies through Canada's commitment to the advancement of democracy and the expansion of the free market.

9

Diplomatic Relations, 1941–1953

Domestic and international pressure was placed on the Canadian government to establish official diplomatic relations with the Latin American and Caribbean nations soon after the Statute of Westminster was implemented in 1931. The emerging economies across the Western Hemisphere wanted to draw Canada into the region and away from its British Commonwealth agenda. The initiative was driven by trade and geopolitical interests; in essence the region saw Canada as a strategic trading partner that could reduce their increasing dependency on the U.S. economy. The United States, on the other hand, wanted to lure Canada into the region in order to distance it from Britain. Meanwhile, domestic pressure was mounted by Canada's private exporting sector that demanded consolidation of a promotional state that could advance business interests across the global market system.

Canadian internationalists welcomed the expansion of Canadian diplomatic relations, but nationalist and loyalist opposition impeded the initiative. By 1939 Canada had been able to establish direct diplomatic relations only with "the United States, France, Japan, Belgium, and the Netherlands."[1] There was no urgency in expanding diplomatic relations across the Americas, for the development of a policy for the region was not a priority. Foreign affairs was left mostly in the hands of the private sector to expand business across the Western Hemisphere.

Colombia was one nation that pushed for establishment of diplomatic relations with Canada. It wanted relations more than Canada did because Canada was the second-largest industrial market in the Western Hemisphere. It represented another potential export market as well as a feasible solution to increasing dependence on the U.S. market. Colombia, and the rest of the Caribbean and Latin American markets, also represented a solution to Canada's economic development constraints of the 1930s that resulted from the Great Depression, but policymakers were absorbed by the urgency of finding domestic solutions to the global crisis.

Colombia and many other regional actors continued to press the Canadian government to establish consular and diplomatic relations throughout the 1930s and into the 1940s, but developments of the Second World War halted the initiative. The pressure resurfaced after the war, this time spearheaded by Canada's exporting business sector, which demanded creation of a promotional state that would help them compete in the international market system and capitalize on President Truman's Point Four Program.

Pressure from Canadian exporters and the Canadian Manufacturers' Association escalated to unprecedented levels in the early stages of the Cold War, as the Latin American and Caribbean nations began to open their markets and restructure their economies in order to comply with the market-driven policies introduced by the United States and the World Bank. Nevertheless, the absence of a Latin American and Caribbean policy and lack of political will prevented the Canadian government from developing a strategy to capitalize on the region's economic liberalization.

Canada's dependence on British representatives stationed across the region and Canadian diplomats stationed in Washington prevented Canadian businesses from dealing directly with regional markets. The dynamics of the first half of the twentieth century allowed some Canadian companies to build leverage in some of these markets, but the dynamics changed during the Cold War. By the late 1940s Canada continued to be a significant supplier of industrial and agricultural goods to some of these markets as well as a significant importer of raw materials and natural resources, but in other markets it had lost ground. Colombia was one market where Canadian businesses lost ground.[2]

After the 1948 incidents that led to La Violencia it was imperative, from the perspective of the U.S. Cold War policy, that Colombia's market-driven economy be strengthened and integrated into the international system. Canada's private sector could contribute to this initiative and therefore it was crucial that it establish diplomatic relations with Colombia.

Washington demanded that Ottawa step up its efforts in the region, contributing to hemispheric security and the promotion of democratic values through establishment of diplomatic relations and expansion of private, cultural, and educational exchange. Nevertheless, the Canadian government lacked the personnel, resources, and institutional capabilities to expand its official presence across the whole region.

The opening of legations "was taken more seriously by the Latin American countries than by Canada itself."[3] This progression slowly changed as the Cold War progressed. In response to domestic and external pressures, Ottawa began to selectively establish diplomatic relations with Latin American nations throughout the early 1940s. Legations of Brazil and Argentina were established in 1941, followed by Chile in 1942, and Peru and Mexico in 1944.[4] Colombia's turn came in November 1952. By that point, nine of the twenty-two Canadian embassies overseas were located in the Americas, a clear sign of the initial development of a Latin American policy.

Diplomatic Relations

The Colombian government had lobbied for diplomatic relations throughout the 1930s and 1940s, claiming that the presence of Canadian corporations and personnel, and an increasing trade relation based on Tropical Oil's exports to Canada, justified the establishment of official relations. During the war, Colombia's bureaucracy, like that of others across Latin America, needed to establish new legations that would provide "employment for diplomats who had been forced to flee from Europe."[5] Ottawa did not become a feasible target for these diplomats, as the Canadian government was not "as inter-American minded as they appeared to Latin Americans." Only the businessmen were.[6]

One year after El Bogotazo, Colombia's foreign minister, Eduardo Zuleta Angel, once again raised the question "of the establishment of direct diplomatic relations between Colombia and Canada."[7] This was the fourth time the Colombian government had approached Canada.[8]

The first request had been made immediately after the Canadian mission to Latin America headed by Trade Minister J.A. MacKinnon in August 1941.[9] The mission's ten-week tour, which included stops in Colombia, Ecuador, Peru, Chile, Argentina, Uruguay, Brazil, Trinidad, and Puerto Rico, had represented a tremendous step forward in the advancement of the promotional state, even though it was cut short in response to MacKinnon's health issues.[10] It had allowed the government to secure continuation of most-favoured nation agreement with Colombia and establishment of similar agreements with other regional partners such as Brazil, but it had failed to advance the specific interests of Canadian investors in each targeted market.[11] It had also failed to realize the expectations of the Colombian government, which wanted to officially link the two countries politically, economically, and diplomatically.

For MacKinnon, the mission was symbolic of a step forward that "had awakened a 'definite interest' in Canada," but for Colombian authorities it meant more than symbolic gestures.[12] The agreement established by the minister of trade and commerce, which was later ratified in Parliament, gave the Colombian government the illusion that Canada was ready to establish diplomatic relations.[13] In 1942 the Colombian government made the official request but Ottawa turned it down.

It was a disappointment for President Eduardo Santos's (1938–42) administration, considering that there was strong Canadian investment in Colombia and that Ottawa had included it as part of the mission's itinerary. Moreover, the Colombian government was well aware that Canada was in need of new markets. MacKinnon himself had said that the mission was designed to further increase trade "and the goodwill between ... nations."[14] The Colombian interpretation that trade was linked directly to diplomatic relations did not fit with the more practical approach of Canadians who saw trade and diplomacy as two separate foreign policy tools. Trade was a private matter, particularly in the absence of a promotional state and a lack of political will to develop a regional policy.

President Eduardo Santos was disappointed to see Canadians establish diplomatic relations with Brazil and Argentina soon after the 1941 trade mission. But these two countries were more strategic for Canadian interests than Colombia. Their economies played a significant role in the global economic system, and the increasing presence of German interests in these two countries represented a threat to regional security. There was a political and economic agenda that justified establishment of diplomatic relations, but not with Colombia.

The United States had established diplomatic relations with Colombia in 1939, and the Colombian government expected other hemispheric industrial powers to follow suit, particularly since the region's trade with Canada had seen an increase as a result of the wartime economy. Canada's trade with the region boomed during the war; imports remained higher than exports, but the volumes of regional trade were "far above those of the pre-war days."[15] Such was the increase in trade that during the first seven months of 1941, Canada's exports increased 93 per cent, in comparison with 1939, and 22 per cent in comparison with 1940 rates.[16] Meanwhile Canada's imports from Latin America increased 267 per cent in relation to 1939 and 74 per cent in relation to 1940.[17] This was the direct result of the "expanded needs of a wartime economy and the elimination of European supplies of manufactured articles."[18]

President Alfonzo López Pumarejo's (1934–8 / 1942–6) administration tried to increase its international relevance by declaring war against

Germany in 1943, following several instances where German U-boats sank several Colombian vessels. Foreign Minister Carlos Lozano y Lozano opted to play the multilateral card, escalating Colombia's participation in the United Nations.[19] Colombia was seeking a much more active role in the international system and even greater recognition, but the Canadian government remained reluctant to establish diplomatic relations with Colombia.

In 1946 MacKinnon returned to the region to finalize his Latin American tour, adding to the itinerary stops in Panama, five Central American republics, and Mexico.[20] Speaking at a Canadian Chamber of Commerce luncheon, MacKinnon emphasized the increasing importance of the Latin American and Caribbean regions and concluded that even though its economy would continue to rely heavily on British and U.S. trade, Canada needed to secure its "fair share" of the Latin American trade.[21]

The Canadian delegation returned home confirming their most favoured nation treaty with Colombia, emphasizing their bilateral commercial exchange "of automobiles, newsprint and pharmaceuticals from Canada and coffee and vegetable products from Colombia."[22] From the point of view of the Colombian government, this represented a closer step toward formalization of diplomatic relations, which was greatly desired by Canada's private sector.

Meanwhile, back in Colombia, the Canadian Manufacturers' Association had been in close contact with Douglas W. Jackson, assistant trade commissioner in Bogotá, trying to lobby for establishment of diplomatic and consular services in Colombia.[23] The need for a Canadian government presence in Colombia was essential if Canadian businesses were to expand their operations in that market, considering the overwhelming presence of U.S. business interests across strategic sectors of the Colombian economy.

That year Colombia extended its second request for establishment of diplomatic relations, but it returned empty-handed.[24] President Mariano Ospina Pérez's (1946–50) administration continued to pursue advancement of bilateral diplomatic relations, but the Canadian government once again stressed its intention to focus on trade and not on diplomacy. Colombia, and the rest of the region, was crucial for implementation of Canada's post-war trade policy. Nevertheless, those against the expansion of diplomatic relations across the region were convinced that trade and not embassies would allow the government to "exploit" the region's markets to the fullest.[25]

Soon after the war, James MacKinnon explained that Canada needed to diversify its trade relations for the survival of its export-based economy and for the sake of reducing its dependence on the United

States.[26] Expanding trade relations with Latin American and other regional markets was crucial for the national economy, because its limited domestic market could not take on the consumption load of the vast natural resources and industrial equipment produced by the national economy.[27] Exports to the region sustained the high volumes of trade experienced during the war years and allowed the domestic economy to preserve high levels of employment and consumption. The government, said MacKinnon, was prepared to develop public investment programs in order to counter a possible decline in private capital expenditure as another way of preserving high levels of export trade.[28] In order to guarantee a more efficient and effective flow of Canadian exports abroad, MacKinnon reassured that his government was committed to international cooperation, particularly with nations that welcomed free trade policies.

The Ospina Pérez administration was moving in that direction and violently oppressing those who did not favour such policies in Colombia. Thus the threat of political leaders like Jorge Eliécer Gaitán and other labour, socialist, and communist organizers who opposed a market-driven model of economic development for Colombia. The state's use of force against its own citizens after El Bogotazo showed the international community that Colombia was committed to protecting free market capitalism, foreign investment, and "democracy" as defined by the U.S. Cold War policies.

From the point of view of the Ospina Pérez administration, diplomatic relations should be extended across the "free world" in reciprocity to those nations that opened their economy to the international market system. The establishment of diplomatic links symbolized the nation's determined path toward modernization and capitalism.

Canada recognized the importance of the Colombian market but did not have the political will or the resources to expand its diplomatic relations. A 1945 report from Canada's *Commercial Intelligence Journal* confirmed Ottawa's interest in expanding trade with Colombia, describing it as "a nation with great economic growth potential" and a vastly diversified food production industry, where "practically the entire essential food requirements of the population" were "met by domestic production."[29] Colombia, said the report, represented an opportunity for Canada to invest in "oil exploration and extraction, particularly in the Llanos region."[30] In industrial production, it was possible that Canada could contribute to the advancement of Colombia's industrialization by "providing machinery and equipment for the ongoing development of a secondary industrial market."[31]

The report recommended that the government enhance its activity in Colombia in order to maintain the commercial influence it had gained as a result of the war. By 1943 Canada had become Colombia's fifth-largest supplier of imports, slowly taking over the market share left behind by the traditional European markets.[32] It was crucial for the Canadian economy to maintain this level of influence, indicated the report, considering that the Latin American market had become more integrated during the interwar period, and all seemed to indicate that it would continue to move more aggressively in that direction.[33] The report warned that regional trade threatened Canada's position in the Latin American market, particularly in nations like Colombia, where it could soon be replaced by exports from Mexico, Venezuela, Brazil, and Argentina.[34]

By the end of the war Canada was the second-largest purchaser of Colombian exports and the fifth-largest exporter to Colombia.[35] From the perspective of Canada's Department of Trade and Commerce, this trade was even more significant, considering that the relationship had been historically underestimated "by import and export statistics" that removed the "Made in Canada" label from certain commodities, as a result of its dependence on American intermediary ports.[36]

Canada's Department of Trade and Commerce was eager to maintain this advantageous position and recognized that, during Europe's reconstruction period, Colombia and other Latin American and Caribbean countries would be eager to purchase the bulk of their imports from nations such as Canada, whose industrial production capacity had not been adversely affected by the war.[37] Speaking on behalf of the private sector, the Department of Trade and Commerce concluded that Colombia would "look to North America for the bulk of its requirements and Canada should profit by the consequent opportunities."[38]

The report exalted the achievements of Canadian exporters and investors in the region, stressing that post-war advancement of Canadian trade interests in Colombia and the rest of the region should remain in the hands of the private sector. Canada's foreign policy in the region was driven by the private sector and should remain so, since Canada's ability to profit from the opportunities of doing business in the region depended largely on the ability of its private sector to open foreign markets. The report concluded that in Colombia the effectiveness of developing new markets depended on the private sector's "first-hand knowledge of the market" and its ability to develop close contacts with domestic policy and economic stakeholders.[39]

The report hinted that the Canadian government should be more active in the region in order to support Canadian businesses but that private actors should continue to spearhead Canada's foreign affairs in the region. The establishment of diplomatic relations was not an urgent item on the agenda.

The Ospina Pérez administration saw things very differently. In 1948 it requested establishment of diplomatic relations for the third time, hoping that this time Canada would also agree to occupy the twenty-second seat at the Pan American Conference in Bogotá. The Canadian government partially accepted the request but opted not to attend, as indicated in the previous chapter.

The Mackenzie King administration accepted "establishment of a Colombian diplomatic mission in Ottawa but it did not reciprocate."[40] The Ospina Pérez administration requested assurance on when the Canadian embassy would be opened in Bogotá, but External Affairs limited itself to reiterating that "insofar as reciprocation was concerned," it was difficult to establish a specific time frame.[41] Development of a promotional state needed to be strategic and responsive to Canadian business interests in the region.

A Canadian government-business partnership could not be effective in an inter-American system that was overly committed to "United States leadership."[42] If the Canadian government wanted to support its exporting business sectors, it needed to patiently wait for the right opportunity. The government was aware that the United States was not going to lay "the golden eggs for Latin America" and that at some point opportunities would rise.[43] In the absence of diplomatic presence, the government would provide logistical support when it was time to fill gaps in the Latin American and Caribbean markets, and in other instances the private sector capitalized upon Canada's exceptional relations with the United States. Canada, according to External Affairs, would indirectly benefit from the acceleration of U.S. investment in the region, since "a more solvent Latin America" would "undoubtedly increase Canadian exports" to the region.[44] This mentality and strategy prevailed throughout the 1940s.

In July 1949 Colombia's foreign minister, Eduardo Zuleta, travelled to Ottawa to raise the question once again, but there was no concrete response from the Canadian government.[45] Zuleta, who initially called to extend his "gratitude to the Canadian Government for the assistance which had been given him in arranging for a group of Canadian officials to visit Colombia to assist … in efforts to improve their electoral system," seized the opportunity to remind Deputy Secretary of State for External Affairs Escott Reid about the agreement reached between the two governments.[46] Zuleta "stressed how important he considered the establishment of closer relations and particularly closer diplomatic relations" between the two countries, particularly since it could allow them to expand their trade relationship and build a stronger partnership multilaterally.[47] Reid assured Zuleta that it was not a matter of willingness, but one of "shortage of personnel and budgetary difficulties."[48] He confirmed to Zuleta that his government hoped to establish "a diplomatic mission in Colombia in the near future."[49] Internally, A.D.P. Henney, under-secretary of state for external affairs, informed Reid that Ottawa was not very "enthusiastic about a recommendation to open a Mission in Colombia in the near future – nor indeed any new Missions anywhere without pretty specific reasons based on pretty evident, tangible and immediate Canadian interest shown."[50]

Later that same year, Minister Zuleta spoke directly with Secretary of State for External Affairs Lester B. Pearson to see if the issue could be clarified.[51] The Colombian government reminded Pearson about its respect and admiration for Canada's "idealistic but sensible approach" to foreign policy, praising the Canadian government and its people, and almost imploring Canada's official recognition.[52] Pearson tactfully responded by explaining that the Colombian government should not interpret the lack of commitment of his government "as an indication of coolness" on its part or lack of respect and admiration for the Colombian people, but simply a reflection of the haphazardness of recent Canadian–Latin American relations.[53] He then assured Zuleta that "he hoped it would be possible ... to make arrangements to establish a diplomatic mission in Colombia in the not too direct future."[54]

Soon after Zuleta's visit, the Department of External Affairs agreed to carry out a "general review ... to open new posts in Latin America."[55] In December 1949, less than a year after El Bogotazo, Under-Secretary of State for External Affairs Arnold Heeney presented Pearson with a report that justified strategic establishment of diplomatic relations in parts of Latin America and the Caribbean. He indicated that of the countries with which they had not yet exchanged missions, three had demanded "serious consideration: Uruguay, Colombia, and Venezuela."[56]

Colombia was strategic because Canada had "substantial economic interests" in it.[57] There was an important presence of Canadian firms operating in Colombia, including Tropical Oil, Andian National Corporation, Royal Bank of Canada, Sun Life Assurance Company, Pato Consolidated Gold Dredging, and Nechi Consolidated Gold Dredging.

Trade with Colombia was significant as well, concluded Heeney's report. By 1948 it had reached US$16 million, which was more than double the trade with Chile and Peru, two nations with which Canada had already established diplomatic exchanges.[58] Bilateral trade had increased significantly, going from a modest US$2.06 million in 1926 to US$16.00 million in twenty-two years.[59] Meanwhile, Canada's Department of Trade and Commerce predicted that Colombia would "eventually prove a more important market for Canadian goods than Cuba, Chile, and Peru."[60]

Speaking on behalf of Canada's exporting sectors, Heeney painted a positive picture of Colombia, indicating that, aside from the disturbances of El Bogotazo, the "nation had a good record of internal stability and democratic government."[61] The report portrayed Colombia not only as a stable nation but also as a committed fighter against totalitarianism; Colombia had a "consistent anti-Axis record ... and [was] one of the first South American republics to sign the United Nations Declaration."[62]

Colombia was a perfect fit for the diplomatic, economic, and political objectives of the overarching Cold War policy designed by the United States and implemented by countries such as Canada. It had declared a frontal war against totalitarianism and communism, had begun to adopt the World Bank recommendations established after the bank's visit in 1950, had consolidated political power under the two traditional elite-driven political parties, and had implemented institutional reforms to establish policies of social control for the adequate transition into capitalist-driven modernization.

The Canadian government was well aware that Colombia had the potential to develop rapidly and it estimated that, in the long run, it would rank "next to Argentina and Brazil among the leading Latin-American republics."[63] The case was made in favour of Colombia, and Pearson was ready to move forward with establishment of bilateral diplomatic relations, but the outbreak of the Korean War forced the two countries to put the diplomatic issue aside.

Between 1950 and 1952 both nations focused their efforts on providing military support to the United Nations Security Council. Canada joined the international conflict in July 1950 and Colombia followed suit in July of 1951 under the new conservative administration of President Laureano Gómez (1950–3). Although Colombia's participation was not as robust as Canada's, it represented the only Latin American presence in the conflict.[64] The Gómez administration had shown the international community that Colombia was committed to fighting communism domestically and abroad. It had also given Canada another reason to consider opening its embassy in Colombia.

While the war unfolded, the two nations resumed diplomatic exchange negotiations, and on 7 November 1952 the Canadian government announced the appointment of Edmond Turcotte as the first ambassador to Colombia.[65] Meanwhile Carlos Martínez Aparicio was designated Colombia's ambassador to Canada, thus formalizing the official bilateral relationship. This strengthened Canada's promotional state in Colombia and sent a clear message to its private sector that the government-business partnership was open for business.

The *Montreal Gazette* indicated that the opening of the Canadian embassies in Colombia and Uruguay were part of an effort to "stimulate trade and improve her markets."[66] It was no secret that the economic agenda was the driving force behind the initiative. The Canadian government was now ready to provide the support necessary to enhance business opportunities in these markets.

Edmond Turcotte was an experienced diplomat who had served as consul-general in Chicago, followed by a similar post in Caracas, Venezuela.[67] He had also been the editor of *Le Canada*, the Quebec Liberal newspaper that promoted free market ideals. Turcotte fulfilled the mission of promoting democracy via Canada's private sector initiatives.

With the presence of Ambassador Turcotte in Colombia, the Canadian government began to disseminate its pragmatic foreign policy that characterized it during the Cold War. After its strong stance against taking the twenty-second seat at the OAS, Turcotte told the Associated Press a few months after his arrival in Bogotá that Canada would join "the Pan American Union if the union tendered an invitation."[68] He became the Canadian voice in the region, saying that Canada's affiliation with the Commonwealth did not prevent it from joining the OAS and assuming a more influential role in the region.[69] He emphasized that Canada wanted to step up its efforts in the region and that it pursued interests and objectives that were completely independent from those of Britain or the Commonwealth.[70] In essence he was distancing Canada from Britain.

Ambassador Turcotte acknowledged that his objective was to increase Canada's presence in Colombia, understanding that his country was already one of the top five purchasers of Colombian goods and the second-largest importer of Colombian coffee.[71] Turcotte remained in Colombia until 1955, laying the groundwork for expansion of bilateral trade relations.

The culmination of ten years of bilateral negotiations toward establishment of diplomatic relations revealed Canada's difficulty in defining a Latin American and Caribbean policy. Contrary to the United States, Canada was handpicking its partnerships in the region in accordance to the needs of its private business sector. This demanded creation of a promotional state tailored to the needs of each market instead of using the more holistic approach implemented by the United States. Ultimately, establishment of diplomatic relations with Colombia indicated that the South American market was strategic for Canadian interests.

During his first year in office Turcotte welcomed Canada's "Goodwill Trade Mission" to Bogotá, part of a South American tour designed by Trade Minister C.D. Howe to facilitate business contacts with Canadian investors and multinational corporations. The 1953 trade mission laid the foundation for expansion of Canadian business interests in Colombia, including the 1956 sale of Canadian military equipment to the Colombian Air Force.

10

The 1953 Goodwill Trade Mission

Prime Minister Louis St. Laurent's administration continued to take incremental steps toward consolidation of a promotional state by sending his minister of trade, C.D. Howe, on a trade mission to the region in 1953. In the absence of a clear-cut line policy for Latin America and the Caribbean, the "Goodwill" Trade Mission was designed to expand trade, market the "Canada" brand, and strengthen the relationship with individual nations. The overarching objective was to tie Canada's "goodwill" to international trade, in hopes of helping its private sector compete against other industrial powers and the regional trade blocs that could surface in the region.[1] Expansion of diplomatic relations and the trade mission that followed were clear indicators that the Canadian government was taking first steps toward development of a promotional state that could facilitate business expansion across the region.

C.D. Howe, who was fighting opposition from the Conservatives who accused Louis St. Laurent's government of "losing its markets abroad" and trading with the wrong countries, attempted to reinforce Canada's position in Latin America, reminding them that under the Liberals, Canada had registered US$33 million in trade with Latin America and the Caribbean and that trade with the region had reached US$560 million.[2] The mission was intended to manage and expand business opportunities in places like Colombia, where there was ample room for market development and expansion.

Part of the new propaganda system of the promotional state was to sell the region to Canadian policymakers and their constituents, who were sceptical about the region's potential. Prior to the mission, Howe emphasized the importance of the region, indicating that it had "the fastest growing population" and an interest in accelerating its industrial development.[3] The Liberals emphasized that countries such as Colombia were going through positive social, structural, legal, economic, political, and institutional transformations, and that Canada needed to take advantage of these changes to advance its own private sector interests. The emerging Latin American markets were diversifying their international commercial relations, and Canada needed to exploit these "changing trade patterns"; they needed to fill market gaps when the opportunity was available.[4]

The adoption of a market-driven economic development model, increasing modernization initiatives, "high production, rising living standards, increasing import requirements," and recent "economic expansion" were enough reasons to justify the tour to Mexico, Venezuela, Brazil, Cuba, Argentina, Chile, and Colombia.[5]

In January 1953 Howe embarked on a five-week tour of nine countries, including Brazil, Argentina, Uruguay, Venezuela, Colombia, Dominican Republic, Haiti, Cuba, and Mexico.[6] The mission included a small group of government officials and seven Canadian business leaders "drawn from widely representative branches of the Canadian economy."[7] Howe and several business representatives were familiar with parts of Latin America and some of them were fluent in Spanish.[8] Representatives included D.W. Ambridge, president and general manager of Abitibi Power & Paper Co., who attended on behalf of the Canadian Chamber of Commerce in Toronto; J.M. Bonin, managing director of La Cooperative Agricole de Granby, representing the Chamber of Commerce of the Province of Quebec; J.S. Duncan, chairman and president of Massey-Harris Co., Ltd., representing the Canadian Manufacturers' Association; Alex Gray, president of Gray-Bonney Tool Co., Ltd., representing the Canadian Exporters' Association; F.L. Marshall, vice-president of export for the House of Seagram, representing the Canadian Inter-American Association; K.F. Wadsworth, president and general manager of Maple Leaf Milling Co., Ltd.; and Clive B. Davidson, secretary of the Canadian Wheat Board.[9]

In Colombia, the mission lasted four days, splitting its time between Bogotá and Barranquilla. The Canadian delegation arrived at a pivotal point in the nation's economic development; the structural recommendations from the 1950 World Bank mission were in the early stages of implementation, foreign direct investment was rising, and regional trade initiatives were being discussed.

During that same January, Venezuelan and Colombian business leaders began talks on greater integration and commercial cooperation between the two nations.[10] At around the same time Air France inaugurated direct flights between Bogotá and Paris, while Pan American World Airways extended its operations into the Colombian market.[11] The Swedish Johnson Line had recently announced expansion of its cargo and passenger fleet to enhance maritime services between Europe and Colombia, while the British government continued to raise concerns about its loss of influence in the region.[12] American and European businesses were aggressively targeting the Colombian market, thanks to the efforts of their respective promotional states, while Canada lagged behind in the absence of a strong promotional state that could catapult its business sector.

On 28 January the Canadian delegates met with Sir Gilbert McKereth, British ambassador to Colombia, followed by a meeting with Colombia's minister of finance and public credit, Antonio Alvarez Restrepo, and the minister of development, Carlos Villaveces, followed by meetings with the minister of external affairs, Juan Uribe Holguín, and the minister of agriculture, Camilo Cabal Cabal.[13] Later that evening they were welcomed by the "staunch anti-communist" Roberto Urdaneta Arbeláez, who was acting president on behalf of Conservative leader Laureano Gómez.

Speaking to the press, C.D. Howe said that Canada was in Colombia "in search of opportunities," ready to listen and learn more about the people and the nation's economic development.[14] The mission generated excitement among Colombian business and policymakers, who were also eager to expand their commercial opportunities with Canada. Colombia's press gave ample coverage to the official visit, calling it a "good neighbor visit," and highlighting the interconnectivity between the two economies, particularly Canada's role as the second-largest buyer of Colombian coffee.[15] In exchange for coffee, Colombia bought from Canada wheat, aluminium, newsprint, and other specialty papers. Ships from the country's merchant fleet Flota Mercante Grancolombiana had been built in Canadian shipyards, proof of collaboration between the two nations.

C.D. Howe emphasized Canada's interest in the Colombian economy and recognized the country's progress in structural adjustments and economic development.[16] He praised Colombia's commitment to a free market model of economic development and said it was in Canada's interest to pair up with nations that "shared similar ideas and perspectives" and were willing to make domestic sacrifices to protect "our way of living in the Western Hemisphere" as well as shared Christian beliefs.[17] Howe concluded by reminding those present that Colombia and Canada shared the same problems and solutions, and that they were honoured to fight shoulder-to-shoulder against communism in Korea.[18]

Canadian delegates also met with the directors of Colombia's central bank, Banco de la República, the president and officials from the Flota

Mercante Grancolombiana, executives from the Colombian Coffee-Producers Federation, and representatives from the powerful business conglomerates that controlled the country's domestic market.[19] That evening, they attended a cocktail party at the Country Club of Bogotá organized by the Flota Mercante Grancolombiana.[20]

In Bogotá they took advantage of the opportunity to meet with delegates from the Canadian Technical Mission who had arrived a year earlier to develop the citizen identification card system and implement Colombia's Decree 2628 of 1951.[21] This was part of early promotional state initiatives of the Canadian government in response to Colombia's efforts to establish bilateral diplomatic relations. In 1951, at the request of the Colombian government, Canada sent a technical mission to recommend a fix for Colombia's troubled electoral system. The Colombian government had awarded the Canadian government the contract to develop a citizen identification card system that removed congressional and presidential elections from the sphere of influence of the executive branch and toward a neutral and independent process. Canada had been chosen over Belgium, Switzerland, Holland, and the United States, perhaps as a result of its neutrality and "goodwill."[22] The trade delegates discussed advancement of the project with their Canadian counterparts, including the training program for local dactylographers and the pilot program in Bogotá.[23]

Delegates also met with government officials to discuss Colombia's wheat import policy, since Canadian wheat producers were eager to sell their excess production to countries across Latin America.[24] Although Colombia was self-sufficient in food production, as attested by the World Bank report of 1950, it was adopting the structural changes recommended by the Bank in order to specialize in agro-industrial production of certain export crops and the import of others that were produced inefficiently.[25] Wheat fell under the list of crops that were inefficiently grown by local farmers and therefore needed to be imported from the international market, where Canada and Argentina competed head-to-head.

Implementation of the report's recommendations under President Laureano Gómez's administration resulted in a decrease in production of domestic wheat and an increase in the import of the commodity. Wheat had been protected under nationalist Colombian policy, therefore the Canadian delegates, and particularly Clive B. Davidson from the Canadian Wheat Board, were interested in discussing deregulation of wheat import policy. The Canadian Wheat Board, created by the Canadian Wheat Board Act of 1935, operated in this case as an instrument of the promotional state, transcending domestic subsidy policies in the international market. Its objective in Bogotá was to ensure that the Colombian government eliminated protectionist policies and increased imports of Canadian and not Argentinean wheat.[26] The new arrangement stipulated that "Colombian importers" would have "a greater opportunity to plan ahead … and be in a position to buy more wheat from Canada in those periods when local production" was insufficient.[27] Why import from the Argentinean market when Colombia could get a much better deal from Canadian suppliers under the Most Favoured Nation agreement. As part of this effort, Davidson met independently with several domestic industrial importers of wheat, including the pasta manufacturer Fábrica de Pastas El Gallo.[28]

During their meeting with Minister Cabal, delegates discussed the impacts of adoption of the 1952 U.S. embargo "against imports of livestock, and fresh and frozen meats from Canada."[29] Canada was interested in renewing its livestock exports to Colombia and wanted to assure the Colombian government that the spread of foot-and-mouth disease had been contained. Minister Cabal informed the delegation that Colombia would lift the embargo when the United States gave them the green light.[30] Canadian businesses wanted to overcome such dependency dynamics with consolidation of a strong promotional state.

One of C.D. Howe's main objectives was to meet with Flota Mercante Grancolombiana executives in Venezuela and Colombia.[31] This was one of the trip's core objectives, considering that Canadian businesses and policymakers had been struggling to overcome their dependence on U.S. ports and merchant ships since early stages of trade relations with Latin America and the Caribbean. Delegates were aware of the importance of strengthening their relationship with the "joint shipping line of Venezuela, Colombia and Ecuador," which already extended its services to Canada's east coast.[32] Consolidation of direct shipping routes strengthened the bilateral relation and reduced their dependency on the United States.

Although no deal was reached on expansion of shipping services to Canada's west coast, the Canadian delegates did take the opportunity to make the point that they would continue to insist on expansion of direct trade routes via the Flota Mercante Grancolombiana. Canada had been deeply involved in development of the merchant fleet; all its ships had been built in Canada, and it had been under the solicitation of Canadian exporters that other negotiations had been carried out "in order to expand the fleet of refrigerated ships" to further promote direct shipments from Canadian ports.[33] The Vickers shipyard in Montreal had built the cargo ships *Ciudad de Maracaibo, Ciudad de Manizales,*

Ciudad de Quito, *Ciudad de Cali*, and *Ciudad de Ibagué*, further linking the two economies.[34]

Three South American nations (Venezuela, Colombia, and Ecuador) were part of an exclusive group of nations that had achieved maritime transportation independence, which was greatly desired by Canadian exporters who continued to depend on intermediaries for their international trade. Coincidentally, talks were taking place between the three partners that same January, and all seemed to indicate that Venezuela and Ecuador would sell their share of the fleet to the Colombian government, leaving it sole proprietor of the Flota Mercante Grancolombiana.[35] Canadian exporters were therefore eager to discuss the future of the merchant fleet.

Delegates also made it a priority to meet with Canadian-owned companies operating in Colombia. In Bogotá they had the opportunity to visit "the modern pharmaceutical laboratories of Frost and Co., of Montreal," which had recently established operations in Colombia.[36] During their stop in Barranquilla they were "guests at a luncheon given by the local branch of the Royal Bank of Canada," and later that evening they attended "two farewell parties … one given by the British embassy and the other by the National City Bank of New York."[37]

On 1 February the delegation departed to the Dominican Republic, with the confidence that trade with countries such as Colombia could "be expanded to still much greater levels."[38] Back in Ottawa, Howe did not hesitate to report to the House of Commons that Canada needed to increase its position in one of the "world's major trading areas," but that effort should continue to be left "primarily" in the hands of "Canadian businessmen."[39] It all seemed to indicate that the government-business partnership would continue to rely on the efforts of the Canadian private sector for development of relationships across the region.

No policy meant zero accountability, and that seemed to be the best strategy for Canadian businesses investing and trading in the region. Leaving matters in the hands of the private sector meant that the public did not need to be informed about Canada's involvement in Latin America and the Caribbean. Discrete intervention of the promotional state, as in the merchant fleet or the citizen identification card program, was effective for some Canadian business sectors, but other exporting sectors wanted more active government intervention to help them promote their own commodities and services across the region. Nevertheless, the status quo prevailed throughout the 1950s and 1960s as a result of the lack of will by the Canadian government to develop a clear-cut line policy for Latin America and the Caribbean.

Sale of F-86 Jet Fighters to Colombia, 1956

Four months after the departure of C.D. Howe's mission, Colombians found themselves mired in General Rojas Pinilla's military coup d'état. His overthrow of President Laureano Gómez's administration, considered by many as the central force behind La Violencia, set a new tone for Colombia's relations abroad. Rojas Pinilla's takeover came in the name of democracy, presenting itself as a temporary political solution to the bipartisan conflict that had engulfed the nation. He assumed power in the name of democracy, promising the international system the eradication of the roots of communism across the country and renewal of peace and harmony among political actors. In the middle of the intense escalation of the Cold War in Colombia, Canadair came to fill the gap left by the U.S. military industry, closing a deal with the Colombian government for the sale of F-86 Sabre jet fighters. Canadair's experience in Colombia showed that the Canadians were willing to contribute to Washington's policies of containment and play its role as a promoter of democracy, as long it benefited its domestic industrial sector. It also revealed Washington's tolerance for the initiatives of the Canadian promotional state in the region and unravelled the increasing levels of interconnectivity and interdependence that were developing between the two North American economies.

The sale of jet fighters to Colombia revealed the effectiveness of the Canadian promotional state. Canadair, with the help of the Canadian government, strengthened the bilateral trade relationship even more. Purchase of the jet fighters by the Colombian Air Force was a clear indication of the success of the 1953 trade mission and the benefits of having bilateral diplomatic relationships. C.D. Howe and his delegates had carried out their tour in a Canadair C-5, using it as a marketing tool to promote Canadian engineering, industrial capacity, and high-quality products. By the 1950s Canadair was an internationally recognized aircraft manufacturer selling its military and commercial products across Europe and the Americas. Its F-86 Sabre had proven itself in the Korean War, both as a jet fighter and a fighter-bomber.

Army General Gustavo Rojas Pinilla, who wanted to modernize the national air force, saw in the F-86 Sabre an optimal solution. Through a letter of intent issued in February 1956, the Colombian government agreed to purchase six F-86 Sabre jet fighters from Canadair.[40]

Negotiations behind the deal showed how Canadair effectively lobbied the Department of Trade and Commerce to close the international sale, and how the Rojas Pinilla administration was able to secure support from the international community by committing to the eradication of communism in Colombia. Sale of the F-86 Sabre jet fighters marked the first sale of Canadian jet aircraft to Latin America and the first time an arms deal took place "outside the Commonwealth and NATO."[41]

The Rojas Pinilla administration first approached Canadair with a request for six F-86 Sabre jet fighters as part of the military build-up to fight leftist guerrilla forces that emanated from La Violencia and the social displacement caused by implementation of agro-industrial production in Colombia. Leveraging on the Canadian promotional state, Canadair eagerly accepted the solicitation and immediately requested a formal export permit from Prime Minster Louis St. Laurent's Cabinet.[42]

The minister of trade and commerce and defence production, C.D. Howe, who had led the 1953 "Goodwill" Trade Mission, agreed to draft the "joint submission to the Cabinet on behalf of Canadair."[43] He was convinced that the sale to Colombia would open doors for other Canadian exports and "stimulate sales to other parts of the world."[44] Expansion of sales of military equipment beyond NATO and the Commonwealth represented an opportunity for Canadair to penetrate the international arms sales market in the Americas and across other markets.[45] It also translated to a reduction of Canadair's overall costs for the production "of similar aircraft for the Royal Canadian Air Force" and reduced costs of all production for Canadian government accounts.[46]

Cabinet approval of the export permit, said C.D. Howe, would also be crucial for expansion of "Canadian commercial relations with Colombia."[47] There was opposition from some members of Cabinet who were unconvinced that this was a good deal, since it could irritate the "great powers," considering that "the role of supplier of military equipment of this nature" had traditionally been under foreign jurisdiction.[48] The Canadian government was also concerned that the sale of jet fighters to Colombia could irritate other hemispheric actors, since the norms for arms sales stipulated by the Rio Treaty did not include Canada as a major actor.[49]

Other Cabinet members were concerned about the impact that this sale could have on Canada's reputation in the region and across the "free world."[50] Negative public relations could result from Canada's bolstering of military equipment across the region, and particularly to a military dictatorship, because that would alienate the "liberal and progressive forces" that Canada supported.[51] Secretary of State for External Affairs Lester B. Pearson indicated that the sale of jet fighters to the military regime of Rojas Pinilla would contradict Canada's Colombo Plan in Southeast Asia, since it had previously negated arm sales to undemocratic regimes.[52] Canada was placed in a Catch-22: its "goodwill" would be questioned by backing Rojas Pinilla but its denial of military support would contradict its commitment to the anti-communist struggle.

Those concerned with the attacks of communist propagandists concluded that the possible sale of military equipment to Colombia would instigate Latin America's Left against Canada.[53] The Left was gaining strength in the region, particularly in places like Colombia, Cuba, Argentina, Chile, and Brazil—curiously some of the top Canadian trade partners in the Western Hemisphere. Therefore, closing the deal with the Colombian government could endanger Canadian capital and business interests.

Other Cabinet members were concerned about backing an unpopular regime through the sale of the six F-86 Sabre jet fighters.[54] Their judgment was that, after almost three years in power, the Rojas Pinilla administration had lost popular support and now "maintained itself in power only through the exercise of increasingly repressive measures backed solely by armed forces."[55] Canada's support for an "unpleasant type" of dictatorship was not good foreign policy, even though Washington recognized the Rojas Pinilla administration.

The raised concerns resulted in a request for further assessment by the Joint Intelligence Bureau, hampering the approval of Canadair's export permit. C.D. Howe continued to advocate on behalf of Canadair by sending his associate deputy minister of trade and commerce, Mitchell Sharp, to negotiate on his behalf. Trade and Commerce, via Sharp and Howe, became the voice of the promotional state in the negotiations.

On 7 March 1956 Mitchell Sharp, who would later head the 1968 ministerial mission to Latin America, explained that Canadair's deal involved more than simply the sale of jet fighters; it represented jobs for Canadians, revenues for the Canadian economy, and a greater opportunity for the expansion of business in Colombia and across the hemisphere.[56]

Beside the six jet fighters, Canadair had negotiated the establishment of "overhaul and service facilities" for the jet aircrafts they sold.[57] This included the management, supervision, and training of personnel, which would result in creation of more than one hundred new jobs for Canadians as well as the need for "large quantities of Canadian equipment" to service the Colombian Air Force.[58] Sharp's department also emphasized that if the deal was closed, there would "be a much larger flow of Canadian equipment into Colombia in the form of replacement parts," and that it would open the door for future purchases of other Canadian military equipment.[59] Trade and Commerce also reminded sceptical Cabinet members that approval of the deal could open new doors for other Canadian businesses, knowing well that Colombia's commercial and military sectors were also in the market for radio beacon stations and telecommunications equipment necessary for the modernization of the country's infrastructure.[60]

Sharp insisted that he did not see a problem in selling these planes to Colombia, considering the fact that in the past the same planes had "been freely offered to Colombia by the United States."[61] He concluded by reminding Pearson that it was commonly agreed among Cabinet members that Colombia was a safe place in which to develop the aircraft export industry.[62] A letter of intent was resting on the desk of the offices of Canadair waiting for authorization from the Canadian government, reiterated Sharp; failure to authorize the export permit would be a "real embarrassment" and a blow to the Canadian industrial sector.[63]

A week later, Secretary of State Pearson told the other Cabinet members "that it would be difficult to refuse to sell to a country which wished to develop its legitimate defense and which was in an area of the world where there was no tension at the moment."[64] Furthermore, said Pearson, it was important to consider the negative implications this would have on the "maintenance of the Canadian aircraft industry."[65] Pearson had shifted his position on the issue, joining the pressure mounted by the promotional state.

Even though Colombia was in the midst of a civil war and under the control of a military government, it was viewed as a "no tension" zone by the Canadian promotional state. Canada slowly joined the United States in recognizing the Rojas Pinilla military government, disregarding the fact that the Colombian government was in a frontal war against communism, and was requesting the F-86 Sabres to fight the leftist guerrillas from the air.

On 20 March 1956, Pearson sent a memorandum to other Cabinet members making a strong case for the sale of jet fighters to the Colombian Air Force. He reiterated Sharp's justifications and added that Colombia would obtain the planes from another supplier if Canada did not release them.[66] He concluded by recommending the "approval … for the issue of an export permit for the export by Canadair of six F-86 aircraft to Colombia."[67]

Soon after, the Cabinet met again to discuss the issue and agreed that the export permit should be issued because, in the event that other South American countries approached Canada to purchase jet fighters, Ottawa would be forced to issue the same refusal given to Colombia.[68] The best option was to sell weapons to Latin America and not deny them the opportunity to fight communism while at the same time enhancing the business dynamics with Canadian companies.

In addition, Pearson added that Colombia "was the best friend that Canada had in South America and it would be difficult to explain why the export of the aircraft could not be permitted."[69] The sale, said Pearson, would result in good business for Canada; it might stimulate sales in other countries and might open doors to other Canadian companies in Colombia.[70]

On 22 March 1956, Cabinet agreed "that an export permit be issued to authorize the transaction."[71] Early that summer, the six F-86 Sabre aircraft were delivered to the Colombian Air Force.[72] Canada had filled another gap in the Colombian market and was now "a supplier of jet aircrafts in Latin America."[73]

Canada's private sector interests had prevailed over politics. Apparently, if the Canadian government wanted to keep its aircraft industry alive and preserve the jobs behind the industry, it needed to sell the equipment overseas because domestic demand was insufficient to keep the industry running. The sale of aircraft abroad made "it far easier to maintain the industry as an up-to-date production facility," allowing it to transition from production of a particular model to "the production of its successor."[74] The sale of the F-86s to Colombia allowed Canadair to manage its inventory more effectively, providing the company the flexibility to move obsolete inventory more efficiently, by selling it to "less advanced countries" where the demand for substandard aircraft was high.[75]

The sale of jet fighters to Colombia also contributed to the hemispheric efforts of containment. The United States was well aware of the escalation of the war against communism in Colombia, and that "Rojas and his military colleagues were not equipped to combat the communist element within the guerrilla movement."[76] Initially, the U.S. embassy "encouraged the U.S. government to materially assist" Rojas Pinilla in his struggle against communism, but in the end it was Canadair that provided the assistance.[77] Canada's government-business partnership had once again played its role as a subordinate state, serving the needs of the U.S. Cold War agenda while at the same time capitalizing on the international business opportunity.

The sale of the F-86 Sabre jets filled the need for military assistance, showing Canada's commitment to the policies of containment in the Western Hemisphere. The Canadian aircraft provided a feasible solution to Colombia's struggle against communism; their effectiveness in the Korean War had shown that they were versatile and reliable. The aircraft could "be used to suppress revolt" in the mountains of Colombia and intimidate the rebel forces.[78]

The same year that the aircraft arrived, La Violencia claimed the lives of 11,000 Colombians.[79] Rojas Pinilla's aggressive anti-communist surge proved somewhat effective, but ultimately failed to curtail the political violence that had brought him to power. Rojas Pinilla was removed from office one year later, unable to use the F-86s for civilian bombardment, which was his intention all along.

The bipartisan political agreement known as *Frente Nacional* (1958–74), which brought the military dictatorship to an end, set a new tone in Canadian-Colombian bilateral relations. Canadair personnel continued to provide training, technical support, and equipment for maintenance of the jetfighters, while new Canadian businesses eagerly set their sights on the Colombian market. Nevertheless, the lack of a clear Latin American and Caribbean policy prevented them from capitalizing on the initiatives of the Canadian promotional state.

The window of opportunity for Canadian businesses was not open for long. Under the John F. Kennedy administration the United States revised their belligerent Cold War policy toward the region and shifted toward ODA to win the hearts and minds of the people. Kennedy's Alliance for Progress initiative, which aimed to establish economic cooperation across the Western Hemisphere, became an obstacle for Canadian business interests in places like Colombia. The robust U.S. government-business partnership once again diminished the capabilities of the Canadian government-business partnership.

The Impact of the Alliance for Progress

President John F. Kennedy's Alliance for Progress initiative of 1961 served as a foreign policy tool to control the U.S. sphere of influence in the Western Hemisphere, at a time when foreign business and ideological interests were inundating the region. Implementation of U.S. external aid policy affected economic development of the Western Hemisphere, and Canada saw its private sector initiatives in the region hampered by both the ODA initiative and its own internal foreign policy decisions. Ultimately, this tempered Canadian-Colombian relations, while at the same time strengthening Colombian-U.S. relations.

The Frente Nacional theoretically put an end to domestic party violence and the expansion of communism, while at the same time establishing the structural conditions necessary for the long-term implementation of capitalist economic development policies recommended by the World Bank. It had generated the political, social, and economic stability necessary for expansion of foreign direct investment, attracting investors and multinational corporations from around the world.

Colombia's political solution to the social crisis was welcomed by the international business sector, yet very few Canadian investors were able to capitalize on a more stable and less risky Colombian economy. Early initiatives of the Canadian promotional state had been compromised with the arrival to power of Prime Minister John Diefenbaker in 1957. His foreign policy agenda had excluded Colombia from the overall Latin American strategy, making it harder for Canadian businesses to compete in that market.[80]

His focus on the 1959 Cuban Revolution and the 1962 Cuban Missile Crisis represented the core of his hemispheric agenda. In the absence of a clear-cut policy on Latin America and the Caribbean, Canadian businesses were forced to accommodate to the new realities of the Cold War introduced by Kennedy's ODA program as well as the change of direction of the Diefenbaker government.

Diefenbaker's regional strategy was limited to Mexico, Brazil, Argentina, and the Commonwealth Caribbean.[81] Colombia was not targeted as a place where Canada could implement policies that would allow it to achieve greater autonomy from the United States, one of the main objectives of the Diefenbaker administration.[82] Canadian exporters and other business interests did not share this view, particularly companies that were already operating in Colombia.

Meanwhile Colombia was high on the United States foreign policy agenda and even more so after the Cuban Revolution. The success of the Castro regime forced President Alberto Lleras Camargo's (1958–62) administration to come up with a land reform initiative that would cater to the Left, and by 1961 his administration had secured U.S. aid for implementation of his program.[83] Kennedy's Alliance for Progress initiative in Colombia, and the military aid initiative known as Plan Lazo, brought the two nations closer together.[84] Canadian, European, and Japanese interests found it more difficult to do business in Colombia, as U.S. influence grew throughout the 1960s. The large number of U.S. Peace Corps volunteers that arrived in Colombia during the early 1960s firmly placed the country under the U.S. sphere of influence.

Colombia's closeness with the United States prevented Diefenbaker from expanding the promotional state into this market,[85] but this did not prevent Canadian companies and investors from pursuing business opportunities in Colombia.

Such was the case of Bank of London and Montreal, which was formed jointly by Bank of Montreal and Bank of London and South America in 1958 in order to take over the fourteen branch offices operated by Bank of London and South America in Colombia, Venezuela, Ecuador, El Salvador, Guatemala, and Nicaragua.[86] By 1963 the operations of Bank of London and Montreal had expanded throughout the region, making Colombia their biggest South American market with six branches.[87] The

new Canadian bank had joined the efforts of Royal Bank and other foreign banks that were eager to finance Colombia's modernization and
other economic development initiatives of the 1960s. Under the stability provided by the Frente Nacional, the branch offices of the Canadian bank were able to finance and promote domestic consumption as
well as imports of luxury and semi-luxury goods by borrowing in other
external markets.[88] Banks such as this became instrumental in generating domestic resources for economic development and the expansion of
a consumer market in Colombia.

The Canadian paper industry was also able to carve a niche market
in Colombia during the 1960s. Gene H. Kruger, a Quebec investor,
took advantage of Colombian stability, expanding his domestic paper
industry into the Colombian market.[89] He established a joint paper
production operation with shared Colombian capital after developing a similar business initiative in Venezuela. Established in 1960,
Papeles Nacionales S.A. became the leading soft paper–producing
company in Colombia, controlling most of Colombia's domestic market. Kruger's operation benefitted from the introduction of top Canadian technology to produce a range of tissue products for multiple
household, industrial, and commercial uses, and helped develop
affiliated companies such as Fibras Nacionales, which was established in 1971 as part of the vertical integration system of Papeles
Nacionales, providing the company with recycled waste paper.[90]
The success of its affiliate eventually reduced Kruger's dependence
on imported pulp and paper, reaching a level of domestic supply of
waste paper that allowed Fibras Nacionales to export raw material
to Central America, the Caribbean, Peru, Ecuador, the United States,
and the United Kingdom.[91]

The experiences of Bank of London and Montreal and Kruger Inc.
illustrated how, in the absence of a robust promotional state, Canadian
businesses flourished in the late 1950s and 1960s, when the Colombian
market was heavily influenced by the United States. Throughout this
period, Canadian-Colombian relations remained dependent on Canada's private sector initiatives.

The economic stability provided by the Frente Nacional policies
offered Canadian and other foreign investors increased participation in
the Colombian market. It enhanced the expansion of capitalism through
implementation of structural adjustment policies and institutional
development programs funded by the Alliance for Progress.[92] By the
late 1960s a market-driven culture of economic development had been
established, together with legal, institutional, and programmatic structural changes that supported the initiatives recommended by the World

Bank back in 1950.[93] One of these structural changes was incorporation of ODA as part of the nation's economic development plan.

Official Development Assistance found its way into the Colombian economy during the 1960s, opening new routes for foreign businesses to enter the market. For example, implementation of the Alliance for Progress initiatives in Colombia became a lucrative opportunity for many U.S. businesses interested in investing in large infrastructure projects. ODA became an integral part of the foreign affairs toolkit of every nation interested in helping its private sector secure new business opportunities in emerging markets such as Colombia's. The Canadian business sector therefore once again demanded that its government also incorporate ODA into the design of the promotional state.

Nevertheless, the Canadian government did not meet the private sector's expectations. Canada's 1960s ODA initiatives under the Colombo Plan kept external aid funding out of Latin America.[94] This slowly changed in response to increasing demand from Canadian foreign investors, exporters, and Left-leaning intellectuals that also found in ODA an alternative to support their own humanitarian and anti-imperialist agendas.

Canadian ODA policies targeted Colombia in 1963 under the administration of Prime Minister Lester B. Pearson, and intensified after 1970 under the administration of Prime Minister Pierre Elliott Trudeau. It was under Trudeau's administration that a clear-cut line policy on Latin America and the Caribbean was finally defined, and the strengthening of the promotional state was identified as a key objective of the regional policy. It was also at that point that ODA became the key component of Canada's Latin American and Caribbean policy.

The 1968 ministerial mission to Latin America helped shape this policy. The hemispheric tour not only confirmed the importance of the region for Canada's economic development; it also revealed the urgent need for a regional policy and a promotional state that could compete not only against U.S. business interests but global business interests as well. The mission became a pivotal point in Canadian–Latin American and Canadian–Colombian relations.

11

The 1968 Ministerial Mission

The Departments of External Affairs and Industry, Trade and Commerce galvanized a clear-cut policy for Latin America and the Caribbean. During the late 1960s and early 1970s they orchestrated the expansion of Canada's promotional state toward the region under the leadership of Prime Minister Pierre Elliott Trudeau, developing and funding new institutions such as the Canadian International Development Agency (CIDA), which replaced the old External Aid Office (EAO). The long-awaited policy, heavily dependent on ODA, followed the 1968 ministerial mission to Latin America. This trade mission reaffirmed the importance of enhancing the promotional state in order to help Canadian companies compete against global investors and businesses. The mission's stop in Colombia set the tone for a more intimate bilateral relationship, which involved development assistance projects, including a growing exchange of human capital, resources, technology, and technical expertise. By 1974, multiple Canadian development programs were well on their way in Colombia; Canada's external aid, like U.S. aid, had begun to make its mark on Colombia's economic development. It shaped the use of land, and natural and human resources. It was responsible for the funding, development, and technical advice behind massive energy and agro-industrial projects that reconfigured landscapes and transformed ecosystems across Colombia.

The mission was "designed to demonstrate the importance" that the Canadian government assigned to strengthening bilateral relations with strategic Latin American partners, such as Colombia.[1] The initiative was selective and strategic; like all other previous missions to Latin America, it reflected not a hemispheric policy, but a sub-regional agenda based on potential bilateral partnerships that best fulfilled the needs and demands of Canadian investors and exporting business sectors.

Three months after the May 1968 announcement, planning of the mission was well on its way. For the first time, planning took place in Ottawa and not in the offices and gathering halls of the Canadian Manufacturers' Association. It was left in the hands of the Department of External Affairs, the Department of Industry, Trade and Commerce, the Export Credits Insurance Corporation, the Department of Finance, and CIDA.[2] These agencies defined the mission's agenda and the nations that would be the focus of the policy.[3] Moreover, the new policy initiative was planned, coordinated, and designed by the offices of the Latin American Division of the Department of External Affairs.[4]

The trade agenda remained the prominent component of the mission, even though private sector representatives were not included in the delegation. The ministerial mission remained committed to the vision of Industry, Trade and Commerce that the new policy initiative toward the region should defend the interests of Canada and more precisely the interests of Canada's private sector.[5]

Promotion and enhancement of Canada's image abroad was another policy objective.[6] The consensus was that capitalizing on Canada's "goodwill" could help Canada's ODA programs distinguish themselves from the other donor nations, and ultimately give it an edge over its competitors. A positive image and greater governmental support, said the deputy minister of industry, trade and commerce, J.F. Grady, was necessary in order to back up Canadian business initiatives in Latin America. Otherwise, Japanese and European investors would find greater space to expand their manoeuvrability in the region.[7]

Britain welcomed plans for the mission. Prime Minister Harold Wilson's government believed that his country should also look more closely at expanding relations across Latin America and the Caribbean since the region was "far more promising in economic terms than ... ex-British colonial territories in Africa."[8] A few weeks before the mission departed, the Canadian embassy in London informed the Department of External Affairs that the British government had approached it to discuss the upcoming tour to the region.[9] The British government welcomed "increased Canadian involvement in Latin America," since it "felt that any increase of economic and political power in the area by Britain or Canada would have a positive effect and would tend to offset the overly strong influence of the USA."[10] The British encouraged the Canadians to take advantage of their "large store of good will in the area" to expand their influence in the region.[11] Trade, they suggested, should be the focus of the policy toward Latin America, while security and containment should be left to the Americans.[12] This view was shared by the nationalist administration of Prime Minister Trudeau.

Communication with the United States prior to the mission's departure was minimal. Washington approached the Canadian government only to ask why U.S. representatives were not invited to participate in official events during the visit.[13]

The mission, as indicated by Secretary of State for External Affairs Mitchell Sharpe, represented the initial step in development of a clear-cut policy toward the region.[14] It was an opportunity to discuss with regional stakeholders the best way to cooperate and strengthen bilateral relations while defining the best options for Canada's economy and its export business sector.[15]

This general feeling was also expressed days before the mission's departure at the twenty-fifth annual meeting of the Canadian Export Association. There the association's president, J.M. McAvity, emphasized its concern about the country's increasing dependence on the U.S. market.[16] He pointed out that close to 65 per cent of Canada's exports went to the United States, and that a possible increase in U.S. protectionist policies and an increasing uncertainty "over the attitude of the U.S. Congress" raised an even greater concern about the "rapidly increasing dependence on the U.S. market."[17] He concluded, on behalf of the Canadian Export Association, that Canada's exports should be more geographically balanced and diversified.[18] Latin America and the Caribbean were targeted as potential markets for implementation of Canada's export diversification strategy.

The mission served as a starting point for the country's export diversification policy. It marked the beginning of a more autonomous regional policy that centred its strategy on ODA initiatives. In Colombia, the visit shed light on the new strategy and revealed the capabilities of the Canadian promotional state under the Pierre Elliott Trudeau government.

Bogotá: 29 October–1 November 1968

Colombia was one of nine strategic destinations of the 1968 ministerial mission to Latin America. Policymakers had studied Colombia's situation and were aware of Canada's private sector interest in continuing to expand operations across that market.[19] Colombia had great potential, and its economy could take off at any moment if the social, economic, and political tensions were resolved. A year before the mission, the Department of Economics and Development reported that Colombia was "potentially Latin America's richest country in coal," fairly self-sufficient in food production, its sugar and tobacco production were slowly taking over Cuba's traditional supply to the free market, and its cattle industry had the potential of entering the global export market system.[20]

Colombia's economic development initiatives, according to the report, offered an opportunity for Canadian investors and multi-national corporations, since Colombia's manufacturing industry depended on "imported raw materials, semi-finished products and capital goods."[21] The report unambiguously recommended doing business in Colombia, considering that it offered political stability under the "unique arrangement" presented by the Frente Nacional.[22] Colombia was committed to opening its economy to the global market system and had been implementing structural adjustments since 1950, as recommended by the World Bank. Moreover, the country was moving forward with constitutional reforms that increased the power of the executive in economic development policy, and was implementing other regulations to stimulate and attract greater foreign investment.[23]

It explains why the Colombian government eagerly welcomed the Canadian initiative of 1968. As in Trudeau's case, Carlos Lleras Restrepo's (1966–70) administration was interested in reducing its dependence on the U.S. market by diversifying Colombia's trade relationships. Colombia, like Canada, was aggressively moving toward market diversification, and it had targeted Canada as part of its trade diversification strategy.[24]

The thirty-seven member delegation left Canada on 27 October 1968 on a mission that took them to nine different countries in one month.[25] The mission included Secretary of State for External Affairs Mitchell Sharp, Minister of Industry, Trade and Commerce, Jean-Luc Pepin, Minister of Energy, Mines and Resources J.J. Greene, Secretary of State Gérard Pelletier, and Minister without Portfolio Otto Lang. It also included Maurice Strong, president of CIDA, and representatives from the Export Credits Insurance Corporation (ECIC), the Canada Council for Arts, Humanities and Social Sciences, the National Gallery of Canada, the National Film Board, and the Canadian Broadcasting Corporation.[26] This not only represented the largest delegation that had ever visited Latin America, but also the first time that a mission included cultural and social agendas—key sectors of the promotional state. These were the initiatives of a more robust promotional state that wanted to market all aspects of the Canada brand abroad, and not just Canadian businesses.[27]

Canadian delegates arrived in Bogotá to demonstrate that Canada had a "genuine interest" in expanding bilateral relations beyond trade, and that they were there to look at ways in which Canada "could adopt a ... clear-cut line of action" that could benefit the bilateral partnership.[28] Delegates knew they were in Colombia to find alternatives that could bring both nations closer together, and were constantly reminded by External Affairs that the government representatives were not interested in discussing Canada's membership to the OAS or any other issue that was irrelevant to the mission's objectives.[29]

Delegates were aware that Colombia was a contested market that had recently been approached by competitors such as Bulgaria, Czechoslovakia, Finland, Denmark, Hungary, Poland, East Germany, Rumania, Spain, Yugoslavia, and the Soviet Union.[30] The Lleras Restrepo administration, under the recommendation of his minister of foreign affairs, Alfonso López Michelsen, had moved forward with a new foreign policy approach that rested on the principles of reducing the country's dependency on the United States, and greater international trade diversification.[31]

The Canadian government wanted to capitalize on Lleras Restrepo's efforts to diversify Colombia's trade relationships across the world, and it sought to secure a place within regional market initiatives such as the Andean Pact that was in the initial negotiations at the time of the mission.[32] It was also aware that the Colombian government had always been interested in strengthening bilateral relations with Canada. It had been reminded earlier that year, during the Latin American Special Coordinating Commission of the Group of 77, when Minister Michelsen emphasized that in the spirit of hemispheric cooperation it was extremely important to involve Canada in hemispheric matters.[33] Colombia, and the rest of the Latin American nations, wanted a closer relationship with Canada in an effort to balance their dependency on the United States, and they envisioned Canada as an alternative economic and diplomatic voice in the region.

This was reflected in the warm greeting received by the Canadian delegation in Colombia. Pépin, Greene, and their staff were prepared to negotiate two specific projects that had been analysed by Industry, Trade and Commerce.[34] The Colombian Interconnection Project was an energy transmission line that was expected to link the cities of Bogotá, Cali, and Medellín; the second was the Barranquilla Thermal Generating Station on the north coast of Colombia.[35] They were also prepared to discuss other issues if raised by the Colombian government, such as participation of the International Development Bank in the Alto

Anchicaya hydroelectric project and the Chocó electrical interconnection project, among others.[36]

Strong was eager to meet with members of the Canadian Universities Services Overseas (CUSO) as well as with the heads of the United Nations Development Program (UNDP) in Colombia, the Departamento Nacional de Planeación (DNP), and the Corporación Autónoma Regional del Valle del Cauca (CVC), in order to discuss social and economic development projects.[37] Meanwhile, Jean Boucher, director-general of the Council of Arts, Humanities and Social Sciences, and Guy Viau, deputy director of the National Gallery of Canada, wanted to advance the cultural agenda. Boucher requested meetings with leading academics from the publicly funded Universidad Nacional and the privately funded Universidad de los Andes; Viau requested a visit to the Museo Arqueológico Nacional, the Museo de Bellas Artes, and the Museo Nacional de Bogotá in order to establish initial contacts for development of future cultural exchange programs.[38]

Ministers and other top officials had the authority to close deals and agreements on behalf of the Canadian government.[39] But External Affairs made it clear that these initiatives had to "contribute to economic development and to the well-being of the people" of Colombia. Moreover, they needed to reflect a positive image of Canada abroad and strengthen the country's branding as a "goodwill" nation.[40] External Affairs indicated that delegates needed to take advantage of "the fact that the United States was losing control in the region as its popularity lost ground," and that they should capitalize on the region's "attitude of goodwill ... toward Canada."[41] New bilateral agreements needed to differentiate Canada from the United States; humanitarian ODA seemed to be the point of differentiation, at least from the perspective of some government officials, such as Strong. Soon after the mission, he was relieved that, for the first time, social policy was a key component of the promotional state.[42]

On the day of their arrival, delegates had the opportunity to meet with counterparts in ministerial posts, as well as officials from Colombia's DNP, representatives from the Colombian business sector, Canadian businessmen operating in the Colombian market, and CUSO members residing Bogotá.[43] Then, on 30 October, Minister Pépin met with President Lleras Restrepo, followed by a round table meeting where the ministers met with counterparts to discuss bilateral trade and commercial issues.[44] Negotiations took place behind closed doors and were not covered in detail by Colombian or Canadian press.

On the following day Pépin and H.T Aitken, president of ECIC, met in a round table with Colombia's minister of mines, oil and development, the superintendent of foreign investment, the minister of external affairs, representatives from Colombia's DNP, members of the Instituto de Fomento Industrial (IFI) and of Banco de la República (Colombia's central bank), and other Cabinet members.[45] During the formal meeting, Pépin indicated that Canada was interested in diversifying bilateral trade relations and used mining as an example of a commercial sector where Canada's experience and expertise would benefit the relationship.[46] He also reminded local representatives that his country was willing to increase coffee imports from Colombia, and that this commercial relationship could benefit even further from implementation of free market policies.[47] On financial development projects, Ottawa was willing to provide funding for specific short- and medium-term projects at an interest rate of 6 per cent.[48] He concluded the meeting by reaffirming his government's interest in bidding for the financing and construction of the Barranquilla Thermal Generating Station, known today as Termobarranquilla.[49]

Pépin opted not to introduce the possibility of bidding for the Colombian Interconnection Project because its private sector had failed to establish a competitive consortium that could bring the 535-kilometre, 220-kilowatt project back to Canada.[50] Instead he pushed the Barranquilla project and waited for other initiatives from the Lleras Restrepo administration.[51]

On 1 November Colombia's minister of development, Hernando Gómez Otálora, Minister of Mines Carlos Gustavo Arrieta, and the superintendent of international trade, Jorge Valencia Jaramillo, met with Pépin and Greene to discuss other development projects.[52] Colombian representatives introduced the possibility of funding the construction of airports across the country, as well as the supply of machinery and equipment for construction of secondary rural roads.[53]

The four-day visit was productive for both nations. Canada agreed to provide the Colombian government with US$12 million for construction of the Barranquilla project.[54] Canada's ECIC agreed to provide Bogotá with an insured line of credit for the export of fire-fighting equipment manufactured in Canada.[55] Mission representatives also agreed that Ottawa would lend to the Fondo Financiero de Proyectos de Desarrollo (FONADE) US$1 million for elaboration of feasibility projects that would bring both nations closer together.[56]

After the mission's return to Ottawa, a second wave of projects and initiatives emerged from the mission's stop in Bogotá. Initial conversations between Strong and Colombia's DNP resulted in a pilot project for a technical assistance program.[57] Meanwhile, Pépin and Greene

The Explorers

The 1968 ministerial mission to Latin America represented an incremental
step toward a more robust promotional state in the region, utilizing ODA
to advance a humanitarian-business agenda.
Source: John Collins, "The Explorer," *Gazette*, 30 October 1968, 6.

established initial contact that led to Canada's involvement in the Alto Anchicaya Hydroelectric Project during the early 1970s.[58]

The mission's preliminary report indicated that trade, political, and cultural exchange were key areas to expand, and that Canada's membership in the OAS was not of immediate relevance to the region.[59] Ministers also spoke about great opportunities for trade expansion, cultural exchanges, and more Canadian investment in South America.[60] Round table negotiations throughout the trip resulted in delegates recommending internal changes to facilitate expansion of relations with the region, as in the Termobarranquilla negotiations, which led Pépin and the Ontario consortium to conclude that the Canadian government should provide the ECIC with greater flexibility and power to make decisions on more robust projects.[61] Key to the success of the promotional state, said Pépin, was to provide the ECIC with greater capabilities to fund "major projects."[62]

By 1970 the Trudeau government had responded with *Latin America: Foreign Policy for Canadians*, part of the broader policy proposition that laid the foundations for Canadian–Latin American and Canadian-Caribbean relations throughout the 1970s and into the 1980s.[63] Within the policy vision, ODA was designed to play an important role in expansion of relations across the region.

Colombia became a key pilot project for implementation of Canada's ODA policy. Increasing numbers of rural ODA projects, allocation of direct ODA funds to Colombia, and growing participation of Canada's private sector in the financing and construction of capital-intensive development projects defined the dynamics of the bilateral relations under the new clear-cut policy.

Canada's promotional state relied heavily on ODA initiatives to strengthen its presence in Colombia and other parts of Latin America and the Caribbean. Nevertheless, the lack of institutional clarity on the objectives and agendas of ODA policies generated conflict within the Canadian government and across Canadian society. An interdepartmental conflict over the agenda of ODA emerged between CIDA and the Department of Industry, Trade and Commerce, raising the debate between market-driven and humanitarian interpretations of ODA, which would rise into Canada's public sphere. Throughout the 1970s implementation of ODA policies for Latin America and the Caribbean oscillated between humanitarian and market-driven agendas. In Colombia, Canadian ODA policies revealed a tendency toward market-driven agendas even though the country was engulfed in a long-lasting and violent civil war.

12
Official Development Assistance to Colombia

In the 1950s Colombia served as a model for implementation of World Bank structural adjustment economic development policies, setting the tone for propagation of this multilateral initiative across the emerging markets. The same took place in Colombia in the 1960s, this time through implementation of market-driven ODA policies. Colombia's political and social instability during the early stages of the Cold War made it a prime target for these Western initiatives. As indicated in chapter 10, the United States was the first nation to allocate ODA funding to Colombia, followed by other Western economies, including Canada. Canada's initial effort lacked a clear vision and depended on international multilateral institutions such as the Inter-American Development Bank (IDB). The strategy changed in the late 1960s with implementation of Pierre Elliott Trudeau's Third Option Policies that aimed to strengthen Canada's sovereignty while reducing the country's dependency on the United States. By the early 1970s the Trudeau government had defined a clear-cut ODA policy for Latin America and the Caribbean, following the 1968 ministerial mission to Latin America. In an effort to differentiate itself from American ODA policies, Canada opted to establish a policy that balanced humanitarian with market-driven aid, but eventually the pressure mounted by Canada's private sector overpowered the initiatives of social, intellectual, religious, and political groups that advocated for a humanitarian agenda.

President John F. Kennedy's Alliance for Progress initiatives in places like Colombia marked the beginning of an ODA race among donor nations, as their governments and private sectors grasped the potential financial and diplomatic benefits that resulted from external aid projects. Most ODA funding received by the Colombian government during the early 1960s came directly from Washington or through multilateral agencies such as the World Bank and the IDB.

President Alberto Lleras Camargo (1958–62) welcomed international development assistance. His administration recognized that Colombia was a good candidate for implementation of ODA pilot programs, because they not only contributed to the political stability of the country through the presence of foreign public and private stakeholders but also because it allowed the government to justify further implementation of aggressive pro-market institutional, social, and economic reforms.

Colombia, Chile, and Brazil became showpieces of the Alliance for Progress in Latin America, but escalation of the conflict in Vietnam eventually diverted external assistance from the region.[1] Financing from the United States and the Washington-based international agencies amounted to $US66 million, US$142 million, US$74 million, and US$27.5 million between 1962 and 1965.[2]

The United States became increasingly concerned as the transfer of capital entering the Colombian economy decreased. American ODA was designed to "hold the line," as development assistance became a crucial diplomatic tool in the policies of containment.[3] A decline in ODA meant an escalating security risk. Therefore there was pressure on the World Bank and the United Nations to diversify the donor base and establish better coordination between the United States and the recipient multilateral agencies.

Increasing the donor pool guaranteed continuation of the transfer of capital necessary to prevent Colombia from falling into social, economic, and political chaos, as the United States shifted its attention to the Southeast Asian conflict. This became an opportunity for Canada to once again fill the gap left by the United States. But Canada was slow to react to this opportunity.

Canadian ODA of the 1950s and early 1960s targeted South and Southeast Asia as part of the Commonwealth's Colombo Plan.[4] In the 1960s Prime Minister Lester Pearson's government slowly began to shift the direction of Canada's external aid, focusing development aid programs on Commonwealth and francophone regions of the world. Haiti and the Commonwealth Caribbean were the first recipients of Canadian ODA in the Western Hemisphere, eventually reaching Colombia in 1963.[5]

Initial Canadian ODA reached Colombia via the IDB. Part of the US$50 million provided by Pearson's government for procurement across the region over a five-year period reached Colombia in the form of economic development projects.[6] The IDB funds, including the Canadian allocation, were used for construction of a soda plant in Cartagena, industrial development of small and medium-size industry, rehabilitation and improvement of port facilities, university teaching and curriculum development, research and development of an African palm industry, development of low-income family housing, hydroelectric projects, sanitation and drinking water infrastructure, expansion of the electric grid in Cali, livestock research and development, construction of a polyethylene plant in Barranquilla, establishment of a synthetic fibre plant in Medellín, and expansion of rural development projects in the Caldas region.[7]

Prime Minister Pearson's 1963 initiative through Canada's External Aid Office (EAO) and the IDB did not experience incremental changes after the initial allocation. The timid approach prevented the Canadian government and private sector from capitalizing on the opportunity, disappointing international and domestic actors who were interested in the expansion of Canadian ODA to the region.

Maurice Strong, head of the EAO, knew the need to expand the geographical scope of ODA beyond the traditional destinations, constantly highlighting the need to move past the "Commonwealth minded" approach to the Western Hemisphere.[8] He also recognized Canada's institutional and programmatic limitations and the need to move away from the multilateral approach, advocating instead for bilateral ODA that could provide Canada with greater "political mileage."[9]

In the absence of support from the Pearson administration, Strong continued to push for transformation of the EAO as a means to better project its institutional objectives across Latin America. He circulated the idea among policymakers in Ottawa that, if Canada wanted to make a lasting impression in Latin America and compete against other donor nations, the EAO's mission, objectives, institutional capability, and budget allocation needed to change.[10] This could be achieved, said Strong, only if ODA centred on specific areas of development where Canada's institutions and private sector could make the most effective contribution and implement "more integrated projects combining capital and technical assistance."[11] The revised ODA policy demanded closer cooperation with other donor countries and multilateral agencies, greater involvement from the Canadian private sector, and much greater participation of the provincial governments.[12]

Prime Minister Trudeau's government capitalized on Strong's vision and used it as a pillar for development of Latin American policy. Strong engineered the look and feel of Canada's multilateral and bilateral aid and the Trudeau government made it politically possible and institutionally feasible.

After the 1968 ministerial mission to Latin America, Trudeau's government presented to the Canadian public the new direction of the nation's foreign policy objectives in the pamphlet series *Foreign Policy for Canadians*.[13] These documents established the strategy for Canada's ability to navigate the international system with greater independence. The government's new vision stressed the importance of Latin America within the revised policy, not only because of its geographical proximity, but also because the region was "destined" to become a "considerable force in the world."[14] International development aid was identified as a key instrument in the foreign policy, a tool through which Canada could tailor a more robust policy toward the region. According to the new vision, development assistance could provide emerging economies with the "extra margin of support" that would enable them to achieve their development goals, while allowing Canada to reach its own development goals.[15]

Trudeau's urgent transformation of the EAO into the more complex CIDA in 1968, as well as the design of a clear-cut policy for Latin America and the Caribbean, revealed a historical shift in the Canadian government.[16] In May 1968 Trudeau explained to his Cabinet that Canada needed to "explore new avenues" in order to increase its political and economic relations with Latin America, because the region represented a market that would surpass 400 million potential consumers by the end of the century.[17] New "avenues," according to his vision, included greater nationalist and autonomous ODA initiatives as well as a shift away from its dependence on multilateral assistance.

Brazil, Peru, Colombia, and the Central American region were chosen as the first recipient markets. Colombia was targeted by the Canadian government-business partnership for its natural resources, untapped economic potential, and increasingly educated and consumer-friendly society.[18] It subsequently became a key recipient of Canadian bilateral and multilateral aid under the Trudeau government.[19] Most external assistance was economic and not humanitarian, fuelling the market-driven agenda. The historical objective remained unchanged: strengthen commercial relations, promote direct trade, and consolidate the bilateral relationship between consumers and producers that had been evolving since the early years of gold mining and oil extraction.

Implementation of more aggressive ODA initiatives coincided with Colombia's eagerness to attract external aid and foreign direct investment in order to fund national modernization projects. Following in the footsteps of the Lleras Camargo administration, the Lleras Restrepo (1966–70) administration doubled the effort to attract ODA funding. His administration pursued funding for commodity-based export projects and infrastructure modernization from other international donors that could fill the gap left by the United States. Canada was among the nations targeted.

The Canadian government-business partnership also found Colombia to be a good fit. Its economy had achieved rates of growth, in real income, considerably above the historical average, registering gross domestic product growth of 6.1 per cent in 1968, 6.5 per cent in 1969, and approximately 7.0 per cent in 1970, compared to growth of less than 5 per cent throughout the 1950s and 1960s.[20] This healthy economic growth pattern was attractive to donor nations such as Canada, particularly those in the private sector interested in capitalizing on lucrative economic development projects. It was therefore no surprise that Colombia became a main target of Canada's ODA policy in the Western Hemisphere.

In the fiscal year 1971–2 the Canadian government reduced its allocation funds for Africa and shifted those resources to Latin America. Fifty per cent of the funding went to Asia, 32 per cent to Africa, 10 per cent to the Commonwealth Caribbean, and 7 per cent to Latin America.[21] There was an 80 per cent increase in the allocation of assistance to Latin America, representative of the new policy for the region.

By an Act of Parliament in 1970 the Canadian government and the Canadian Crown corporation created the International Development Research Centre (IDRC), a new state-owned enterprise designed to advance research and public policy across the emerging markets of the world. Directors of the new Crown corporation chose Bogotá as IDRC's Latin American headquarters, strengthening the presence of the promotional state in Colombia.[22]

Through the IDRC, Canada funded and expanded technical assistance programs that focused on grassroots initiatives. One focused on cassava research and development. The IDRC partnered with the Ford, Kellogg, and Rockefeller Foundations, as well as the United States and the Netherlands, to advance cassava research and development at the Centro Internacional de Agricultura Tropical (CIAT), which had been created by the Consultative Group on International Agricultural Research in 1967.[23] IDRC's funding for CIAT projects came to represent the core of Canada's multilateral ODA to Colombia in the 1970s. CIAT, on the other hand, became one of the greatest promoters of agroindustry in Colombia and an advocate of UN economic development initiatives, particularly those focusing on food security. Canadian ODA channelled through CIAT helped accelerate Colombia's transition from food self-sufficiency to the international commercialization of food production and consumption.[24]

Food-related technical assistance programs made up just a fraction of Canada's ODA funding. The majority was aimed at capital-intensive technical assistance programs and tied aid projects. The objective was to guide and support the recipient nation as it tapped its underutilized natural resources through technical assistance programs that provided the Canadian private sector a window of opportunity for direct involvement in the economic development policies and processes of the recipient nation.[25] Meanwhile tied aid projects forced the recipient nation to procure Canadian goods, technology, "know-how," and services. Canada's bilateral and multilateral ODA funding eventually constructed another layer of bilateral relationships with industrial and food production sectors across Colombia, creating new spatial and temporal dimensions of history between donor and recipient nation, while opening new business opportunities for the Canadian economy. Ultimately, ODA allowed the Canadian government to strengthen its promotional state. This allowed the Canadian government-business partnership to compete effectively against other donor nations.

By 1972, CIDA had allocated US$2.0 million to Colombia from US$9.5 million assigned to Latin America.[26] This bilateral assistance was aimed at education, forestry, fisheries, and community development programs.[27] Multilateral aid was channelled through the IDRC, and capital-intensive projects were funded through the IDB. This included funding for feasibility and pre-investment projects, telecommunications facilities, port facilities, airport facilities, technical universities, and the financing and construction of energy projects.[28]

The revamped promotional state pulled new sectors of the Canadian economy into the Latin American market. In Colombia, middle-level government officials responsible for managing the Canadian government-business partnership made their way into the Colombian economy. This external assistance bureaucracy was accompanied by academics from Canadian universities and non-state actors collaborating through Canadian and international NGOs. The private sector received the biggest boost, including engineers, middle and upper management, and highly educated technicians working in telecommunications, transportation, construction, energy, extractive industries, and infrastructure. Meanwhile, tied aid projects indirectly linked other Canadian business sectors to the Colombian economy, including suppliers of technology, parts, services, and "know-how."

These private and public stakeholders joined Canadian companies that were participating in the Colombian economy. They included Papeles Nacionales S.A., Kruger Inc.'s subsidiary that controlled large portions of the commercial paper, and pulp and paper industries, as well as Alcan's subsidiary, Aluminio de Colombia, the Montreal-based company that controlled 54 per cent of the domestic aluminium market and 41 per cent of copper imports to Colombia.[29]

Canada's private sector also became heavily involved in development of Colombia's energy grid. By that point, Canadian "know-how" and experience in hydro and thermal power gave it a comparative advantage in the international market. The Canadian government-business partnership capitalized on the 1950 World Bank recommendation to Colombia, linking the country's water resources to the "know-how" and capabilities of Canadian hydroelectric companies. Through multilateral ODA, Canadian energy companies could circumvent the market for open bidding, landing key tied aid contracts for the export of boiling equipment, non-aircraft gas turbines, electric power machinery, and technical "know-how."[30] Throughout the 1970s Canadian energy companies were directly involved in construction of energy infrastructure projects such as the Alto Anchicayá Hydroelectric project and the Termobarranquilla project on Colombia's Atlantic coast.[31]

Throughout the 1970s, the Trudeau government attempted to balance technical market-driven aid with humanitarian aid, to distinguish Canadian from American ODA initiatives. Nevertheless, bilateral ODA funding for humanitarian and social projects was limited not only by budget constraints but also because there was lack of political will in Canadian government institutions, such as the Department of Industry, Trade and Commerce, and sectors of External Affairs, which were more interested in advancing a market-driven ODA agenda.

Between 1970 and 1975 CIDA allocated US$7.8 million to Colombia, ranking it among the top ten recipients of Canadian ODA.[32] Half of this bilateral assistance was directed at social policy programs, while another 30 per cent went to food-production projects managed by CIAT.[33] Meanwhile multilateral aid via the IDB continued to be directed toward capital-intensive tied aid projects. Throughout the 1970s bilateral ODA slowly transitioned from humanitarian projects toward market-driven projects, as external assistance policy leaned closer to a market-driven agenda that favoured Canada's private sector. Humanitarian aid continued to pour into emerging markets but in Colombia and other Latin American and Caribbean nations the market-driven agenda predominated.

The Canadian promotional state was reinforced in the 1970s, not to solve Colombia's internal social and economic problems but to advance Canadian business interests. This was institutionally reaffirmed in 1973 by Jean-Luc Pépin, minister of industry, trade and commerce, who reminded policymakers that ODA was meant to focus on Canada's domestic economic development and prosperity.[34] Future bilateral ODA, suggested the document, "should be structured in large measure around specific actual and potential fields of excellence based on the knowledge and experience of internationally competitive

Canadian companies."[35] It stipulated that Latin American recipients of aid "should be selected according to their capacity and success in using Canada's technical and capital assistance," and not based on their social or economic needs.[36]

The argument that Canada's ODA strategy should be left in the hands of the private sector and not humanitarian NGOs gained ground throughout the 1970s. The change in policy was confirmed by CIDA's *Strategy for International Development Cooperation 1975–1980*, which reaffirmed that ODA should shift from multilateral social and community development projects to market-driven bilateral technical assistance projects.[37]

The Canadian assistance awarded to Colombia during the 1970s revealed Canada's internal institutional conflict over the ODA agenda. This resulted in fragmentation of Canadian external aid, eventually forcing NGOs and other civil society stakeholders to pursue their own humanitarian initiatives juxtaposed against the government's market-driven agenda.[38]

By 1977 CIDA's initiatives in Colombia were essentially market-driven, to push Colombia toward the modernization and economic development model envisioned by the World Bank and demanded by the advanced industrial markets of the world.[39] By this point, Trudeau's government had crafted an effective promotional state that secured market opportunities for Canadian businesses, researchers, scientists, and consumers. His nationalist agenda had carved out niche markets for Canadian companies in places like Colombia. By 1979, before he narrowly lost the national election to the Conservatives, Canadians were drinking Colombian coffee and vacationing in Colombia's Caribbean island of San Andres. Canadian businesses were extracting resources across Colombia, building hydroelectric plants, and selling paper products and aluminium to an emerging consumer market, while its scientists and researchers were using Colombia as a laboratory for agricultural experimentation.

Pierre Elliott Trudeau's refocus on the national scene after 1979, following an electoral defeat that left him with a minority government, detracted his attention from his foreign policy agenda, which directly affected the effectiveness of the Canadian promotional state. This, combined with intensification of the Cold War conflict in Colombia and the escalation of the War on Drugs, decelerated the bilateral relationship between the two countries. Colombia's isolation from the international community, as a result of its escalating internal conflicts, and Canada's departure from its Third Option policies after the end of Trudeau's government marked the end of an era in Canadian-Colombian business relations. A shift toward neoliberalism in both countries set the tone for a new chapter in their bilateral relations in the late 1980s.

Conclusion

Canada's limited domestic market and its dependence on commodity exports forced business elites to search for new global markets that would provide the national economy with raw materials, imported commodities, and alternative markets for Canadian exports. The lack of a promotional state, in its early nation-building stages, forced its business sector to navigate around British and U.S. business interests in regions such as Latin America and the Caribbean, while capitalizing on its exceptional relationships with the two imperial powers. Their early business expansion into Latin America and the Caribbean was therefore opportunistic, filling market gaps left by British and American business interests, as power changed hands between these two empires during the first half of the twentieth century. This strategy became obsolete after the Second World War when the United States redefined a new world order based on free market initiatives supported by strong government–business partnerships. Canada's private sector pressured its government to enhance the promotional state, as it engaged in a highly competitive international market system. It was not until the late 1960s that the Canadian government could provide its private sector with a revamped promotional state that allowed it to compete across Latin America and the Caribbean. The history of Canadian-Colombian relations illustrates the challenges faced by Canada's business expansionism. This close look at how Canadian companies and capital entered the Colombian market unravels a part of Canadian business and economic history that has been relatively untapped.

Since Confederation, Canada's nation-building depended on the global market system. Its dependence on Britain and the United States was a detriment to the objective of constructing an independent and sovereign economic development model. The search for sovereignty led the Canadian government-business partnership to explore new markets that had not been aggressively tapped by the empires that were competing for control in the Americas.

Colombia was an untapped market. Internally, it was politically unstable and therefore a high risk for international investors, but it was blessed with abundant natural resources, potential undeveloped internal markets, and a strategic geographical location that connected it to South America, Central America, and the Caribbean. The relative absence of British and American business interests, compared, for example, to British involvement in Argentina or U.S. involvement in Mexico, influenced Canada's decision to target the relatively untapped Colombian market. The country became a strategic objective when carving out a niche for Canadian exporters and foreign investors.

It was hard for Canadian business interests to gain a foothold in this market because it had limited capital and lacked the support of a robust promotional state. As indicated in Part Two of this book, it was through opportunism that Canadian businesses were able to navigate their way into the Colombian market. Serving as American subsidiaries, Canadian companies, such as La Troco, secured a source of oil for Canadian domestic consumption. Moreover, they were able to negotiate new deals and develop new partnerships that allowed other Canadian companies to enter the Colombian market. The Andian National Corporation, a Canadian subsidiary that spun off from Tropical Oil's operation in Barrancabermeja, became the leading constructor of pipeline and port infrastructure on the Atlantic coast during early stages of Colombia's oil export industry.

Canadian mining "know-how" also provided its private sector an opportunity to become involved in gold mining in Colombia. Canadian business interests were able to gain a foothold in the Colombian market, serving initially as subsidiaries for British gold-mining companies. Canadian engineers, managers, and other professionals became pioneers who created the foundations of Canadian-Colombian relations.

Canadian financial institutions also entered Colombia's unexplored market in order to serve Canadian and other foreign personnel in need of financial services and insurance. Opportunism was once again the strategy, taking advantage of Canada's unregulated financial market in order to allow its banks and insurance companies to take risks overseas. The services of the Royal Bank of Canada and Sun Life Assurance, among others, became indispensable for multinational corporations operating in Colombia in the first half of the twentieth century. Moreover, Canadian financial institutions capitalized on Colombia's undeveloped financial market, introducing branch services as well as banking and insurance products that created the foundations for Colombia's domestic financial market.

Rising global competition and the emergence of the United States as a superpower closed these windows of opportunity during the early stages of the Cold War. Limited capital and lack of corporate capabilities for subsidiaries prevented Canadian companies from maintaining their position in the Colombian market. Meanwhile, Canadian banks and insurance companies were overpowered by their American counterparts, forcing them out the market. By the end of the Second World War Canadian interests in Colombia had dissipated.

Canada's private sector once again mounted pressure on its government to strengthen the promotional state, as global competitors began to target Colombia for its natural resources and emerging consumer markets. The establishment of diplomatic relations in 1953 and the subsequent "Goodwill" Trade Mission were clear signs of government efforts to revamp the promotional state, but the lack of a clear regional policy slowed the process. It was not until the late 1960s, under the government of Pierre Elliott Trudeau, that Canada's private sector finally obtained the political and institutional support necessary to compete in Latin America and the Caribbean. Not only did the government establish a clear-cut policy for the region but it also identified ODA as the strategic mechanism to re-enter the Colombian market.

The 1968 ministerial mission, and the policy initiatives that followed, placed Colombia at the epicentre of Canada's Latin American strategy. In the 1970s Colombia became a significant recipient of Canadian bilateral and multilateral assistance. This affected the nation's economic development in significant ways. Canadian ODA shaped Colombia's energy policy, making it dependent on hydroelectric power. External aid also contributed to Colombia's transition from food independence to agro-industrial production models that turned the country into a food-importing nation. Meanwhile, tied aid strengthened the bond between Canada's private sector and the Colombian market, particularly through development of transportation, industrial, communication, social, and food production projects.

The strengthening of Canada's promotional state in the Americas transformed the relationship between Canada and the region. It broke the history of Canadian–Latin American and Canadian-Caribbean relations into two long chapters that unfolded throughout the twentieth century. A third chapter rose after implementation of neoliberal policies of the 1980s that laid the foundations for the second era of globalization, a history that merits a book of its own.

The history of the development of Canadian-Colombian relations is intended to encourage other historians to dig up other histories that make up the unresolved puzzle of Canadian–Latin American and Canadian-Caribbean relations. Further work of this kind will help historians reconstruct a more holistic understanding of the dynamics that shaped the economic, political, social, cultural, environmental, and business history of the Americas. Ultimately, evidence like this showed that Canada's economic development and the hemisphere's economic development were and will continue to be interdependent, beyond the dynamics of imperial powers.

Notes

Introduction

1 Emily S. Rosenberg, *Spreading the American Dream: American Economic and Cultural Expansion, 1890–1945* (New York: Hill and Wang, 1982), 38.

2 Rosenberg, *Spreading the American Dream*, 7.

3 As leader of the Liberal Party, Pierre Elliott Trudeau would lead the government Canada from 1968 to 1979 and again from 1980 to 1984.

4 For more on Canadian development aid to Latin America see, for example, Stefano Tijerina, "Canadian Official Development Aid to Latin America: The Struggle over the Humanitarian Agenda, 1963–1977," *Journal of Canadian Studies / Revue d'études canadiennes* 51, no. 1 (Winter 2017): 217–43.

5 For more on the ideas, principles, and history of neoliberalism, see, for example, David Harvey. *A Brief History of Neoliberalism* (New York: Oxford University Press, 2005), 1.

6 John Holmes, "Canadian Security: A Historical Perspective," speech to Collège Militaire Royale, 11 April 1987, file 13, box 9, Holmes Papers, Trinity College Archives, Toronto.

7 For more on liberal views of the theory of empires, see, for example, Bernard Semmel, *The Liberal Ideal and the Demons of Empire* (Baltimore, MD: Johns Hopkins University Press, 1993).

8 See, for example, Todd Gordon and Jeffery R. Webber, *Blood of Extraction: Canadian Imperialism in Latin America* (Winnipeg: Fernwood Publishing, 2016); and Radhika Desai, "Canadian Capitalism and Imperialism: A Brief Note," paper presented at the Society for Socialist Studies Conference, Ryerson University, Toronto, June 2017.

9 Through the creation of the Organization of American States (OAS) in 1948, the nations of the Western Hemisphere, with the exception of Canada, authorized the implementation of containment policies across

the Americas on behalf of democracy and free market capitalism. The outcome was half a century of human rights atrocities and the violation of sovereignty across the region. For more on the Cold War in Latin America, see, for example, Gilbert M. Joseph and Daniela Spenser, eds. *In from the Cold: Latin America's New Encounter with the Cold War* (Durham, NC: Duke University Press, 2008).

10 Brian Bow and Patrick Lennox, eds., *An Independent Foreign Policy for Canada? Challenges and Choices for the Future* (Toronto: University of Toronto Press, 2008), 35. See also Patrick Lennox, "John W. Holmes and Canadian International Relations Theory," *International Journal* 65, no. 2 (Spring 2010): 381–9.

11 For more information on Canada's asymmetrical relations, see, for example, Michael B. Dolan and Brian W. Tomlin, "Foreign Policy in Asymmetrical Dyads: Theoretical Reformulation and Empirical Analysis, Canada–United States Relations, 1963–1972," *International Studies Quarterly* 28, no. 3 (September 1984): 349–68.

12 For more information on Lennox's structural specialization theory, see Lennox, "John W. Holmes."

13 For a robust historiography on the theory of empires, see Philip Pomper, "The History and Theory of Empires," in "Theorizing Empire," theme issue, *History and Theory* 44, no. 4 (December 2005): 2.

14 Pomper, "History of Theory of Empires," 2.

15 For example, see Dermot O'Connor and Juan Pablo Bohórquez Montoya, "Neoliberal Transformation in Colombia's Goldfields: Development Strategy or Capitalist Imperialism?," in "Contemporary Colombia: The Continuity of Struggle / Numéro Thématique: Colombie Contemporaine: Persistance des conflicts," special issue, *Labour, Capital and Society / Travail, capital et société* 43, no. 2 (2010): 85–118.

16 For example, see Brian Stevenson, *Canada, Latin America and the New Internationalism: A Foreign Policy Analysis, 1968–1990* (Montreal and Kingston: McGill-Queen's University Press and the Centre for Security and Foreign Policy Studies, 2000); James Rochlin, *Discovering the Americas: The Evolution of Canadian Foreign Policy toward Latin America* (Vancouver: UBC Press, 1994); María Teresa Aya Smitmans, *Canada-Colombia, 50 Años de Relaciones* (Bogotá: Universidad Externado de Colombia, 2003); and Gordon and Webber, *Blood of Extraction*. Rosana Barbosa, *Brazil and Canada: Economic, Political and Migratory Ties, 1820s to 1970s* (London: Lexington Books, 2017) is one of the few exceptions that links Canada's connections to the region back to the 1800s; for more on Canadian–Latin American historiography, see Stefano Tijerina, "One Cinderblock at a Time: Historiography of Canadian–Latin American and Canadian-Colombian Relations," *Desafíos* 1, no. 24 (2012): 275–92.

17 For more on Colombia's early economic development and dependency on staples such as coffee, see, for example, Charles Berquist, *Café y Conflicto en Colombia (1886–1910): La Guerra de los Mil Días, sus Antecedentes y Consecuencias* (Bogotá: Ancora Editores, 1981). For more on Canada's early economic development and its dependency on the export of staples, see, for example, Harold Adams Innis, *The Fur Trade in Canada: An Introduction to Canadian Economic History* (New Haven, CT: Yale University Press, 1930).

1. The Jamaican Entrepôt

1 Janet Burke and Ted Humphrey, eds., *Nineteenth-Century Nation Building and the LatinAmerican Intellectual Tradition* (Indianapolis: Hackett Publishing, 2007), 268.

2 By the mid-1700s the Spanish colonies in the Americas were politically organized into four viceroyalties: the Viceroyalty of New Spain, Viceroyalty of New Granada, Viceroyalty of Peru, and Viceroyalty of the Rio de la Plata. The Viceroyalty of New Granada had jurisdiction over the region of northern South America, corresponding to present-day Colombia, Ecuador, Venezuela, and Panama.

3 "A list of ships and vessels that have entered the port of Kingston in the Island of Jamaica between the 25th day of September and the 25th day of December 1756," *Naval Office Shipping Lists for Jamaica, 1683–1818*, 111, reel 3, microfilm A5840, OCLC no. 11451263, University of Maine Fogler Library, Orono; "A list of ships and vessels that have entered the port of Kingston in the Island of Jamaica between 25th day of January and the 25th day of March 1765. *Naval Office Shipping Lists for Jamaica, 1683–1818*, 26, reel 4.

4 *Naval Office Shipping Lists for Jamaica, 1683–1818*, reels 1–7.

5 *Naval Office Shipping Lists for Jamaica, 1683–1818*, reels 1–7.

6 "A list of ships and vessels that have entered the port of Kingston in the Island of Jamaica between the 25th day of July and the 25th day of September 1767," *Naval Office Shipping Lists for Jamaica, 1683–1818*, 73–125, reel 4.

7 Burke and Humphrey, *Nineteenth-Century Nation Building*, 268.

8 For more on the War of Jenkins' Ear, see, for example, Patricia T. Young and Jack S. Levy, "Domestic Politics and the Escalation of Commercial Rivalry: Explaining the War of Jenkins' Ear, 1739–48," *European Journal of International Relations* 17, no. 2 (2011): 209–32.

9 J.C.M. Ogelsby, "England vs. Spain in America, 1739–1748: The Spanish Side of the Hill," *Historical Papers / Communications Historiques* 5, no. 1 (1970): 157.

10 J.H. Parry, P.M. Sherlock, and A.P. Maingot, eds., *A Short History of the West Indies* (New York: St. Martin's, 1987): 111–13. For more on the British

Free Ports Act of 1766 and its impact on Jamaica, see, for example, Nadine Hunt, "Expanding the Frontiers of Western Jamaica through Minor Atlantic Ports in the Eighteenth Century," *Canadian Journal of History* 45, no. 3 (Winter 2010): 485–501.

11 Parry, Sherlock, and Maingot, *Short History of the West Indies*, 111.
12 Robert Walsh, "British Colonial and Navigation System," *American Quarterly Review*, 2 (1827): 293.
13 Parry, Sherlock, and Maingot, *Short History of the West Indies*, 120.
14 Parry, Sherlock, and Maingot, *Short History of the West Indies*, 120.
15 Parry, Sherlock, and Maingot, *Short History of the West Indies*.
16 For more on the Bourbon Reforms, see, for example, Allan J. Kuethe and Kenneth J. Andrien. *The Spanish Atlantic World in the Eighteenth Century: War and the Bourbon Reforms, 1713–1796* (New York: Cambridge University Press, 2014).
17 Born in what is now known as Venezuela, Simón Bolívar was a military and political leader who led the revolution against Spanish colonialism in South America between 1810 and 1919. The victory in the Battle of Boyacá in 1819 resulted in the independence of the Viceroyalty of New Granada.
18 Pares, *War and Trade in the West Indies*, 288.
19 The liberated Viceroyalty of New Granada was renamed Gran Colombia, which included what is currently known as Colombia, Ecuador, Panama, Venezuela, parts of Peru, western Guyana, and northwestern Brazil. Gran Colombia would remain consolidated until 1831, when Ecuador and Venezuela seceded. Panama seceded in 1903, reducing the territory to what is now known as the Republic of Colombia.
20 Kenneth Morgan, *Bristol and the Atlantic Trade in the Eighteenth Century* (Cambridge: Cambridge University Press, 1993), 9.
21 Walsh, "British Colonial and Navigation System," 283.
22 Walsh, "British Colonial and Navigation System," 292.
23 Walsh, "British Colonial and Navigation System," 294–6.
24 Walsh, "British Colonial and Navigation System," 296.
25 Walsh, "British Colonial and Navigation System," 282.

2. Joining the International System

1 *New York Times*, "Colombia's Riches Reviewed by Bank," 3 July 1925, 24.
2 Tratado de Amistad, Comercio, y Nabegación, entre la República de Colombia, y su Majestad el Rey del Reyno Unido de la Gran Bretaña e Irlanda, 1825, https://babel.hathitrust.org/cgi/pt?id=uiuo.ark:/13960 /t39059f58;view=1up;seq=1.
3 Chester Brown, ed., *Commentaries on Selected Model Investment Treaties* (Oxford: Oxford University Press, 2013), 5.

4 Carlos Marichal, *A Century of Debt Crises in Latin America: From Independence to the Great Depression, 1820–1930* (Princeton, NJ: Princeton University Press, 1989), 32.

5 Francisco de Paula Santander was a leader of the independence movement and a strong defender of the rule of law, an issue that would later distance him from Bolivar. José Antonio Páez also fought next to Bolivar during the era of independence but would later be instrumental in the break-up of Gran Colombia, advocating for Venezuela's independence.

6 William Paul McGreevey. *An Economic History of Colombia, 1845–1930* (Cambridge: Cambridge University Press, 1971), 34.

7 Luis Ospina Vásquez, *Industria y Protección en Colombia, 1810–1930* (Bogotá: Editorial Santafé, 1955), 95–6.

8 Vásquez, *Industria y Protección en Colombia*, 97.

9 Vásquez, *Industria y Protección en Colombia*, 102.

10 Vásquez, *Industria y Protección en Colombia*, 121.

11 Vásquez, *Industria y Protección en Colombia*, 121.

12 Dominions such as Canada "had no direct treaty-making powers, and their ministers were not parties to the negotiation of treaties even when their interests were immediately concerned. For the purposes of commercial treaties the whole of the British possessions were regarded as coming within the sphere covered by the negotiations of British ministers." Finance Committee, "Reciprocity with Canada: Compilation of 1911, part 3C," United States Senate, 28 April 1911, 4355.

13 Vásquez, *Industria y Protección en Colombia*, 101.

14 Vásquez, *Industria y Protección en Colombia*, 101.

15 Vásquez, *Industria y Protección en Colombia*, 101.

16 The new country, encompassing present-day Colombia and Panamá, was named the Republic of New Granada, a name that would be preserved until 1863 when it was changed to the United States of Colombia. Short-lived state-driven federalism came to an end in 1886 under the new constitution that renamed the country the Republic of Colombia.

17 It was determined that Venezuela was responsible for 28 per cent and Ecuador 22 per cent of the total debt. Marichal, *Century of Debt Crises in Latin America*, 29.

18 Marichal, *Century of Debt Crises in Latin America*, 32–43.

19 Vásquez, *Industria y Protección en Colombia, 1810–1930*, 128.

20 Vásquez, *Industria y Protección en Colombia, 1810–1930*, 68.

21 Vásquez, *Industria y Protección en Colombia, 1810–1930*, 131.

22 After the breakup of Gran Colombia, the Republic of Colombia experienced a series of civil wars that extended to the turn of the twentieth century. This included the War of the Supremes (1839–41), the Civil War of 1860 (1860–2), the Civil War of 1863, the Civil War of 1876, the Civil War of 1895, and the Thousand Days War (1899–1902).

23 Charles Bergquist, *Café y Conflicto en Colombia (1886–1910): La Guerra de los Mil Días, sus Antecedentes y Consecuencias* (Bogotá: Ancora Editores, 1981), 40.
24 Vásquez, *Industria y Protección en Colombia*, 153.
25 McGreevey, *Economic History of Colombia*, 41.
26 Caudillos were regional political leaders who used their political, military, and popular influence to preserve and strengthen regionalism across Colombia. In many instances their power and influence would catapult them into national politics as in the case of Sergio Arboleda, Tomás Cipriano de Mosquera, Jorge Eliécer Gaitán, Alfonso López Pumarejo, Aquileo Parra, and Rafael Uribe Uribe, among others.
27 Bergquist, *Café y Conflicto en Colombia (1886–1910)*, 35.
28 Vásquez, *Industria y Protección en Colombia*, 173.
29 The Resguardo, legitimized by colonial titles granted to Indigenous communities residing in Colombia's territory, was a policy that regulated Indigenous lands. It determined territoriality and the authority of Indigenous communities to administer the land. For more on Resguardos, see, for example, Joanne Rappaport. *The Politics of Memory: Native Historical Interpretation in the Colombian Andes* (New York: Cambridge University Press, 1990).
30 McGreevey, *Economic History of Colombia*, 2.
31 For more on the 1854 Reciprocity Agreement between Canada and the United States, see, for example, Desmon Morton, "The Divisive Dream: Reciprocity in 1854; Fifteen Years Ago, the Free Trade Debate Divided the Country. It wasn't the First Time. When It Comes to Trading with America, Canada Has a History of Ambivalence," *Beaver* 82, no. 6 (December 2002): 16–21; and Randall White. *Fur Trade to Free Trade: Putting the Canada-U.S. Trade Agreement in Historical Perspective* (Toronto: Dundurn, 1989).
32 Michael Hart, *A Trading Nation: Canadian Trade Policy from Colonialism to Globalization* (Vancouver: UBC Press, 2003), 54–6. The Cayley-Galt Tariff was the first Canadian protective tariff, designed to boost domestic manufacturing industries.
33 For more contemporary interpretations of Confederation, see, for example, Jacqueline D. Krikorian, Marcel Martel, and Adrian Shubert. *Globalizing Confederation: Canada and the World in 1867* (Toronto: University of Toronto Press, 2017).

3. Institutionalizing International Trade, 1867–1904

1 Mary O. Hill, *Canada's Salesman to the World: The Department of Trade and Commerce, 1892–1939* (Montreal and Kingston: McGill-Queen's University Press, 1971), 1.

2 John Hamilton Gray, *Confederation, or, the Political and Parliamentary History of Canada (Microfilm): From the Conference at Quebec in October, 1864, to the Admission of British Columbia, in July, 1871* (Toronto: Copp, Clark, 1872), microfiche CIHM no. 06500, 357, University of Maine Fogler Library Archives, Orono.

3 Gray, *Confederation, or, the Political and Parliamentary History of Canada*, 358.

4 Hill, *Canada's Salesman to the World*, 7.

5 In 1969, under the Pierre Elliott Trudeau administration, the department's name was changed to the Department of Industry, Trade and Commerce.

6 Hill, *Canada's Salesman to the World*, 1.

7 O.J. Firestone, "Canada's External Trade and Net Foreign Balance, 1851–1900," in *Trends in the American Economy in the Nineteenth Century*, ed. Conference on Research in Income and Wealth (Princeton, NJ: Princeton University Press, 1960), 757–71.

8 Firestone, "Canada's External Trade and Net Foreign Balance, 766.

9 Richard Harris, Ian Keay, and Frank Lewis, "Protecting Infant Industries: Canadian Manufacturing and the National Policy, 1870–1913," *Explorations in Economic History* 56 (2015): 15–31.

10 *New York Times*, "Protection Fails in Canada," 26 October 1893, 3.

11 Hill, *Canada's Salesman to the World*, 44.

12 Hill, *Canada's Salesman to the World*, 45.

13 Hill, *Canada's Salesman to the World*, 46–8.

14 Hill, *Canada's Salesman to the World*, 62.

15 *New York Times*, "General Debate to Close Today: Mills to Make Last Speech for the Bill-Washburn on Reciprocity," 24 April 1894, 2.

16 *New York Times*, "General Debate to Close Today."

17 *New York Times*, "General Debate to Close Today."

18 *New York Times*, "General Debate to Close Today."

19 *New York Times*, "Hints for Our Merchants: Figs from State Department Thistles," 26 January 1880, 3. For more information on the American promotional state, see, for example, Rosenberg, *Spreading the American Dream*.

20 *New York Times*, "Hints for Our Merchants," 3.

21 *New York Times*, "Hints for Our Merchants," 3.

22 *New York Times*, "General Debate to Close Today."

23 Daniel Jay Baum, *The Banks of Canada in the Commonwealth Caribbean: Economic Nationalism and Multinational Enterprises of a Medium Power* (New York: Praeger, 1974), 155.

24 Ivanhoe Gadpaille, "Manufacturer's Life Insurance Company of Canada: Positive Protection to Policyholders," *Daily Gleaner*, 29 April 1902, 6.

25 For more on Colombia's transition from tobacco to coffee exports, see Berquist, *Café y Coflicto en Colombia (1886–1910)*.

26 According to American consular officials, 1880 data showed that the value of the annual exports of Colombia totaled US$12 million, gained mostly from the trade of quinoa, tobacco, and coffee; and that from the imports totaling US$10 million, "two-thirds ... paid for cotton, wool, hemp, linen, and silk goods." Therefore control of the cotton market led to greater dependency on the American market. *New York Times*, "General Debate to Close Today."

27 Marcelo Bucheli, *Bananas and Business: The United Fruit Company in Colombia, 1899–2000* (New York: New York University Press, 2005), 20. The War of a Thousand Days (1899–1903) was yet another civil war between liberals and conservatives, where liberals pushed for liberalization of the economy in opposition to the protectionist initiatives of conservatives. For more on the War of a Thousand Days, see Geoffrey Demarest, "War of the Thousand Days," *Small Wars and Insurgencies* 12, no. 1 (Spring 2001): 1–30.

28 For more on U.S. gun diplomacy, see, for example, Robert D. Schulzinger. *U.S. Diplomacy since 1900* (New York: Oxford University Press, 2008).

29 Hill, *Canada's Salesman to the World*, 69.

30 Hill, *Canada's Salesman to the World*, 69.

31 Hill, *Canada's Salesman to the World*, 139.

32 Hill, *Canada's Salesman to the World*, 139.

33 Hill, *Canada's Salesman to the World*, 139.

34 For example, by 1914, British consular presence in the Americas included offices in twenty-nine cities in Mexico, three in Costa Rica, three in Guatemala, five in Honduras, two in El Salvador, three in Nicaragua, three in Panama, thirteen in Argentina, six in Bolivia, twenty-three in Brazil, seven in Colombia, four in Ecuador, twenty-five in Chile, seven in Peru, five in Uruguay, seven in Venezuela, and one in Paraguay. A.E. Southall, ed. *Imperial Year Book for Dominion of Canada, 1914–1915* (Montreal: John Lovell & Son, 1914), 44–6.

35 Southall, *Imperial Year Book for Dominion of Canada, 1914–1915*, 49.

36 W.F.E., "Our trade with Colombia: It Might Amount to Something If Our Manufacturers Were Businesslike," *New York Times*, 24 February 1895, 12.

37 *New York Times*, "Learn Spanish and Prosper: An American Consul's Advice to Merchants and Students," 28 June 1896, 9.

38 *New York Times*, "Learn Spanish and Prosper."

39 *New York Times*, "Canada's Trade Relations: The Dominion Government Will Seek New Markets Abroad," 9 April 1891, 5.

40 *New York Times*, "The Pan-Anglican Idea," 17 September 1888, 4.

41 *New York Times*, "Direction of Trade Currents," 8 March 1879, 4.

42 *New York Times*, "Direction of Trade Currents."

43 Southall, *Imperial Year Book for Dominion of Canada, 1914–1915*, 48.

4. Colombia and the Emerging Latin American Market, 1904–1910

1 Pan American Union, *Fourth Pan American Commercial Conference: Foreign Trade of Latin America, 1910–1929* (Washington DC: U.S. Government Printing Office, 1931), 1.
2 McGreevey, *Economic History of Colombia,* 78–90.
3 Bergquist, *Café y Conflicto en Colombia (1886–1910),* 71. For more on the Baring Panic of 1890 and its impact on Latin America, see, for example, Kris James Mitchener and Marc D. Weidenmier, "The Baring Crisis and the Great Latin American Meltdown of the 1890s." National Bureau of Economic Research working paper no. 13403, September 2007.
4 Bergquist, *Café y Conflicto en Colombia (1886–1910),* 319.
5 Bergquist, *Café y Conflicto en Colombia (1886–1910),* 341–9.
6 That same year Colombia was removed from the international list of debtor countries. Bergquist, *Café y Conflicto en Colombia (1886–1910).*
7 Vásquez, *Industria y Protección en Colombia,* 324.
8 As indicated by Ospina Vásquez, the system was designed to connect regions and not the nation. It was so inefficient that by the turn of the century it remained more cost-effective for regions like Antioquia to import flour from the United States than from neighboring Boyacá, only a few hundred miles away. Vásquez, *Industria y Protección en Colombia,* 325.
9 Bergquist, *Café y Conflicto en Colombia,* 365.
10 Bergquist, *Café y Conflicto en Colombia,* 357.
11 Vásquez, *Industria y Protección en Colombia,* 341–3.
12 Bergquist, *Café y Conflicto en Colombia,* 56 and 345.
13 McGreevey, *Economic History of Colombia,* 201.
14 McGreevey, *Economic History of Colombia,* 201.
15 Vásquez, *Industria y Protección en Colombia,* 346.
16 Canada's demographic growth had reached seven million 1911, compared to the ninety-two million of the United States and the forty-five million in the top Latin American and Caribbean markets of the time (Brazil, Argentina, Chile, Mexico, and Cuba).
17 For more on Canada's triangular relations with Britain and the United States, see: Bartlet Brebner, *Canada: A Modern History* (Ann Arbor: University of Michigan Press, 1960).
18 Edward Marshall, "Fight for South America's Great Trade," *New York Times,* 4 December 1910, SM10.
19 Marshall, "Fight for South America's Great Trade."
20 Pan American Union, *Fourth Pan American Commercial Conference,* iv.
21 Marshall, "Fight for South America's Great Trade."
22 For more information on Argentina's history of economic development, see, for example, Mario Rapaport. *Las Políticas Económicas de la Argentina, Una Breve Historia* (Buenos Aires: Editorial Booket, 2010).

23 For more on the history of rubber extraction in Brazil see, for example, Barbara Weinstein, *The Amazon Rubber Boom, 1850–1920* (Stanford, CA: Stanford University Press, 1983); for more on Cuba and sugar, see, for example, César J. Ayala, *American Sugar Kingdom: The Plantation Economy of the Spanish Caribbean, 1898–1934* (Chapel Hill: University of North Carolina Press, 1999); for more on Mexico's oil industry, see, for example, Catherine E. Jayne. *Oil, War and the Anglo-American Relations: American and British Reactions to Mexico's Expropriation of Foreign Oil Properties, 1937–1941* (Westport, CT: Greenwood, 2001).

24 Pan American Union, *Fourth Pan American Commercial Conference*, iv.

25 Allen Morrison, "The Tramways of Bogotá," 2007, http://www.tramz .com/co/bg/t/te.html.

26 *New York Times*, "Back from Colombia and Jungle Mines," *New York Times*, 16 July 1910, 10.

27 *New York Times*, "Back from Colombia and Jungle Mines," 10.

28 *New York Times*, "Back from Colombia and Jungle Mines," 10.

29 *New York Times*, "Back from Colombia and Jungle Mines," 10.

30 *New York Times*, "Back from Colombia and Jungle Mines," 10.

31 *New York Times*, "Back from Colombia and Jungle Mines," 10.

32 George H. Harris, *The President's Book: The Story of the Sun Life Assurance Company of Canada* (Montreal: Sun Life Assurance Company, 1928), 87.

33 Pan American Union, *Fourth Pan American Commercial Conference*, 39.

34 Pan American Union, *Fourth Pan American Commercial Conference*, 1.

35 For more on the Good Neighbor policy, see, for example, Irwin F. Gellman, *Good Neighbor Diplomacy: United States Policies in Latin America, 1933–1945* (Baltimore, MD: Johns Hopkins University Press, 1979).

36 For more information on the Balfour Declaration, see, for example, Peter Marshall, "The Balfour Formula and the Evolution of the Commonwealth," *Commonwealth Journal of International Affairs* 90, no. 361 (2001): 541–53.

37 Canadian Gazette, "Trade between Dominion and West Indies," *Daily Gleaner*, 29 December 1922, 6.

38 Canadian Gazette, "Trade between Dominion and West Indies," 6.

39 Canadian Gazette, "Trade between Dominion and West Indies," 6.

40 Canadian Gazette, "Trade between Dominion and West Indies," 6.

41 *New York Times*, "Colombia's Riches Reviewed by Bank," 3 July 1925, 24.

42 Hill, *Canada's Salesman to the World*, 411.

43 *Daily Gleaner*, "Trade Mission from Canada Is Planned," 19 May 1927, 1.

44 *Daily Gleaner*, "Trade Mission from Canada Is Planned," 1.

45 *Manitoba Free Press*, "A Time to Go Forward," 18 April 1927, 13.

46 *Manitoba Free Press*, "A Time to Go Forward," 13.

47 *Manitoba Free Press*, "A Time to Go Forward," 13.

48 E.C. Austin, "Need of Trade Agents in South America," *Manitoba Free Press*, 18 June 1927, 33.
49 Austin, "Need of Trade Agents in South America," 33.
50 Austin, "Need of Trade Agents in South America," 33.
51 Austin, "Need of Trade Agents in South America," 33.
52 Austin, "Need of Trade Agents in South America," 33.
53 Austin, "Need of Trade Agents in South America," 33.
54 Austin, "Need of Trade Agents in South America," 33.

5. Internationalizing Banking and Insurance, 1886–1939

1 Neil C. Quigley, "The Bank of Nova Scotia in the Caribbean, 1889–1940," *Business History Review* 63, no. 4 (Winter 1989): 799.
2 Quigley, "Bank of Nova Scotia in the Caribbean, 1889–1940," 797.
3 Frank Safford, "Foreign and National Enterprise in Nineteenth-Century Colombia," special Latin American issue, *Business History Review* 39, no. 4 (Winter 1965): 521.
4 Royal Bank faced domestic and international competition from institutions such as Bank of London, Banco de Bogotá, Banco Alemán Antioqueño, Anglo South American Bank Limited of London, and the French and Italian Bank.
5 Gregory P. Marchildon, "Canadian Multinationals and International Finance: Past and Present," *Business History* 34, no. 3 (July 1992): 3.
6 Quigley, "Bank of Nova Scotia in the Caribbean, 1889–1940," 797.
7 Quigley, "Bank of Nova Scotia in the Caribbean, 1889–1940," 802.
8 For more on the National Bank Act of 1864, see "National Bank Act of 1864; an Act to Provide a National Currency, Secured by a Pledge of United States Bonds, and to Provide for the Circulation and Redemption Thereof. Approved June 3, 1864," Washington (1865), https://babel .hathitrust.org/cgi/pt?id=hvd.hnv8fx&view=1up&seq=1.
9 Quigley, "Bank of Nova Scotia in the Caribbean, 1889–1940," 798.
10 Quigley, "Bank of Nova Scotia in the Caribbean, 1889–1940," 799.
11 Quigley, "Bank of Nova Scotia in the Caribbean, 1889–1940," 799.
12 Quigley, "Bank of Nova Scotia in the Caribbean, 1889–1940," 803.
13 Quigley, "Bank of Nova Scotia in the Caribbean, 1889–1940," 803.
14 Adolfo Meisel Roca, *¿Por Qué Perdió la Costa Caribe el Siglo XX? Y Otros Ensayos* (Bogotá: Banco de la República, 2011), 133–68.
15 Graeme Mount, "Canadian Investment in Colombia: Some examples, 1919–1939," *North/South: The Canadian Journal of Latin American Studies* 1, no. 1 and 2 (1976): 46.
16 Vernon Lee Fluharty, *Dance of the Millions: Military Rule and the Social Revolution in Colombia* (Pittsburgh: University of Pittsburgh Press, 1957), 23.

17 Canada, Toronto Head Office, "Manufacturers Life Insurance Company," 7.
18 Quigley, "Bank of Nova Scotia in the Caribbean, 1889–1940," 800.
19 Canada, Toronto Head Office, "Manufacturers Life Insurance Company," 7.
20 Canada, Toronto Head Office, "Manufacturers Life Insurance Company," 7.
21 Canada, Toronto Head Office, "Manufacturers Life Insurance Company," 7.
22 Canada, Toronto Head Office, "Manufacturers Life Insurance Company," 7.
23 Manufacturers' operations in other parts of the Caribbean and South America were initially based in Jamaica. Ivanhoe Gadpaille, "Manufacturers Life Insurance Company of Canada," *Daily Gleaner*, April 29, 1902, 6.
24 *Daily Gleaner*, "Empty hands!" advertisement, 8 May 1926, 17.
25 This includes Latin American and Caribbean nations such as Cuba, Haiti, Jamaica, Mexico, Nicaragua, Peru, Puerto Rico, Santo Domingo, Chile, and Argentina. See Harris, *President's Book*, viii–ix.
26 Mount, "Canadian Investment in Colombia," 46.
27 Harris, *President's Book*, 83.
28 Harris, *President's Book*, 83.
29 Harris, *President's Book*, 84.
30 According to company records, Colombia was seen as an untapped market; for more information see Harris, *President's Book*, 87.
31 Harris, *President's Book*, 87.
32 Harris, *President's Book*, 87.
33 *Titusville Herald*, "Oil Jungles of Colombia, South America," 19 May 1920, 4.
34 *Titusville Herald*, "Oil Jungles of Colombia, 4.
35 *Titusville Herald*, "Oil Jungles of Colombia, 26.
36 Mount, "Canadian Investment in Colombia," 47.
37 By 1927 Sun Life Assurance was present in the United States, Great Britain, Mexico, Chile, Colombia, Cuba, Argentina, Peru, Nicaragua, Guatemala, Puerto Rico, Santo Domingo, Haiti, British West Indies, Japan, India, China, Egypt, Philippines, and South Africa. *Daily Gleaner*, "Sun Life Assurance Company of Canada: A Great International Institution," 3 March 1928, 17.
38 Mira Wilkins, "Multinational Enterprise in Insurance: An Historical Overview," *Business History* 51, no. 3 (May 2009): 343.
39 For more information on the "dance of the millions," see Fluharty, *Dance of the Millions*.
40 J. Fred Rippy indicated that U.S. direct investment in Colombia experienced a rapid expansion, going from "11 million dollars in 1910 to 23 million in 1913, more than 112 million in 1920, and over 153 million in 1929"; for more detail, see Fred J. Rippy, *The Capitalists and Colombia* (New York: Vanguard, 1931), 14. In the case of United Fruit, investments in Colombia had escalated from an initial $2 million to $125 million by 1928; see *Daily Gleaner*, "Progress Made by United Fruit Company in the Caribbean," 27 March 1928, 6.

41 Numerous American and Canadian cruise lines used newspaper advertisements as a means to market their product. A 1924 ad in the *Manitoba Free Press* showed the key destinations of the Canadian Red Star Line, the White Star, and the Dominion Line. In this case, as in many others, Cartagena was included as a key destination in the Caribbean. See *Manitoba Free Press*, "Winter Cruises," 2 December 1924, 16.

42 Mount, "Canadian investment in Colombia," 47.

43 Fluharty, *Dance of the Millions*, 43.

44 Wilkins, "Multinational Enterprise in Insurance," 344.

45 *New York Times*, "Assets of Sun Life Rise $36,000,000," 10 February 1932, 35.

46 For more on Frente Nacional conflict resolution policies, see, for example, Sven Schuster, "Las Políticas de la Historia en Colombia: El Primer Gobierno del Frente Nacional y el 'Problema' de la Violencia (1958–1962)," *Iberoamericana* 9, no. 6 (2009): 9–26.

47 James L. Darroch, "Global Competitiveness and Public Policy: The Case of Canadian Multinational Banks," *Business History* 34, no. 3 (July 1992): 153.

48 The Bank of London and Montreal was jointly formed by the Bank of Montreal and the Bank of London and South America; for more detail, see Duncan McDowall, *Quick to the Frontier: Canada's Royal Bank* (Toronto: McClelland & Stewart, 1993), 409.

49 Scott W. See, *The History of Canada* (Westport, CT: Greenwood, 2001), 116.

50 See, *History of Canada*, 108.

51 See, *History of Canada*, 154.

52 Darroch, "Global Competitiveness and Public Policy."

53 *New York Times*, "Banks as Agents in South America: O.H. Fuerth Advises Financiers Here Also to Get Local Capital in Branches," 23 May 1915, 29.

54 *New York Times*, "Banks as Agents."

55 Herbert Holt, "Forty-Eighth Annual Meeting of the Royal Bank of Canada," *Manitoba Free Press*, 19 January 1917, 12.

56 Holt, "Forty-Eighth Annual Meeting."

57 Holt, "Forty-Eighth Annual Meeting."

58 Holt, "Forty-Eighth Annual Meeting."

59 Holt, "Forty-Eighth Annual Meeting."

60 *Daily Gleaner*, "The Royal Bank of Canada Has Formed a Close Working Association with the London County Westminster and Parr's Bank, Limited," 11 July 1919, 7.

61 The Urrutia-Thompson Treaty was eventually signed on 20 April 1921, awarding the Colombian government a reparation payment of US$25 million that resolved the tensions over Panama's independence, and that unleashed the Dance of the Millions in Colombia.

62 United States, Department of Commerce, *Banking Opportunities in South America*, Special Agents Series no. 106, ed. William H. Lough (Washington, 1915), 65–6.

63 *New York Times*, "Bank to Specialize in Latin America," 15 September 1922, 31.

64 *New York Times*, "Bank to Specialize in Latin America."

65 *New York Times*, "Colombia's Riches Reviewed by Bank."

66 *New York Times*, "Colombia's Riches Reviewed by Bank."

67 *New York Times*, "Colombia's Riches Reviewed by Bank."

68 *New York Times*, "Colombia's Riches Reviewed by Bank."

69 *New York Times*, "Colombia's Riches Reviewed by Bank," 24.

70 *Daily Gleaner*, "Bank of Canada Is Spreading Out," 30 March 1925, 19.

71 *Daily Gleaner*, "Bank of Canada Is Spreading Out."

72 *Daily Gleaner*, "Bank of Canada Is Spreading Out."

73 *New York Times*, "Bank of Canada Adds to Holdings," 4 February 1925, 33.

74 Herbert Holt, "Fifty-Ninth Annual Meeting of the Royal Bank of Canada," *New York Times*, 17 January 1928, 47.

75 Holt, "Fifty-Ninth Annual Meeting."

76 In the 1960s, Quebec and British interests came together to form the Bank of London and Montreal. The partnership absorbed the branch offices of Bank of London and South America in Colombia, and operated in that market until 1970. It took another forty-two years before another Canadian bank penetrated the Colombian consumer market. In January 2012, Scotiabank purchased 51 per cent of Banco Colpatria de Colombia, adding to its Latin American operations, which also included Chile, Peru, and Mexico.

77 For more information on Kemmerer's missions to Latin America and their impact on the region's financial markets, see, for example, Paul W. Drake, *The Money Doctor in the Andes* (Durham, NC: Duke University Press, 1989).

78 *New York Times*, "Kemmerer to Leave Soon: Commission to Study Finances in Colombia, Plans Start This Month," 3 August 1930, 30.

79 AP, "Banking Group Headed by the National City Plans Loans to Regional Departments," *New York Times*, 18 February 1931, 7.

80 *New York Times*, "Banking Concerns Merge," 14 August 1936, 33.

81 Charles E. Egan, "Economic Advance Is Seen in Colombia: Head of Banking Group Says Rapid Expansion Brings Need for More Capital," *New York Times*, 22 January 1950, 117.

82 *New York Times*, "Canadian Bank at Cali Closed," 14 November 1948, 22.

6. Tropical Oil and the Andian National Corporation, 1918–1945

1 *Titusville Herald*, "Oil Jungles of Colombia."

2 *New York Times*, "South American Oil Needed Badly Now," 16 March 1920, 22.

3 The Barco oil concession and the De Mares oil concession marked the early development of Colombia's oil industry. For more information on the De Mares concession, see, for example, Marcelo Bucheli, "Negotiating under the Monroe Doctrine: Weetman Pearson and the Origins of U.S. Control of Colombian Oil," *Business History Review* 82 (Autumn 2008): 529–53.

4 For more on the American reparation payment to Colombia, see, for example, Fluharty, *Dance of the Millions*.

5 Bucheli, "Negotiating under the Monroe Doctrine," 537.

6 Graham D. Taylor, "From Branch Operation to Integrated Subsidiary: The Reorganization of Imperial Oil under Walter Teagle, 1911–17," *Business History* 34, no. 3 (July 1992): 57–61.

7 *New York Times*, "Buys Oil Land in Colombia," 16 September 1919, 26.

8 For more on the Pearson and Son's negotiations, see, for example, Bucheli, "Negotiating under the Monroe Doctrine."

9 Bucheli, "Negotiating under the Monroe Doctrine," 546.

10 Bucheli, "Negotiating under the Monroe Doctrine," 544.

11 Bucheli, "Negotiating under the Monroe Doctrine," 545.

12 Bucheli, "Negotiating under the Monroe Doctrine," 547.

13 Bucheli, "Negotiating under the Monroe Doctrine," 545.

14 Alvaro T. Mejía, "Rivalidades por Colombia a Comienzos Del Siglo XX," *Colombia en la Repartición Imperialista (1870–1914)*, (2002), http://www .lablaa.org/blaavirtual/historia/corim/corim3.htm. ,2.

15 Bucheli, "Negotiating under the Monroe Doctrine," 550.

16 Bucheli, "Negotiating under the Monroe Doctrine," 550.

17 Bucheli, "Negotiating under the Monroe Doctrine," 548.

18 Bucheli, "Negotiating under the Monroe Doctrine," 552.

19 Lord Cowdray (Marconi), "Says Press Beat Colombia Oil Plan: Lord Cowdray Blames American Papers for His Failure to Get Concessions," *New York Times*, 28 November 1913, 2.

20 Lord Cowdray (Marconi), "Says Press Beat Colombia Oil Plan."

21 Eduardo Saenz Rovner, "La Industria Petrolera En Colombia: Concesiones, Reversión y Asociaciones," *Revista Credencial Historia*, January 1994, http:// www.lablaa.org/blaavirtual/revistas/credencial/enero94/enero2.htm, 1.

22 The De Mares concession, also known as the Barco oil concession, was one of the major concessions in the early stages of Colombia's oil industry. For more on the oil agreement, see, for example, Bucheli, "Negotiating under the Monroe Doctrine."

23 Marcelo Bucheli, "Canadian Multinational Corporations and Economic Nationalism: The Case of Imperial Oil Limited in Alberta (Canada) and Colombia, 1899–1938," *Enterprises et Histoire* 54 (April 2009): 76.

24 Bucheli, "Negotiating under the Monroe Doctrine," 552.

25 *Titusville Herald*, "International Petroleum," 25 December 1919, 7.

26 Taylor, "From Branch Operation to Integrated Subsidiary," 50.
27 Taylor, "From Branch Operation to Integrated Subsidiary," 51.
28 Taylor, "From Branch Operation to Integrated Subsidiary," 51.
29 Taylor, "From Branch Operation to Integrated Subsidiary," 51.
30 Taylor, "From Branch Operation to Integrated Subsidiary," 62.
31 Arthur Neal, "Canada's Trade Ties with Latin America," *Canadian Geographical Journal* 31, no. 2 (August 1945): 82.
32 Neal, "Canada's Trade Ties with Latin America," 87.
33 Neal, "Canada's Trade Ties with Latin America," 92.
34 *New York Times*, "Imperial Oil Company Will Keep Drilling," 27 February 1923, 30.
35 Bucheli, "Canadian Multinational Corporations and Economic Nationalism," 68.
36 *Bradford Era*, "Tropical Oil Co. Makes First Shipment of Gas," 6 October 1921, 1.
37 *Bradford Era*, "Tropical Oil Co. Makes First Shipment of Gas."
38 Bucheli, "Canadian Multinational Corporations and Economic Nationalism," 68.
39 Bucheli, "Canadian Multinational Corporations and Economic Nationalism," 68.
40 F. Ayearst, "G. Harrison Smith: The Power behind the South American Oil Fields," *Financial Post*, 7 May 1926, 10.
41 Ayearst, "G. Harrison Smith."
42 *New York Times*, "Imperial Oil Company Will Keep Drilling."
43 *Bradford Era*, "Imperial Oil Increases South American Output," 12 March 1923, 7.
44 Bucheli, "Canadian Multinational Corporations and Economic Nationalism," 80.
45 Colombia, Ministerio de Minas y Petróleos, *Memoria 1944* (Bogotá: Imprenta Nacional, 1944), 44–88.
46 Colombia, Ministerio de Minas y Petróleos, *Memoria 1944*.
47 Cartagena's urban development benefited from the company town investments of the Andian National Corporation, which, together with the Royal Bank of Canada and local elites, expanded and modernized the port infrastructure, constructed the Manga port and the Cartagena-Mamonal-Pasacaballo connector, and built the Bocagrande urban development project, which would house most of the foreign executives and employees. This last project led to other secondary services like education and health, and entertainment facilities, including the Club Campeste de Cartagena.
48 *Bradford Era*, "Building of Colombian Pipe Line Is under Way, Capacity 25,000 Bbls.," 22 January 1925, 3.
49 *Bradford Era*, "Building of Colombian Pipe Line."

50 *Bradford Era*, "Building of Colombian Pipe Line."

51 *Bradford Era*, "Building of Colombian Pipe Line."

52 For more on early labour relations between *La Troco* and local labour, see, for example, Stefano Tijerina, "The Zero-Sum Game of Early Oil Extraction Relations in Colombia: Workers, Tropical Oil, and the Police State, 1918–1938," in *Working for Oil: Comparative Social Histories of Labor in Petroleum*, ed. Tourah Atabaki, Kaveh Ehsani, and Elisabetta Bini, 37–67 (Basingstoke, UK: Palgrave Macmillan, 2018).

53 Prior to the Second World War, Colombia was the eighth-largest importer to Canada. Bucheli, "Canadian Multinational Corporations and Economic Nationalism," 80.

54 Robert C. Fisher, "'We'll Get Our Own': Canada and the Oil Shipping Crisis of 1942," *Northern Mariner / Le Marin du Nord* 3, no. 2 (April 1993): 34.

55 Fisher, "'We'll Get Our Own,'" 34.

56 Fisher, "'We'll Get Our Own,'" 36.

57 Phyllis R. Griess, "Colombia's Petroleum Resources," *Economic Geography* 22, no. 4 (October 1946): 251.

58 Griess, "Colombia's Petroleum Resources," 251.

59 Griess, "Colombia's Petroleum Resources," 251.

60 Bucheli, "Negotiating under the Monroe Doctrine," 529.

61 Bucheli, "Negotiating under the Monroe Doctrine," 529.

62 Bucheli, "Negotiating under the Monroe Doctrine," 529.

7. Canadian Gold Dredging Operations, 1909–1962

1 Instituted by the Rafael Núñez administration in the early 1890s, the Regeneration period included a series of social, political, and economic reforms that restored the power of the Catholic church, strengthened centralization of government, and later, under the Rafael Reyes administration, incorporated economic policies that allowed the nation to consolidate an import-export economy. For more on this period, see, for example, Nola Reinhardt, "The Consolidation of the Import-Export Economy in Nineteenth-Century Colombia: A Political-Economic Analysis," *Latin American Perspectives* 13, no. 1 (Winter 1986): 75–98.

2 *New York Times*, "Colombia Invites Our Trade," 24 November 1898, 5.

3 *New York Times*, "Colombia Invites Our Trade."

4 *New York Times*, "Colombia Invites Our Trade."

5 V. Lévine, *South American Handbook: Colombia, Physical Features, Natural Resources, Means of Communication, Manufactures, and Industrial Development* (New York: D. Appleton, 1914), 115.

6 *New York Times*, "Harry Stuart Derby: Prospector Who Won Fortune in Colombia Gold Field Dies," 30 July 1929, 13.

7 *New York Times*, "Harry Stuart Derby."

8 *New York Times*, "To Seek Gold in Colombia," 13 May 1901, 2.

9 Eric K. Craig, "Gold Mining in Colombia," *Engineering and Mining Journal* 113, no. 12 (March 1922): 479.

10 Arnold Hoffman, *Free Gold: The Story of Canadian Mining* (Toronto: Rinehart, 1947), 97.

11 World Mining Corporation, "Significant Adjacent Mining History," 2005, http://www.wmcus.com/mnrlprop.html.

12 José Medina, "Los problemas mineros," *El Tiempo*, 4 March 1939, 4.

13 Medina, "Los problemas mineros," *El Tiempo*, 4 March 1939.

14 Medina, "Los problemas mineros," *El Tiempo*, 4 March 1939.

15 Frederick W. Baker, "Oroville Dredging Company Limited – Meeting Held on December 30 at Salisbury House, London Wall, E.G., Mr. Frederick Baker (Chairman of the Company) Presiding," Internet Archive, http://www.archive.org/stream/statist83londuoft/statist83londuoft_djvu.txt, 3.

16 The price of one ounce of gold was $304 in December 1929; it reached a high of $663 in April 1934 and ended the decade at $624. For more information on the historic price of gold, see, for example, *Macrotrends*, "Gold Prices: 100 Year Historical Chart," 2018, accessed July 1, 2018, https://www.macrotrends.net/1333/historical-gold-prices-100-year-chart.

17 President Enrique Olaya Herrera had been minister to Washington in the late 1920s. During his assignment in Washington he established the Colombian-American Chamber of Commerce and expanded credit relations with the United States.

18 *New York Times*, "End of Exploitation in Colombia Pledged: Dr. Lopez, Honored at Dinner Here, Says His New Deal Will Abolish Privilege," 29 June 1934, 4.

19 *New York Times*, "End of Exploitation in Colombia."

20 *New York Times*, "Developing Colombia's Resources," 27 December 1921, 11.

21 Medina, "Los problemas mineros," 4.

22 Canadian Press, "Placer Turns Record Profits," *Winnipeg Free Press*, 4 August 1956, 42.

23 *Sydney Morning Herald*, "Placer Development," 25 July 1929, 13.

24 *Sydney Morning Herald*, "Placer Development."

25 Canadian Press, "Placer Turns Record Profits," 42.

26 Jairo Patiño Suárez, *Compañías Extranjeras y Fiebre de Oro en Zaragoza, 1880–1952* (Medellín: IDEA, 1997), 54.

27 Minera Timmins Ochali had exploited the Berlín Mine in the Antioquia region between 1920 and 1932, producing over 500,000 ounces of gold. J.W. Asociados y Compañía Limitada, "Oronorte Project Area," Webspawner.com, accessed 20 January 2013, http://www.webspawner.com/users/oronorte (site discontinued).

28 Canadian Press, "Placer Turns Record Profits," 42.
29 *Montreal Gazette*, "Nechí Shareholders Vote Merger plan," 1 July 1953, 28.
30 *New York Times*, "Colombia Allows Free Sale of Gold," 16 October 1953.
31 *New York Times*, "Mining Concern Gets New Top Team," 25 May 1954.
32 *New York Times*, "Mining Concern Moves to Expand: South American Gold Obtains One-Third of Capital Stock of Pato Dredging, Ltd.," 18 November 1954, 56.
33 *New York Times*, "Mining Concern Moves to Expand."
34 Today the mines that were taken over by the American mining firm are under the control of the Canadian company Gran Colombia Gold, currently the largest underground gold and silver producer in Colombia. For more information, see Gran Colombia Gold, "About Us," Gran Colombia Gold Corp, 2017, http://www.grancolombiagold.com/about -us/default.aspx.
35 *New York Times*, "South American Gold," 13 June 1962, 55.
36 *New York Times*, "International Mining," 25 July 1963, 46.
37 Hector Melo, *La Maniobra del Oro en Colombia* (Medellín: Editorial La Pulga, 1975), 68.
38 *New York Times*, "U.S. Capital Lured to Latin America: Even Smaller Countries Are Investing in Nations Where Outside Funds Are Needed," 5 January 1955, 78.
39 *New York Times*, "U.S. Capital Lured to Latin America."
40 Colombia's use of force on civilians for the protection of Canada's Tropical Oil interests illustrates this point. For more detail, see Tijerina, "Zero-Sum Game of Early Oil Extraction Relations."
41 *New York Times*, "U.S. Capital Lured to Latin America," 78.

8. Limitations under the Cold War

1 For more on the assassination of Jorge Eliécer Gaitán, see Herbert Braun, *The Assassination of Gaitán: Public Life and Urban Violence in Colombia* (Madison: University of Wisconsin Press, 1985).
2 Canada would continue to grapple with the idea of full OAS membership for the next four decades, and finally joined the multilateral organization in 1990, as the region transitioned into neoliberalism.
3 Peter McKenna, *Canada and the OAS: From Dilettante to Full Partner* (Montreal and Kingston: McGill-Queen's University Press, 1995), 120.
4 For more on the banana massacre debates, see, for example, Jorge Eliécer Gaitán, "La Zona Bananera: Una Nicaragua Colombiana," *El Debate de las Bananeras*, 1929, https://www.scribd.com/doc/52035148/Jorge-Eliecer -Gaitan-El-Debate-de-las-Bananeras.
5 Gaitán, "La Zona Bananera," 91.

6 Gaitán, "La Zona Bananera," 91

7 United States, Department of State. "A Positive Program of United States Assistance for Latin America," *Foreign Relations of the United States 1948: The Western Hemisphere – Foreign Relations* (Washington, 1948), 9:6.

8 Rochlin, *Discovering the Americas*, 37.

9 Rochlin, *Discovering the Americas*, 33–49.

10 Rochlin, *Discovering the Americas*, 7.

11 Rochlin, *Discovering the Americas*, 7.

12 James D. Henderson, *Modernization in Colombia: The Laureano Gómez Years, 1889–1965* (Gainesville: University Press of Florida, 2001), 303.

13 AP, "Historic Treaty: Hemisphere Defense to Be Planned," *News Palladium*, 15 August 1947, 9.

14 *Lethbridge Herald*, "Argentina Wants Claims Approved," 9 April 1948, 2.

15 *Lethbridge Herald*, "Argentina Wants Claims Approved."

16 For more on this issue, see C.P. Stacey, *Canada and the Age of Conflict*, vol. 2, *1921–1948* (Toronto: University of Toronto Press, 1981).

17 *Lethbridge Herald*, "Pan-American Conference Opens at Bogota, Colombia, on Thursday," 27 March 1948, 1.

18 *Lethbridge Herald*, "Pan-American Conference Opens at Bogota."

19 *Lethbridge Herald*, "Pan-American Conference Opens at Bogota."

20 *Lethbridge Herald*, "Pan-American Conference Opens at Bogota."

21 Chester Bloom, "Canada's Share in the Marshall Plan," *Winnipeg Free Press*, 10 April 1948, 1.

22 Bloom, "Canada's Share in the Marshall Plan."

23 Bloom, "Canada's Share in the Marshall Plan."

24 United States, Department of State. "Positive Program of United States Assistance for Latin America," 6.

25 United States, Department of State. "Positive Program of United States Assistance for Latin America," 6.

26 United Press, "Text of President's Latin Loan Message," *New York Times*, 9 April 1948, A1.

27 United Press, "Text of President's Latin Loan Message."

28 United Press, "Text of President's Latin Loan Message."

29 *Toronto Telegram*, "Collective Snub Given U.S. by 20 American Republics, Dead Silence Follows Talks," 10 April 1948, 1.

30 *Toronto Telegram*, "Collective Snub Given U.S."

31 For more on *El Bogotazo*, see, for example, Braun. *Assassination of Gaitán*. A tentative peace agreement was reached between the state and the guerrilla group Fuerzas Armadas Revolucionarias de Colombia (FARC) in 2017, but social, political, and structural violence still prevails.

32 "Remarks of William McChesney Martin, Jr., President of the Export-Import Bank of Washington before Committee IV of the Ninth International

Conference of American States," *Foreign Relations of the United States 1948: Western Hemisphere* (Washington, 1972), 37.

9. Diplomatic Relations, 1941–1953

1 D.R. Murray, "Canada's First Diplomatic Missions in Latin America," *Journal of Interamerican Studies and World Affairs* 16, no. 2 (May 1974): 154.
2 Throughout the 1940s and 1950s oil imports turned Venezuela into Canada's most important trading partner in Latin America and the Caribbean. This trade relation remained insignificant for Canada, representing less than 5 per cent of Canada's global trade, while Canada became a crucial market for Venezuelan exports. This was also the case for Colombia and other Latin American and Caribbean nations that traded with Canada. Throughout the 1940s and 1950s, Canada ranked as one of the top ten trading partners for Colombia. For example, in 1950, Canada's exports to Colombia represented only 0.5 per cent of exports. This represented 1.5 per cent of Colombia's imports at a time when the United States controlled more than 50 per cent of imports entering the Colombian market. United Nations, *Yearbook of International Trade Statistics 1950*, ed. Statistical Office of the United Nations (New York: United Nations, 1951), 195 and 229.
3 Murray, "Canada's Diplomatic Missions in Latin America," 169.
4 Initially the Canadian government established diplomatic relations at the level of legation, with a high commissioner as the head of the diplomatic office. Under this status Canadian representatives could not "come into official relations with ambassadors of other countries because technically they did not have the status of an ambassador." This problem was "alleviated" in 1944 when "the Canadian government decided to elevate the rank of several foreign posts from legation to embassy," including their post in Brazil, Argentina, Chile, Peru, and Mexico. Linwood DeLong, *A Guide to Canadian Diplomatic Relations, 1925–1983* (Ottawa: Canadian Library Association, 1985), 5.
5 Murrray, "Canada's Diplomatic Missions in Latin America," 169.
6 Murrray, "Canada's Diplomatic Missions in Latin America," 170.
7 Escott Reid, memorandum from deputy under-secretary of state of external affairs to under-secretary for external affairs, 20 July 1949, Documents on Canadian External Relations (Ottawa), 1821, University of Maine Fogler Library, Orono.
8 Reid, memorandum, 20 July 1949.
9 Canadian Press, "Canada Resuming Trade Mission to South," *Daily Gleaner*, 14 August 1941, 1.
10 Canadian Press, "Canada Resuming Trade Mission to South."

11 Reid, memorandum, 20 July 1949.
12 Canadian Press, "Canada, Brazil Sign Trade Agreement," *Winnipeg Free Press*, 18 October 1941, 3.
13 C.D. Howe, memorandum from minister of trade and commerce to Cabinet: Proposed trade negotiations with Venezuela, Colombia, Ecuador, Costa Rica and Honduras, 14 September 1950, 1, Ministry of Foreign Affairs, University of Maine Fogler Library, Orono.
14 *Lethbridge Herald*, "Seek Trade South America: Mackinnon to Lead Five-Man Mission to Eight Countries," 25 July 1941, 1.
15 James Montagnes, "Canada's Latin-American Trade Booms: Imports and Exports Far Above Those of the Pre-War Days," *Lethbridge Herald*, 27 October 1941, 2.
16 Montagnes, "Canada's Latin-American Trade Booms."
17 Montagnes, "Canada's Latin-American Trade Booms."
18 Montagnes, "Canada's Latin-American Trade Booms."
19 Associated Press, "Colombia at War with Germany," *Winnipeg Free Press*, 17 November 1943, 7.
20 J.C.M. Ogelsby, *Gringos from the Far North: Essays in the History of Canadian–Latin American Relations, 1866–1968* (Toronto: MacMillan of Canada, 1976), 24.
21 Canadian Press, "Mackinnon Forecasts Loosening of British Import Regulations," *Lethbridge Herald*, 22 January 1946, 1.
22 *New York Times*, "Colombian-Canadian Pact Signed," 21 February 1946, 3.
23 *Winnipeg Free Press*, "Trade Commissioner from Colombia Arriving," 25 October 1945, 18.
24 Reid, memorandum from deputy under-secretary of state for external affairs, 1821.
25 *Winnipeg Free Press*, "$1.55 Wheat: 200,000,000 Bushels Yearly to Britain," 28 January 1946, 4.
26 *New York Times*, "Exports Declared Vital for Canada," 2 January 1946, 30.
27 *New York Times*, "Exports Declared Vital for Canada."
28 *New York Times*, "Exports Declared Vital for Canada."
29 Canada, Department of Trade and Commerce, *Postwar Trade Reviews: Colombia and Venezuela* (Ottawa: Department of Trade and Commerce, 1946), 1–2.
30 Department of Trade and Commerce, *Postwar Trade Reviews*, 5.
31 Department of Trade and Commerce, *Postwar Trade Reviews*, 5.
32 Department of Trade and Commerce, *Postwar Trade Reviews*, 5.
33 Department of Trade and Commerce, *Postwar Trade Reviews*, 5.
34 Department of Trade and Commerce, *Postwar Trade Reviews*, 5.
35 Department of Trade and Commerce, *Postwar Trade Reviews*, 7.
36 Department of Trade and Commerce, *Postwar Trade Reviews*, 8.

37 Department of Trade and Commerce, *Postwar Trade Reviews*, 9.
38 Department of Trade and Commerce, *Postwar Trade Reviews*, 9.
39 Department of Trade and Commerce, *Postwar Trade Reviews*, 9.
40 A.D.P. Heeney, memorandum from under-secretary of state for external affairs to secretary of state for external affairs, 5 December 1949, 18, Documents on Canadian External Relations.
41 Heeney, memorandum from under-secretary of state for external affairs.
42 Arthur Blanchette, memorandum from American and Far Eastern Division to head, American and Far Eastern Division, Documents on Canadian External Relations (Ottawa, 1948), 1868.
43 Blanchette, memorandum from American and Far Eastern Division.
44 Blanchette, memorandum from American and Far Eastern Division.
45 Heeney, memorandum from under-secretary of state for external affairs, 16.
46 Reid, memorandum from deputy under-secretary of state for external affairs, 1821.
47 Reid, memorandum from deputy under-secretary of state for external affairs, 1822.
48 Reid, memorandum from deputy under-secretary of state for external affairs, 1821.
49 Reid, memorandum from deputy under-secretary of state for external affairs, 1822.
50 Reid, memorandum from deputy under-secretary of state for external affairs, 1822.
51 Heeney, memorandum from under-secretary of state for external affairs, 18.
52 A.R. Menzies, memorandum by acting head, American and Far Eastern Division, 21 July 1949, Documents on Canadian External Relations, 1823.
53 Menzies, memorandum by acting head, 1824.
54 Menzies, memorandum by acting head, 1824.
55 Heeney, memorandum from under-secretary of state for external affairs, 16.
56 Heeney, memorandum from under-secretary of state for external affairs, 18.
57 Heeney, memorandum from under-secretary of state for external affairs, 19.
58 Heeney, memorandum from under-secretary of state for external affairs, 19.
59 Heeney, memorandum from under-secretary of state for external affairs, 19.
60 Heeney, memorandum from under-secretary of state for external affairs, 19.
61 Heeney, memorandum from under-secretary of state for external affairs, 19.
62 Heeney, memorandum from under-secretary of state for external affairs, 19.
63 Heeney, memorandum from under-secretary of state for external affairs, 19.
64 David Bushnell, *The Making of a Modern Colombia: A Nation in Spite of Itself* (Berkeley: University of California Press, 1993), 212.
65 Canadian Press Dispatch, "Canada Names Ray Lawson to New York Post," *Winnipeg Free Press*, 7 November 1952, 26.

66 Canada Press, "Canada Names 2 Ambassadors in South America,"
    Montreal Gazette, 22 November 1952, 1.
67 Canadian Press Dispatch, "Canada Names Ray Lawson to New York
    Post," 26.
68 Associated Press, "Canada May Join 'Union,'" *Ottawa Citizen*, 25 March
    1953, 20.
69 Associated Press, "Canada May Join 'Union,'"
70 Associated Press, "Canada May Join 'Union,'"
71 Associated Press, "Canada May Join 'Union,'"

10. The 1953 Goodwill Trade Mission

 1 Canada, Department of External Affairs Information Division, "Canadian
    Goodwill Trade Mission to Latin America: Statement by the Minister of
    Trade and Commerce, Mr. C.D. Howe, Made in the House of Commons,
    February 26, 1953," 3, Department of External Affairs, Statements and
    Speeches, Dr. John Archer Library, University of Regina.
 2 N.R.D., "The Facts about Prosperity: Mr. Howe on Trade," *Winnipeg Free
    Press*, 4 August 1953, 1.
 3 Canadian Press, "Trade with Latin America Well Founded," *Winnipeg Free
    Press*, 9 January 1953, 32.
 4 Canadian Press, "Trade with Latin America Well Founded."
 5 Canada Department of External Affairs Information Division, "Canadian
    Goodwill Trade Mission to Latin America," 2.
 6 Canada Department of External Affairs Information Division, "Canadian
    Goodwill Trade Mission to Latin America," 2.
 7 Canada Department of External Affairs Information Division, "Canadian
    Goodwill Trade Mission to Latin America," 2.
 8 Howe was particularly familiar with Argentina since he had worked as
    a commercial engineer, selling grain elevators in the region during the
    1930s. See *Lethbridge Herald*, "Howe Plans Seek Trade South America," 8
    November 1952, 2.
 9 Canada Department of External Affairs Information Division, "Canadian
    Goodwill Trade Mission to Latin America," 3.
10 *El Tiempo*, "Habrá Trueque de Productos entre Colombia y Venezuela en
    Este Año," 2 January 1953, 1.
11 *El Tiempo*, "Inauguración: Nuevo Servicio de Primera Clase a Nueva
    York," 14 January 1953, 15–19.
12 *El Tiempo*, "La Johnson Line Amplía sus Servicios a Colombia," 16 January
    1953, 5.
13 *El Tiempo*, "Misión Canadiense Llegará Hoy en las Horas de la Tarde a
    Bogotá," 28 January 1953, 9.

14 *El Tiempo*, "Canadá Pagará en Dólares Todas las Importaciones," 29 January 1953, 1 and 13.

15 *El Tiempo*, "Canadá Pagará en Dólares Todas las Importaciones," 1 and 13.

16 *El Tiempo*, "Canadá Pagará en Dólares Todas las Importaciones," 13.

17 *El Tiempo*, "Canadá Pagará en Dólares Todas las Importaciones," 13.

18 *El Tiempo*, "Canadá Pagará en Dólares Todas las Importaciones," 13.

19 Canada Department of External Affairs Information Division, "Canadian Goodwill Trade Mission to Latin America," 8.

20 *El Tiempo*, "Misión Canadiense Llegará Hoy en las Horas de la Tarde a Bogotá."

21 As a result of the violent incidents of *El Bogotazo* and in order to adopt a system that would guarantee free elections, the government issued Decree 2628 of 1951 with the objective of developing the citizen I.D. card. The identification system, designed by a Canadian technical mission, not only kept track of citizenship but also developed a centralized database that included citizens' fingerprints and other vital statistics.

22 *El Tiempo*, "10,000 Cédulas Diarias Tomará en Bogotá la Misión Canadiense," 18 January 1953, 1.

23 *El Tiempo*, "10,000 Cédulas Diarias Tomará en Bogotá la Misión Canadiense."

24 Canada Department of External Affairs Information Division, "Canadian Goodwill Trade Mission to Latin America," 8.

25 See World Bank's report on agriculture: *The Basis of a Development Program for Colombia*, ed. Lauchlin Bernard Currie (Washington, 1950), 8–16.

26 Canada Department of External Affairs Information Division, "Canadian Goodwill Trade Mission to Latin America," 8.

27 Canada Department of External Affairs Information Division, "Canadian Goodwill Trade Mission to Latin America," 8.

28 *El Tiempo*, "Parte Mañana la Misión del Canadá, y el Príncipe Danes," 29 January 1953, 4.

29 Ronald H.E. Krystynak, "Canada's Experience with Foot-and-Mouth Disease," *Canadian Veterinary Journal* 28, no. 8 (August 1987): 541.

30 The U.S. government lifted the trade restrictions in March 1953, soon after Canada's visit to Colombia. Krystynak, "Canada's Experience with Foot-and-Mouth Disease," 542.

31 Canada Department of External Affairs Information Division, "Canadian Goodwill Trade Mission to Latin America," 7.

32 Canada Department of External Affairs Information Division, "Canadian Goodwill Trade Mission to Latin America," 7.

33 Canada Department of External Affairs Information Division, "Canadian Goodwill Trade Mission to Latin America," 7.

34 Tim Colton, "General Cargo Ships Built in Canada since WWII," 22 August 2017, http://shipbuildinghistory.com/canadaships/freighters.htm.

35 Horacio Franco, "Una Realidad: La Flota Grancolombiana," *El Tiempo*, 14 January 1953, p.4; see also *El Tiempo*, "4 Nuevos Buques Adquiere la Flota Grancolombiana," 13 January 1953, 1 and 19.

36 Canada Department of External Affairs Information Division, "Canadian Goodwill Trade Mission to Latin America," 7.

37 United Press, "Mission Quits Colombia: Canadian Group Heads for Ciudad Trujillo of Dominican Republic," *New York Times*, 2 February 1953, 34.

38 Canada Department of External Affairs Information Division, "Canadian Goodwill Trade Mission to Latin America," 11.

39 Canada Department of External Affairs Information Division, "Canadian Goodwill Trade Mission to Latin America," 11.

40 L.B. Pearson, memorandum from secretary of state for external affairs to Cabinet: Proposed export of F-86 aircraft to Colombia, 20 March 1956, Documents on Canadian External Relations (Ottawa), 1.

41 Canada Department of Trade and Commerce, memorandum by head, American Division: Export of military jet aircraft to countries in Latin America, 19 October 1956, Documents on Canadian External Relations (Ottawa), 1.

42 Canada, Department of Trade and Commerce, "Sale of F86s to Colombia," ed. Department of External Affairs, 27 February 1956 (Ottawa), 1, University of Maine Fogler Library, Orono.

43 Canada, Department of Trade and Commerce, "Sale of F86s to Colombia."

44 Canada, Department of Trade and Commerce, "Sale of F86s to Colombia."

45 For more detail on Canada's role in NATO, see John Gellner, *Canada in NATO* (Toronto: Ryerson, 1970).

46 Canada Department of Trade and Commerce, "Sale of F86s to Colombia."

47 Canada Department of Trade and Commerce, "Sale of F86s to Colombia."

48 Jules Leger, under-secretary of state for external affairs to deputy minister of trade and commerce: Possible sale to Colombia of F-86 aircraft, 28 February 1956, Documents on Canadian External Relations (Ottawa), 1.

49 Leger to deputy minister of trade and commerce: Possible sale.

50 Leger to deputy minister of trade and commerce: Possible sale.

51 Leger to deputy minister of trade and commerce: Possible sale.

52 Leger to deputy minister of trade and commerce: Possible sale.

53 Leger to deputy minister of trade and commerce: Possible sale.

54 Leger to deputy minister of trade and commerce: Possible sale.

55 Leger to deputy minister of trade and commerce: Possible sale.

56 Canada Department of Trade and Commerce, "Sale of F86s to Colombia."

57 Canada Department of Trade and Commerce, "Sale of F86s to Colombia."

58 Canada Department of Trade and Commerce, "Sale of F86s to Colombia."

59 Canada Department of Trade and Commerce, "Sale of F86s to Colombia."

60 Canada Department of Trade and Commerce, "Sale of F86s to Colombia."

61 Mitchell Sharp, associate deputy minister of trade and commerce to under-secretary of state for external affairs: Possible sale of F-86 aircraft to Colombia, 7 March 1956, Documents on Canadian External Relations (Ottawa), 1.

62 Sharp to under-secretary of state for external affairs: Possible sale.

63 Sharp to under-secretary of state for external affairs: Possible sale.

64 Canada Department of Trade and Commerce, "Extract from Cabinet Conclusions," 15 March 1956, Documents on Canadian External Relations (Ottawa), 1.

65 Canada Department of Trade and Commerce, "Extract from Cabinet Conclusions."

66 Pearson, memorandum to Cabinet: Proposed export of F-86 aircraft to Colombia, 1.

67 Pearson, memorandum to Cabinet: Proposed export of F-86 aircraft to Colombia, 1

68 Canada Department of Trade and Commerce, "Extract from Cabinet conclusions," 1.

69 Canada Department of Trade and Commerce, "Extract from Cabinet conclusions," 1.

70 Pearson, memorandum to Cabinet: Proposed export of F-86 aircraft to Colombia, 1.

71 Canada Department of Trade and Commerce, "Extract from Cabinet conclusions," 1.

72 Canada Department of Trade and Commerce, memorandum by head, American Division: Export of military jet aircraft, 1.

73 Canada Department of Trade and Commerce, memorandum by head, American Division: Export of military jet aircraft.

74 Canada Department of Trade and Commerce, memorandum by head, American Division: Export of military jet aircraft.

75 Canada Department of Trade and Commerce, memorandum by head, American Division: Export of military jet aircraft.

76 Henderson, *Modernization in Colombia*, 370.

77 Henderson, *Modernization in Colombia*, 370.

78 Canada Department of Trade and Commerce, memorandum by head, American Division: Export of military jet aircraft 1.

79 Henderson, *Modernization in Colombia*, 374.

80 For more detail on John Diefenbaker's policy on Latin America, see Jason Gregory Zorbas, "Diefenbaker, Latin America and the Caribbean: The Pursuit of Canadian Autonomy" (PhD diss., University of Saskatchewan, 2009).

81 Zorbas, "Diefenbaker, Latin America and the Caribbean," 21.

82 Zorbas, "Diefenbaker, Latin America and the Caribbean," 21

83　Henderson, *Modernization in Colombia*, 391.

84　For an assessment of the Alliance for Progress initiative in Colombia, see Jeffrey F. Taffet, *Foreign Aid as Foreign Policy: The Alliance for Progress in Latin America* (New York: Routledge, 2007); for more detail on *Plan Lazo* see Bradley Lynn Coleman, *Colombia and the United States: The Making of an Inter-American Alliance, 1939–1960* (Kent, OH: Kent State University Press, 2008).

85　Zorbas, "Diefenbaker, Latin America and the Caribbean," 5.

86　Baum, *Banks of Canada in the Commonwealth Caribbean*, 23.

87　Baum, *Banks of Canada in the Commonwealth Caribbean*, 23.

88　Baum, *Banks of Canada in the Commonwealth Caribbean*, 84.

89　Gene C. Kruger, son of Joseph Kruger I, a successful American paper merchant from New York who moved to Montreal in the early 1900s, built Kruger Inc. into a major producer of publication paper for the international market. In South America it specialized in the tissue business, and at the present time controls a large part of the markets in Venezuela and Colombia. For more detail, see Hugh O'Brian, "Kruger Takes a Long-Term Outlook for Steady Growth in Consumer Products," *Perini Journal*, n.d., http://www.perinijournal.it/Items/en-US/Articoli /PJL-28/Kruger-takes-a-longterm-outlook-for-steady-growth-in-consumer -products.

90　Papeles Nacionales S.A., "Quienes somos," accessed 23 November 2010, www.papelesnacionales.com.

91　Papeles Nacionales S.A., "Quienes somos."

92　"Over the life of the program the United States and international lending agencies lent Colombia more than US$1,000,000,000," which represented 11 per cent of total Alliance for Progress funding. See Henderson, *Modernization in Colombia*, 391.

93　Ricardo Sánchez, *Estado y Planeación en Colombia* (Bogotá: Editorial la Rosa Roja, 1984), 82.

94　For more detail on Canada's ODA policy, see David R. Morrison, *Aid and Ebb Tide: A History of CIDA and Canadian Development Assistance* (Waterloo, ON: Wilfrid Laurier University Press, 1998); for more on Canada's ODA policy to Latin America, see Tijerina, "Canadian Official Development Aid to Latin America."

11. The 1968 Ministerial Mission

1　Canada, Department of External Affairs, Ministerial Mission to Latin America, memorandum to Cabinet: Ministerial Mission to Latin America, 10 October 1968, 1, file 20-204-1 pt. 3.1, vol. 3, RG 20, Library and Archives Canada (LAC), Ottawa.

2 Canada, Department of External Affairs, Ministerial Mission to Latin America, "Ministerial Mission to Latin America: Inter-Departmental Meeting; Acting as Secretary of Meeting: F.W.O. Morton, Latin American Division," 21 August 1968, 3, file 20-204-2-1 pt. 3.1, vol. 3, RG 20, LAC.

3 The heavily bureaucratic-driven agenda meant that other Canadian social actors deeply involved by the late 1960s in Latin American matters were excluded from policy design and definition, including intellectuals, academics, labour groups, and religious organizations.

4 Canada, Department of External Affairs, Ministerial Mission to Latin America, "Ministerial Mission to Latin America," 3.

5 J.F. Grady, deputy minister, Department of Industry, Trade and Commerce, to Paul Gérin-Lajoie, president CIDA, memorandum, "Ref.: Latin America Aid Program," November 1972, 2, document no. 11784, file 38-1, CIDA vol. 7, RG 25, LAC.

6 Canada, Department of External Affairs, Ministerial Mission to Latin America, "Ministerial Mission to Latin America," 7.

7 Grady to Gérin-Lajoie, memorandum, "Ref.: Latin America Aid Program," 2.

8 Canada, Department of External Affairs, "Correspondence (Telex) – From: London Post; to: External Affairs (Canadian Ministerial Mission to Latin America – British Views)," 15 October 1968, 2, document no. 42111, file 20-204-2-1 pt. 3.1, vol. 3, LAC.

9 Canada, Department of External Affairs, "Correspondence (Telex) – From: London Post."

10 Canada, Department of External Affairs, "Correspondence (Telex) – From: London Post."

11 Canada, Department of External Affairs, "Correspondence (Telex) – From: London Post."

12 Canada, Department of External Affairs, "Correspondence (Telex) – From: London Post."

13 Canada, Department of External Affairs, *Correspondence-From: Mexico Post; to: External Affairs / Ref. Ministerial Mission to Guatemala*, 14 October 1968, 2, document no. 42566, file 20-204-2-1 pt. 3.1, vol. 3, LAC.

14 AFP, "Misión Canadiense vendrá a Colombia el 30 de octubre," *El Tiempo*, 25 October 1968, 1.

15 For more detail on nationalist policies under the Trudeau administration, see John Herd Thompson and Stephen Randall, *Canada and the United States: Ambivalent Allies* (Montreal and Kingston: McGill-Queen's University Press, 1994); and *Pierre Elliott Trudeau Memoirs: Episode III*, directed by Brian McKenna (Canadian Broadcasting Company, 1990), VHS.

16 Canadian Press, "Exporters Aim for Markets Other Than U.S.," *Telegram*, 21 October 1968, 22.

17 Canadian Press, "Exporters Aim for Markets Other Than U.S.," 22.

18 Canadian Press, "Exporters Aim for Markets Other Than U.S.," 22.

19 Canada's private sector continued to pressure Ottawa through the Canadian Manufacturers' Association and through other NGOs designed to advance business interests across the international system.

20 Office of the Chief Economist, Applied Economics Branch, *Colombia: A Market for Canadian Products* (Ottawa: Department of Economics and Development, 2 December 1968), 5–11.

21 Office of the Chief Economist, Applied Economics Branch, *Colombia*, 14.

22 Office of the Chief Economist, Applied Economics Branch, *Colombia*, 4.

23 *El Tiempo*, "Se estimula ingreso de capital extranjero," 31 October 1968, 1.

24 Others countries that were targeted by the new foreign policy included European countries such as Germany, Britain, Denmark, Netherlands, and France; Eastern European countries such as Poland, Czechoslovakia, East Germany, and Rumania; and regional neighbours such as Brazil and the Andean nations. See República de Colombia, Ministerio de Relaciones Exteriores, *Memorias: Tomo 2* (Bogotá: Imprenta Nacional, 1970), 286–99.

25 The following was the mission's itinerary: Caracas (27–9 October), Bogotá (29 October–1 November), Lima (2–4 November), Santiago de Chile (5–7 November), Buenos Aires (8–11 November), Rio de Janeiro (12–18 November), Ciudad de México (19–23 November), Ciudad de Guatemala (24–6 November) and San José (26–7 November). See Canada, Department of External Affairs, "Cabinet Visit to Latin America," *Canada Weekly Bulletin*, 13 November 1968, 5.

26 M. Cadieux, under secretary of Treasury Board, to S.S. Reisman, secretary of the Treasury Board, "Ref. Ministerial Mission to Latin America, 2 October 1968, 1, document no. 43005, file 20-204-2-1 pt. 3.2, vol. 2586, RG 20.

27 Canadian Press, "Cabinet Team Set: Latin Tour Planned," *Gazette*, 25 October 1968, 4.

28 Canadian Press, "Cabinet Team Set," 3.

29 Canadian Press, "Cabinet Team Set," 3.

30 Office of the Chief Economist, Applied Economics Branch, *Colombia*, 25.

31 Juan Gabriel Tokatlian and Rodrigo Pardo, *Política Exterior Colombiana: De la Subordinación a la Autonomía?* (Bogotá: Tercer Mundo Editores, 1989), 104.

32 Trudeau as well as Restrepo and many other leaders across the hemisphere had been influenced by the Interdependent school as well as the Structuralist thesis coming out of the United Nations Economic Commission for Latin America and the Caribbean. Juan Gabriel Tokatlian and Rodrigo Pardo, *Política Exterior Colombiana* 103.

33 República de Colombia, Ministerio de Relaciones Exteriores, *Memorias: Tomo 1*, 28.

34 External Affairs also instructed delegates to refrain from initiating discussion of all possible topics set in the agenda, and that they should proceed to do so only after Colombian ministers and officials brought specific projects and topics to the negotiating table. See Canada, Department of External Affairs, Ministerial Mission to Latin America, "Correspondence (Telex): From: External Affairs; to: Bogota Post – Ref. Ministerial Mission: Subjects for Discussion," 20 October 1968, 2, document no. 42465, file 20-204-2-1 pt. 3.2, vol. 2586, RG-20, LAC.

35 Canada, Department of Industry, Trade and Commerce, Ministerial Mission to Latin America, "Ministerial Mission Briefing Message no. 14131; From: Valentine De Hart (Trade and Commerce); To: Trade and Commerce Bogotá," 30 October 1968, 1–2, file 20-204-2-1 pt. 3.2, vol. 2586, RG-20, LAC.

36 These included bilateral trade arrangements, an International Development Bank loan to the recently created Fondo Financiero de Proyectos de Desarrollo (FONADE), the proposed Bogotá water and power supply projects, sister city project between Winnipeg and Bogotá, and Instituto Colombiano Agropecuario (ICA) rural development projects. See Canada, Department of External Affairs, "Correspondence (Telex); From: External Affairs; To: Bogotá Post – Ref. Ministerial Mission: Subjects for Discussion," 2.

37 Canada, Department of External Affairs, "Correspondence (Telex); From: External Affairs; To: Bogotá Post – Ref. Ministerial Mission to Colombia," 2.

38 Canada, Department of External Affairs, "Correspondence (Telex); From: External Affairs; To: Bogotá Post – Ref. Ministerial Mission to Colombia," 2.

39 Canada, Department of External Affairs, "Draft for Ministerial Meeting of October 23, 1968 Held at the East Block: The Ministerial Mission to Latin America – Policy Guidelines," 22 October 1968, 4, file 20-204-2-1 pt. 3.2, vol. 2586, RG-20, LAC.

40 Canada, Department of External Affairs, "Draft for Ministerial Meeting," 4.

41 Canada, Department of External Affairs, "Draft for Ministerial Meeting," 3.

42 For more detail on Strong's perception of the role of Canadian ODA, see, for example, Morrison, *Aid and Ebb Tide*, 57–99.

43 Canada, Department of External Affairs, "Correspondence (Telex); From: External Affairs; To: Bogotá Post – Ref. Ministerial Mission," 2.

44 Canada, Department of External Affairs, "Correspondence (Telex); From: External Affairs; To: Bogotá Post – Ref. Ministerial Mission," 2.

45 República de Colombia, Ministerio de Relaciones Exteriores, *Memorias: Tomo 2*, 299.

46 República de Colombia, Ministerio de Relaciones Exteriores, *Memorias: Tomo 2*, 299.

47 República de Colombia, Ministerio de Relaciones Exteriores, *Memorias: Tomo 2*, 299.

48 Pépin was referring to projects of no less than five years and no more than fifteen years. República de Colombia, Ministerio de Relaciones Exteriores, *Memorias: Tomo 2*, 299.

49 Canada's private sector experience with domestic and international thermo and hydroelectric projects led Canada to focus its efforts on bidding on such development projects across Latin America. República de Colombia, Ministerio de Relaciones Exteriores, *Memorias: Tomo 2*, 299.

50 Canada, Department of Trade and Commerce, , Ministerial Mission to Latin America, "Ministerial Mission Briefing Message No. 14131," 1.

51 In the case of the Barranquilla project, two consortiums were created – one from Ontario and the other from Quebec. The Ontario consortium was headed by Foundation Company and CDN Comstock Company, which joined forces with CGE and Acres International Limited. The Montreal consortium was headed by Montreal Engineering Company and Combustion Engineering Company, which partnered with Associated Electrical Industries of Britain. Canada, Department of Trade and Commerce, Ministerial Mission to Latin America, "Ministerial Mission Briefing Message No. 14131," 2.

52 *El Tiempo*, "Financiación de Proyectos Ofrece la Misión Canadiense," 5A.

53 *El Tiempo*, "Financiación de Proyectos Ofrece la Misión Canadiense," 5A.

54 *El Tiempo*, "Financiación de Proyectos Ofrece la Misión Canadiense," 5A.

55 *El Tiempo*, "Financiación de Proyectos Ofrece la Misión Canadiense," 5A.

56 *El Tiempo*, "Financiación de Proyectos Ofrece la Misión Canadiense," 5A.

57 This initial idea led to the establishment of IDRC's Latin American operations headquarters in Colombia in 1970.

58 Canada, Department of External Affairs, *Ministerial Mission to Latin America: Preliminary Report of the Ministerial Mission to Latin America, October 27–November 27* (Ottawa: Queen's Printer, 11 July 1969), 28.

59 Gordon Pape, "Sharp, Pepin Discuss Mission: Closer Latin-American Ties Forecast," *Gazette*, 30 November 1968, 8.

60 Pape, "Sharp, Pepin Discuss Mission," 8.

61 Canada, Department of Trade and Commerce, Ministerial Mission to Latin America, "Ministerial Mission Briefing Message No. 14131," 1.

62 Pape, "Sharp, Pepin Discuss Mission," 8.

63 For more detail on Trudeau's Latin American policy, see Canada, Department of External Affairs. *Latin America: Foreign Policy for Canadians* (Ottawa: Queen's Publisher, 1970).

12. Official Development Assistance to Colombia

1 Harvey S. Perloff, *Alliance for Progress: A Social Invention in the Making* (Baltimore, MD: Johns Hopkins University Press, 1969), 223.

2 Perloff, *Alliance for Progress*, 223.
3 Perloff, *Alliance for Progress*, 223.
4 Keith Spicer, "Clubmanship Upstaged: Canada's Twenty Years in the Colombo Plan," *International Journal* 25, no. 1 (Winter 1969): 23.
5 Stefano Tijerina, "One Size Fits All? Canadian Development Assistance to Colombia, 1953–1972," in *A Samaritan State Revised: Historical Perspectives on Canadian Foreign Aid, 1950–2016*, ed. Greg Donaghy and David Webster, 121–4 (Calgary: University of Calgary Press, 2018).
6 Morrison, *Aid and Ebb Tide*, 55.
7 Inter-American Development Bank, IDB. "Projects," accessed 5 February 2011, www.iadb.org.
8 Spicer, "Clubmanship Upstaged," 25.
9 Spicer, "Clubmanship Upstaged," 26.
10 Canadian International Development Agency, "Minutes; Office of the Director General, External Aid Office; Ref. Minutes of the Meeting of the External Aid Board Held on Wednesday, February 8, 1967," 2, document no. 11784, file 38-1 CIDA vol. 5, RG 25, LAC.
11 Canadian International Development Agency, "Minutes," 1.
12 Canadian International Development Agency, "Minutes," 2.
13 For more details on Trudeau's foreign policy vision, see Canada, Department of External Affairs, *Foreign Policy for Canadians* (Ottawa: Queen's Publisher, 1970).
14 Canada, Department of External Affairs, "Latin America: Foreign Policy for Canadians," 5.
15 Canada, Department of External Affairs, "International Development: Foreign Policy for Canadians," *Foreign Policy for Canadians* (Ottawa: Queen's Publisher, 1970), 7.
16 Morrison, *Aid and Ebb Tide*, 57.
17 Canada, Department of External Affairs, Ministerial Mission to Latin America, memorandum to the Cabinet: Ministerial Mission to Latin America, 10 October 1968, 1.
18 Tijerina, "One Size Fits All?" 124.
19 Tijerina, "One Size Fits All?" 124
20 Dragoslav Avromovic, ed., *Economic Growth of Colombia: Problems and Prospects – Report of a Mission Sent to Colombia in 1970 by the World Bank* (Baltimore, MD: Johns Hopkins University Press, 1970), 1.
21 Canadian International Development Agency (CIDA), "Memorandum to the Cabinet: The Allocation of Canadian Development Assistance Funds for the Fiscal Year 1971–1972," February 1971, document no. 11784, file 38-1 CIDA vol. 6, RG 25, LAC.
22 International Development Research Centre (IDRC), *IDRC at 40: A Brief History* (Ottawa: IDRC, 2010), 6.

23 The Consultative Group on International Agricultural Research was in itself
    a multilateral initiative funded by numerous nations, including Canada,
    Belgium, Denmark, Germany, Japan, Netherlands, Norway, Sweden,
    Switzerland, the United Kingdom, and the United States. For more details,
    see Consultative Group on International Agricultural Research, "Summary
    of Proceedings: Third Meeting of the Consultative Group on International
    Agricultural Research," 1 and 2 November 1972, 1, document no. 11784,
    file 38-1, CIDA vol. 7, RG 25, LAC, 1.
24 Tijerina, "One Size Fits All?" 142.
25 IDRC, *IDRC at 40*, 13.
26 CIDA, "Memorandum to the Cabinet," 22.
27 IDRC, *IDRC at 40*, 15.
28 Canada, Department of External Affairs, "Latin America," 13.
29 Office of the Chief Economist, Applied Economic Branch, *Colombia*, 50.
30 Office of the Chief Economist, Applied Economic Branch, *Colombia*, 50.
31 República de Colombia, Departamento Nacional de Planeación, *Las Cuatro
    Estratégias* (Bogotá, 1972), 303–11.
32 Morrison, *Aid and Ebb Tide*, 457.
33 IDRC, *International Development Research Centre Projects 1970–1981* (Ottawa:
    IDRC, 1982), 53–359.
34 Canada, Department of Industry, Trade and Commerce, "Notes on a Revised
    Canadian Aid Program, 22 January 1973, 1, file 38-1 CIDA, vol. 11784, RG-25,
    LAC.
35 Canada, Department of Industry, Trade and Commerce, "Notes," 2.
36 Tijerina, "Canadian Official Development Aid to Latin America," 233.
37 Tijerina, "Canadian Official Development Aid to Latin America," 233–4.
38 Tijerina, "Canadian Official Development Aid to Latin America," 219.
39 Cranford Pratt, *Canadian International Development Assistance Policies:
    An Appraisal* (Montreal and Kingston: McGill-Queen's University Press,
    1994), viii.

Bibliography

Archives

Fogler Library, University of Maine, Orono
Library and Archives Canada, Ottawa
Trinity College Archives, Toronto

Primary Sources and Microfilm

Avramovic, Dragoslav, ed. *Economic Growth of Colombia: Problems and Prospects – Report of a Mission Sent to Colombia in 1970 by the World Bank*. Baltimore, MD: Johns Hopkins University Press, 1972.

Canada, Department of External Affairs. *Foreign Policy for Canadians*. Ottawa: Queen's Printer, 1970.

– *International Development: Foreign Policy for Canadians*. Ottawa: Queen's Printer, 1970.

– *Latin America: Foreign Policy for Canadians*. Ottawa: Queen's Printer, 1970.

– *Ministerial Mission to Latin America: Preliminary Report of the Ministerial Mission to Latin America, October 27–November 27*. Ottawa: Queen's Printer, 11 July 1969.

– "Possible Sale to Colombia of F-86 Aircrafts." 28 February 1950.

Canada, Department of Trade and Commerce. *Extract from Cabinet Conclusions*. Ed. Department of External Affairs, Documents on Canadian External Relations. Ottawa, 15 March 1956.

– *Post War Trade Reviews: Colombia and Venezuela*. Ottawa, 1946.

– *Sale of F86s to Colombia*. Edited by Department of External Affairs, 1–2. Ottawa, 27 February 1956.

Gray, John Hamilton. *Confederation, or, the Political and Parliamentary History of Canada (Microfilm): From the Conference at Quebec in October, 1864, to the Admission of British Columbia, in July, 1871*. Toronto: Coop, Clark, 1872. CIHM microfiche series no. 06500, University of Maine Fogler Library Archives, Orono.

International Development Research Centre (IDRC). *IDRC at 40: A Brief History*. Ottawa: IDRC, 2010.

– *International Development Research Centre Projects 1970–1981*. Ottawa: IDRC, 1982.

Lévine, V. *South American Handbook: Colombia, Physical Features, Natural Resources, Means of Communication, Manufactures, and industrial Development*. New York: D. Appleton, 1914.

Ministerio de Relaciones Exteriores, República de Colombia. *Memorias: Tomo 1*. Edited by Ministerio de Relaciones Exteriores. Bogotá: Imprenta Nacional, 1970.

– *Memorias: Tomo 2*. Edited by Ministerio de Relaciones Exteriores. Bogotá: Imprenta Nacional, 1970.

Office of the Chief Economist, Applied Economics Branch. *Colombia: A Market for Canadian Products*. Ottawa: Department of Economics and Development, 2 December 1968.

Pan American Union. *Fourth Pan American Commercial Conference: Foreign Trade of Latin America, 1910–1929*. Washington, DC: U.S. Government Printing Office, 1931.

Pierre Elliott Trudeau Memoirs: Episode III. Directed by Brian McKenna. Canadian Broadcasting Company, 1990. VHS.

Remarks of William McChesney Martin, Jr., President of the Export-Import Bank of Washington before Committee Iv of the Ninth International Conference of American States. Washington: Foreign Relations of the United States 1948: Western Hemisphere, 1972.

República de Colombia, Departamento Nacional de Planeación. *Las Cuatro Estratégias*. Edited Departamento Nacional de Planeación. Bogotá, 1972.

República de Colombia, Ministerio de Minas y Petróleos. *Memorias 1944*. Bogotá, Imprenta Nacional, 1944.

United States, Department of Commerce. *Banking Opportunities in South America*. Special Agents Series No. 106, ed. William H. Lough. Washington, 1915.

United States, Department of State. "A Positive Program of United States Assistance for Latin America." *Foreign Relations of the United States 1948: The Western Hemisphere – Foreign Relations*, vol. 9. Washington, 1948.

United States Senate. *Reciprocity with Canada: Compilation of 1911, part 3C*, prepared by the Finance Committee. Washington, April 28, 1911.

World Bank. *The Basis of a Development Program for Colombia*. Ed. Lauchlin Bernard Currie. Washington, 1950.

Secondary Sources

AFP. "Misión Canadiense Vendrá a Colombia El 30 de octubre." *El Tiempo*, 25 October 1968.

Associated Press. "Banking Group Headed by the National City Plans Loans to Regional Department." *New York Times*, 18 February 1931.

– "Canada May Join 'Union.'" *Ottawa Citizen*, 25 March 1953, 20.

– "Colombia at War with Germany." *Winnipeg Free Press*, 17 November 1943.

– "Historic Treaty: Hemisphere Defense to Be Planned." *News Palladium*, 15 August 1947.

Austin, E.C. "Need of Trade Agents in South America." *Manitoba Free Press*, 18 June 1927.

Ayala, César J. *American Sugar Kingdom: The Plantation Economy of the Spanish Caribbean, 1898–1934*. Chapel Hill: University of North Carolina Press, 1999.

Ayearst, F. "G. Harrison Smith: The Power behind the South American Oil Fields." *Financial Post*, 7 May 1926.

Baker, Frederick W. "Oroville Dredging Company Limited – Meeting Held on December 30 at Salisbury House, London Wall, E.G., Mr. Frederick W. Baker (Chairman of the Company) Presiding." Internet Archive. http://www .archive.org/stream/statist83londuoft/statist83londuoft_djvu.txt.

Barbosa, Rosana. *Brazil and Canada: Economic, Political and Migratory Ties, 1820s to 1970s*. London: Lexington Books, 2017.

Baum, Daniel Jay. *The Banks of Canada in the Commonwealth Caribbean: Economic Nationalism and Multinational Enterprises of a Medium Power*. New York: Praeger, 1974.

Berquist, Charles. *Café y Conflicto en Colombia (1886–1910): La Guerra De los Mil Días, sus Antecedentes Y Consecuencias*. Bogotá: Ancora Editores, 1981.

Bloom, Chester. "Canada's Share in the Marshall Plan." *Winnipeg Free Press*, 10 April 1948.

Bow, Brian, and Patrick Lennox, eds. *An Independent Foreign Policy for Canadians? Challenges and Choices for the Future*. Toronto: University of Toronto Press, 2008.

Bradford Era. "Building of Colombian Pipe Line Is under Way Capacity 25,000 Bbls." 22 January 1925.

– "Imperial Oil Increases South American Output." 12 March 1923.

– "Tropical Oil Co. Makes First Shipment of Gas." 6 October 1921.

Braun, Herbert. *The Assassination of Gaitán: Public Life and Urban Violence in Colombia*. Madison: University of Wisconsin Press, 1985.

Brebner, Bartlet. *Canada: A Modern History*. Ann Arbor: University of Michigan Press, 1960.

Brown, Chester, ed. *Commentaries on Selected Model Investment Treaties*. Oxford: Oxford University Press, 2013.

Bucheli, Marcelo. *Bananas and Business: The United Fruit Company in Colombia, 1899–2000*. New York: New York University Press, 2005.

– "Canadian Multinational Corporations and Economic Nationalism: The Case of Imperial Oil Limited in Alberta (Canada) and Colombia, 1899–1938." *Enterprises et Histoire* 54 (April 2009): 67–85.

– "Negotiating under the Monroe Doctrine: Weetman Pearson and the Origins of U.S. Control of Colombian Oil." *Business History Review* 82 (Autumn 2008): 529–53.

Burke, Janet, and Ted Humphrey, eds. *Nineteenth-Century Nation Building and the Latin American Intellectual Tradition*. Indianapolis: Hackett Publishing, 2007.

Bushnell, David. *The Making of Modern Colombia: A Nation in Spite of Itself*. Berkeley: University of California Press, 1993.

Canada, Toronto Head Office. "Manufacturers Life Insurance Company." *Daily Gleaner*, 20 March 1901.

Canadian Gazette. "Trade between Dominion and West Indies." *Daily Gleaner*, 29 December 1922.

Canadian Press. "Cabinet Team Set: Latin Tour Planned." *Gazette*, 25 October 1968.

– "Canada, Brazil Sign Trade Agreement." *Winnipeg Free Press*, 18 October 1941, 3.

– "Canada Names 2 Ambassadors in South America." *Montreal Gazette*, 22 November 1952, 1.

– "Canada Resuming Trade Mission to South." *Daily Gleaner*, 14 August 1941.

– "Exporters Aim for Markets Other Than U.S." *Telegram*, 21 October 1968.

– "Mackinnon Forecasts Loosening of British Import Regulations." *Lethbridge Herald*, 22 January 1946, 1.

– "Placer Turns Record Profits." *Winnipeg Free Press*, 4 August 1956.

– "Trade with Latin America Well Founded." *Winnipeg Free Press*, 9 January 1953.

Canadian Press Dispatch. "Canada Names Ray Lawson to New York Post." *Winnipeg Free Press*, 7 November 1952, 26.

Coleman, Lynn Bradley. *Colombia and the United States: The Making of an Inter-American Alliance, 1939–1960*. Kent, OH: Kent State University Press, 2008.

Collins, John. "The Explorer." *Gazette*, 30 October 1968, 6.

Colombia, Ministerio de Minas y Petróleos. *Memoria 1944*. Bogotá: Imprenta Nacional, 1944.

Colton, Tim. "General Cargo Ships Built in Canada since WWII." 22 August 2017. http://shipbuildinghistory.com/canadaships/freighters.htm.

Cowdray, Lord. "Says Press Beat Colombia Oil Plan: Lord Clowdray Blames American Papers for his Failure to get Concessions." *New York Times*, 28 November 1913.

Craig, Eric K. "Gold Mining in Colombia." *Engineering and Mining Journal* 113, no. 12 (March 1922): 479.

Daily Gleaner. "Bank of Canada Is Spreading Out." 30 March 1925.

– "Empty Hands!" Advertisement. 8 May 1926.

– "Progress Made by United Fruit Company in the Caribbean," 27 March 1928.

- "The Royal Bank of Canada Has Formed a Close Working Association with the London County Westminster and Parr's Bank, Limited." 11 July 1919.
- "Sun Life Assurance Company of Canada: A Great International Institution." 3 March 1928.
- "Trade Mission from Canada Is Planned." 19 May 1927.

Darroch, James L. "Global Competitiveness and Public Policy: The Case of Canadian Multinational Banks." *Business History* 34, no. 3 (July 1992): 153–75.

DeLong, Linwood. *A Guide to Canadian Diplomatic Relations.* Ottawa: Canadian Library Association, 1985.

Demarest, Geoffrey. "War of the Thousand Days." *Small Wars and Insurgencies* 12, no. 1 (Spring 2001): 1–30.

Desai, Radhika. "Canadian Capitalism and Imperialism: A Brief Note." Paper presented at the Society for Socialist Studies Conference. Ryerson University, Toronto, June 2017.

Dolan, Michael B., and Brian W. Tomlin. "Foreign Policy in Asymmetrical Dyads: Theoretical Reformulation and Empirical Analysis, Canada–United States Relations, 1963–1972." *International Studies Quarterly* 28, no. 3 (September 1984): 349–68.

Drake, Paul W. *The Money Doctor in the Andes.* Durham, NC: Duke University Press, 1989.

Egan, Charles E. "Economic Advance Is Seen in Colombia: Head of Banking Group Says Rapid Expansion Brings Need for More Capital." *New York Times*, 22 January 1950.

El Tiempo. "4 Nuevos Buques Adquiere la Flota Grancolombiana." 13 January 1953.
- "10,000 Cédulas Diarias Tomará en Bogotá la Misión Canadienses." 18 January 1953.
- "Canadá Pagará en Dólares todas las Importaciones." 29 January 1953.
- "Financiación de Proyectos Ofrece La Misión Canadiense." 1 November 1968.
- "Habrá Trueque de Productos entre Colombia y Venezuela en este Año." 2 January 1953.
- "Inauguración: Nuevo Servicio de Primera Clase a Nueva York." 14 January 1953.
- "La Johnson Line Amplía sus Servicios a Colombia." 16 January 1953.
- "Misión Canadiense Llegará Hoy en las Horas de la Tarde a Bogotá." 28 January 1953.
- "Parte Mañana la Misión del Canadá, y el Príncipe Danes." 29 January 1953.
- "Se Estimula Ingreso de Capital Extranjero." 31 October 1968.

Firestone, O.J. "Canada's External Trade and Net Foreign Balance, 1851–1900." In *Trends in the American Economy in the Nineteenth Century*, edited by the

Conference on Research in Income and Wealth, 757–71. Princeton, NJ: Princeton University Press, 1960.

Fisher, Robert C. "'We'll Get Our Own': Canada and the Oil Shipping Crisis of 1942." *Northern Mariner / Le Marin du Nord* 3, no. 2 (April 1993): 33–9.

Fluharty, Vernon Lee. *Dance of the Millions: Military Rule and the Social Revolution in Colombia.* Pittsburgh: University of Pittsburgh Press, 1957.

Franco, Horacio. "Una Realidad: La Flota Grancolombiana." *El Tiempo*, 14 January 1953.

Gadpaille, Ivanhoe. "Manufacturers Life Insurance Company of Canada." *Daily Gleaner*, 29 April 1902.

Gaitán, Jorge Eliécer. "La Zona Bananera: Una Nicaragua Colombiana." *El Debate de las Bananeras.* 1929. https://www.scribd.com/doc/52035148/Jorge-Eliecer-Gaitan-El-Debate-de-las-Bananeras.

Gellman, Irwin F. *Good Neighbor Diplomacy: United States Policies in Latin America, 1933–1945.* Baltimore, MD: Johns Hopkins University Press, 1979.

Gellner, John. *Canada in NATO.* Toronto: Ryerson, 1970.

Gordon, Todd, and Jeffery R. Webber. *Blood of Extraction: Canadian Imperialism in Latin America.* Winnipeg: Fernwood Publishing, 2016.

Gran Colombia Gold. "About Us." Gran Colombia Gold Corp. 2017. http://www.grancolombiagold.com/about-us/default.aspx.

Griess, Phyllis R. "Colombia's Petroleum Resources." *Economic Geography* 22, no. 4 (October 1946): 245–54.

Harris, George. *The President's Book: The Story of the Sun Life Assurance Company of Canada.* Montreal: Sun Life Assurance, 1928.

Harris, Richard, Ian Keay, and Frank Lewis. "Protecting Infant Industries: Canadian Manufacturing and the National Policy, 1870–1913." *Explorations in Economic History* 56 (2015): 15–31.

Hart, Michael. *A Trading Nation: Canadian Trade Policy from Colonialism to Globalization.* Vancouver: UBC Press, 2003.

Harvey, David. *A Brief History of Neoliberalism.* New York: Oxford University Press, 2005.

Henderson, James D. *Modernization in Colombia: The Laureano Gómez Years, 1889–1965.* Gainesville: University Press of Florida, 2001.

Hill, Mary O. *Canada's Salesman to the World: The Development of Trade and Commerce, 1892–1939.* Montreal and Kingston: McGill-Queen's University Press, 1977.

Hoffman, Arnold. *Free Gold: The Story of Canadian Mining.* Toronto: Rinehart, 1947.

Holt, Herbert. "Fifty-Ninth Annual Meeting of the Royal Bank of Canada." *New York Times*, 17 January 1928.

– "Forty-Eighth Annual Meeting of the Royal Bank of Canada." *Manitoba Free Press*, 19 January 1917.

Hunt, Nadine. "Expanding the Frontiers of Western Jamaica through Minor Atlantic Ports in the Eighteenth Century." *Canadian Journal of History* 45, no. 3 (Winter 2010): 485–501.

Innis, Harold Adam. *The Fur Trade in Canada: An Introduction to Canadian Economic History*. New Haven, CT: Yale University Press, 1930.

Inter-American Development Bank. "Projects." Accessed 5 February 2011. www.iadb.org.

J.W. Asociados y Compañía Limitada. "Oronorte Project Area." Webpawner. com. Accessed 20 January 2013. http://www.webspawner.com/users /oronorte (site discontinued).

Jayne, Catherine E. *Oil, War and the Anglo-American Relations: American and British Reactions to Mexico's Expropriation of Foreign Oil Properties, 1937–1941*. Westport, CT: Greenwood, 2001.

Joseph, Gilbert M., and Daniela Spenser, eds. *In from the Cold: Latin America's New Encounter with the Cold War*. Durham, NC: Duke University Press, 2008.

Krikorian, Jacqueline D., Marcel Martel, and Adrian Shubert. *Globalizing Confederation: Canada and the World in 1867*. Toronto: University of Toronto Press, 2017.

Krystynak, Ronald H.E. "Canada's Experience with Foot-and-Mouth Disease." *Canadian Veterinary Journal* 28, no. 8 (August 1987): 540–2.

Kuethe, Allan J., and Kenneth J. Andrien. *The Spanish Atlantic World in the Eighteenth Century: War and the Bourbon Reforms*. New York: Cambridge University Press, 2014.

Lennox, Patrick. "John W. Holmes and Canadian International Relations Theory." *International Journal* 65, no. 2 (Spring 2010): 381–9.

Lethbridge Herald. "Argentina Wants Claims Approved." 9 April 1948.

– "Howe Plans Seek Trade South America." 8 November 1952.

– "Pan-American Conference Opens at Bogotá, Colombia, on Thursday." 27 March 1948.

– "Seek Trade South America: Mackinnon to Lead Five-Man Mission to Eight Countries." 25 July 1941.

Macrotrends. "Gold Prices: 100 Year Historical Chart." 2018. https://www .macrotrends.net/1333/historical-gold-prices-100-year-chart.

Manitoba Free Press. "A Time to Go Forward." 18 April 1927.

– "Winter Cruises." 2 December 1924.

Marchildon, Gregory P. "Canadian Multinationals and International Finance: Past and Present." *Business History* 34, no. 3 (July 1992): 1–15.

Marichal, Carlos. *A Century of Debt Crises in Latin America: From Independence to the Great Depression, 1820–1930*. Princeton, NJ: Princeton University Press, 1989.

Marshall, Edward. "Fight for South America's Great Trade." *New York Times*, 4 December 1910.

Marshall, Peter. "The Balfour Formula and the Evolution of the Commonwealth." *Commonwealth Journal of International Affairs* 90, no. 361 (2001): 541–53.

McDowall, Duncan. *Quick to the Frontier: Canada's Royal Bank*. Toronto: McClelland & Stewart, 1993.

McGreevey, William Paul. *An Economic History of Colombia, 1845–1930*. Cambridge: Cambridge University Press, 1971.

McKenna, Peter. *Canada and the OAS: From Dilettante to Full Partner*. Montreal and Kingston: McGill-Queen's University Press, 1995.

Medina, José. "Los Problemas Mineros." *El Tiempo*, 4 March 1939.

Mejía, Alvaro T. "Rivalidades por Colombia a Comienzos del Sligo XX." *Colombia en la Repartición Imperialista (1870–1914)*. 2002. http://www.lablaa .org/blaavirtual/historia/corim/corim3.htm.

Melo, Hector. *La Maniobra del Oro en Colombia*. Medellín: Editorial La Pulga, 1975.

Mining Watch Canada. "Publications." 2017. http://miningwatch.ca/.

Mitchener, Kris James, and Marc D. Weidenmier. "The Baring Crisis and the Great Latin American Meltdown of the 1890s." National Bureau of Economic Research working paper no. 13403, September 2007.

Montagnes, James. "Canada's Latin-American Trade Booms: Imports and Exports Far above Those of the Pre-War Days." *Lethbridge Herald,* 27 October 1941.

Montreal Gazette, "Nechi Shareholders Vote Merger Plan." 1 July 1953.

Morgan, Kenneth. *Bristol and the Atlantic Trade in the Eighteenth Century*. Cambridge: Cambridge University Press, 1993.

Morrison, Allen. "The Tramways of Bogotá." 2007. http://www.tramz.com /co/bg/t/te.html.

Morrison, David R. *Aid and Ebb Tide: A History of CIDA and Canadian Development Assistance*. Waterloo, ON: Wilfrid Laurier University Press, 1998.

Morton, Desmon. "The Divisive Dream: Reciprocity in 1854; Fifteen Years Ago, the Free Trade Debate Divided the Country. It wasn't the First Time. When It Comes to Trading with America, Canada Has a History of Ambivalence." *Beaver* 82, no. 6 (December 2002): 16–21.

Mount, Graeme. "Canadian Investment in Colombia: Some Examples, 1919–1939." *North/South: The Canadian Journal of Latin American Studies* 1, no. 1 and 2 (1976): 46–61.

Murray, D.R. "Canada's First Diplomatic Missions in Latin America." *Journal of Interamerican Studies and World Affairs* 16, no. 2 (1974): 153–72.

N.R.D. "The Facts about Prosperity: Mr. Howe on Trade." *Winnipeg Free Press,* 4 August 1953.

Neal, Arthur. "Canada's Trade Ties with Latin America." *Canadian Geographical Journal* 31, no. 2 (August 1945): 79–95.

New York Times. "Assets of Sun Life Rise $36,000,000." 10 February 1932.
- "Back from Colombia and Jungle Mines." 16 July 1910.
- "Banking Concerns Merge." 14 August 1936.
- "Bank of Canada Adds to Holdings." 4 February 1925.
- "Banks as Agents in South America: O.H. Fuerth Advises Financiers Here Also to Get Local Capital in Branching." 23 May 1915.
- "Bank to Specialize in Latin America." 15 September 1922.
- "Buys Oil Land in Colombia." 16 September 1919.
- "Canada's Trade Relations: The Dominion Government Will Seek New Markets Abroad." 9 April 1891.
- "Canadian Bank at Cali Closed." 14 November 1948.
- "Colombia Allows Free Sale of Gold." 16 October 1953.
- "Colombia Invites Our Trade." 24 November 1898.
- "Colombian-Canadian Pact Signed." 21 February 1946.
- "Colombia's Riches Reviewed by Bank." 3 July 1925.
- "Developing Colombia's Resources." 27 December 1921.
- "Direction of Trade Current." 8 March 1879.
- "End of Exploration in Colombia Pledged: Dr. Lopez, Honored at Dinner Here, Says His New Deal Will Abolish Privilege." 29 June 1934.
- "Exports Declared Vital for Canada." 2 January 1946.
- "General Debate to Close Today: Mills to Make Last Speech for the Bill-Washburn on Reciprocity." 24 April 1894.
- "Harry Stuart Derby: Prospector Who Won Fortune in Colombia Gold Field Dies." 30 July 1929.
- "Hints for Our Merchants: Figs from State Department Thistles." 26 January 1880.
- "Imperial Oil Company Will Keep Drilling." 27 February 1923.
- "International Mining." 25 July 1963.
- "Kemmerer to Leave Soon: Commission to Study Finances in Colombia, Plans Start This Month." 3 August 1930.
- "Learn Spanish and Prosper: An American Consul's Advice to Merchants and Students." 28 June 1896.
- "Mining Concern Gets New Top Team." 25 May 1954.
- "Mining Concern Moves to Expand: South American Gold Obtains One-Third of Capital Stock of Pato Dredging, Ltd." 18 November 1954.
- "The Pan-Anglican Idea." 17 September 1888.
- "Protection Fails in Canada." 26 October 1893.
- "South American Gold." 13 June 1962.
- "South American Oil Needed Badly Now." 16 March 1920.
- "To Seek Gold in Colombia." 13 May 1901.
- "U.S. Capital Lured to Latin America: Even Smaller Countries Are Investing in Nations Where Outside Funds Are Needed." 5 January 1955.

O'Brian, Hugh. "Kruger Takes a Long-Term Outlook for Steady Growth in Consumer Products." *Perini Journal*, n.d. http://www.perinijournal.it /Items/en-US/Articoli/PJL-28/Kruger-takes-a-longterm-outlook-for -steady-growth-in-consumer-products.

O'Connor, Dermot, and Juan Pablo Bohórquez Montoya. "Neoliberal Transformation in Colombia's Goldfields: Development Strategy or Capitalist Imperialism?" In "Contemporary Colombia: The Continuity of Struggle / Numéro Thématique: Colombie Contemporaine: Persistance des conflicts," special issue, *Labour, Capital and Society / Travail, capital et société* 43, no. 2 (2010): 85–118.

Ogelsby, J.C.M. "England vs. Spain in America, 1739–1748: The Spanish Side of the Hill." *Historical Papers / Communications Historiques* 5, no. 1 (1970): 147–57.

– *Gringos from the Far North: Essays in the History of Canadian–Latin American Relations, 1866–1968.* Toronto: MacMillan of Canada, 1976.

Pape, Gordon. "Sharp, Pepin Discuss Mission: Closer Latin-American Ties Forecast." *Gazette*, 30 November 1968.

Papeles Nacionales S.A., "Quienes somos." Accessed 23 November 2010. www.papelesnacionales.com.

Pares, Richard. *War and Trade in the West Indies, 1739–1763.* Oxford: Oxford University Press, 1936.

Parry, J.H., P.M. Sherlock, and A.P. Maingot, eds. *A Short History of the West Indies.* New York: St. Martin's, 1987.

Perloff, Harvey S. *Alliance for Progress: A Social Invention in the Making.* Baltimore, MD: Johns Hopkins University Press, 1969.

Pomper, Philip. "The History and Theory of Empires." In "Theorizing Empire," theme issue, *History and Theory* 44, no. 4 (December 2005): 1–27.

Pratt, Cranford. *Canadian International Development Assistance Policies: An Appraisal.* Montreal and Kingston: McGill-Queen's University Press, 1994.

Quigley, Neil C. "The Bank of Nova Scotia in the Caribbean, 1889–1940." *Business History Review* 63, no. 4 (Winter 1989): 797–838.

Rapaport, Mario. *Las Políticas Económicas de la Argentina, Una Breve Historia.* Buenos Aires: Editorial Booklet, 2010.

Rappaport, Joanne. *The Politics of Memory: Native Historical Interpretation in the Colombian Andes.* New York: Cambridge University Press, 1990.

Reinhardt, Nola. "The Consolidation of the Import-Export Economy in Nineteenth-Century Colombia: A Political-Economic Analysis." *Latin American Perspectives* 13, no. 1 (Winter 1986): 75–98.

Rippy, Fred J. *The Capitalists and Colombia.* New York: Vanguard, 1931.

Roca, Adolfo Meisel. *¿Por Qué Perdió la Costa Caribe el Siglo XX?* Bogotá: Banco de la República, 2011.

Rochlin, James. *Discovering the Americas: The Evolution of Canadian Foreign Policy toward Latin America.* Vancouver: UBC Press, 1994.

Rosenberg, Emily S. *Spreading the American Dream: American Economic and Cultural Expansion, 1890–1945.* New York: Hill and Wang, 1982.

Rovner, Eduardo Saenz. "La Industria Petrolera En Colombia: Concesiones, Reversión y Asociaciones." *Revista Credencial Historia* (January 1994). http://www.lablaa.org/blaavirtual/revistas/credencial/enero94/enero2.htm.

Safford, Frank. "Foreign and National Enterprise in Nineteenth-Century Colombia." In special Latin American issue, *Business History Review* 39, no. 4 (Winter 1965): 503–26.

Sánchez, Ricardo. *Estado y Planeación En Colombia.* Bogotá: Editorial La Rosa Roja, 1984.

Schulzinger, Robert D. *U.S. Diplomacy since 1900.* New York: Oxford University Press, 2008.

Schuster, Sven. "Las Políticas de la Historia en Colombia: El Primer Gobierno del Frente Nacional y el 'Problema' de la Violencia (1958–1962)." *Iberoamericana* 9, no. 6 (2009): 9–26.

See, Scott W. *The History of Canada.* Westport, CT: Greenwood, 2001.

Semmel, Bernard. *The Liberal Ideal and the Demons of Empire.* Baltimore, MD: Johns Hopkins University Press, 1993.

Smitmans, María Teresa Aya. *Canadá-Colombia, 50 Años de Relaciones.* Bogotá: Universidad Externado de Colombia, 2003.

Southhall, A.E., ed. *Imperial Year Book for Dominion of Canada, 1914–1915.* Montreal: John Lovell & Son, 1914.

Spicer, Keith. "Clubmanship Upstaged: Canada's Twenty Years in the Colombo Plan." *International Journal* 25, no. 1 (Winter 1969): 23–33.

Stacey, C.P. *Canada and the Age of Conflict.* Vol. 2, *1921–1948.* Toronto: University of Toronto Press, 1981.

Stevenson, Brian. *Canada, Latin America and the New Internationalism: A Foreign Policy Analysis, 1968–1990.* Montreal and Kingston: McGill-Queen's University Press and the Centre for Security and Foreign Policy Studies, 2000.

Suárez, John Jairo Patiño. *Compañías Extranjeras y Fiebre de Oro En Zaragoza, 1880–1952.* Medellín: IDEA, 1997.

Sydney Morning Herald. "Placer Development." 25 July 1929.

Taffet, Jeffrey F. *Foreign Aid as Foreign Policy: The Alliance for Progress in Latin America.* New York: Routledge, 2007.

Taylor, Graham D. "From Branch Operation to Integrated Subsidiary: The Reorganization of Imperial Oil under Walter Teagle, 1911–17." *Business History* 34, no. 3 (July 1992): 49–68.

Thompson, John Herd, and Steven Randall. *Canada and the United States: Ambivalent Allies.* Montreal and Kingston: McGill-Queen's University Press, 1994.

Tijerina, Stefano. "Canadian Official Development Aid to Latin America: The Struggle over the Humanitarian Agenda, 1963–1977." *Journal of Canadian Studies / Revue d'études canadiennes* 51, no. 1 (Winter 2017): 217–43.

– "One Cinderblock at a Time: Historiography of Canadian–Latin American and Canadian-Colombian Relations." *Desafíos* 1, no. 24 (2012): 275–92.

– "One Size Fits All? Canadian Development Assistance to Colombia, 1953–1972." In *A Samaritan State Revised: Historical Perspectives on Canadian Foreign Aid, 1950–2016*, edited by Greg Donaghy and David Webster, 123–44. Calgary: University of Calgary Press, 2018.

– "The Zero-Sum Game of Early Oil Extraction Relations in Colombia: Workers, Tropical Oil, and the Police State, 1918–1938." In *Working for Oil: Comparative Social Histories of Labor in Petroleum*, edited by Tourah Atabaki, Kaveh Ehsani, and Elisabetta Bini, 37–67. Basingstoke, UK: Palgrave Macmillan, 2018.

Titusville Herald. "International Petroleum." 25 December 1919.

– "The Oil Jungles of Colombia, South America." 19 May 1920.

Tokatlian, Juan Gabriel, and Rodrigo Pardo. *Política Exterior Colombiana: De la Subordinación a la Autonomía?* Bogotá: Tercer Mundo Editores, 1989.

Toronto Telegram. "Collective Snub Given U.S. by 20 American Republics, Dead Silence Follows Talks." 10 April 1048.

United Press. "Mission Quits Colombia: Canadian Group Heads for Ciudad Trujillo of Dominican Republic." *New York Times*, 2 February 1953.

– "Text of President's Latin Loan Message." *New York Times*, 9 April 1948.

United Nations. *Yearbook of International Trade Statistics 1950.* Edited by Statistical Office of the United Nations. New York: United Nations Publishing Division, 1951.

Vásquez, Luis Ospina. *Industria y Protección en Colombia, 1810–1930.* Bogotá: Editorial Santafé, 1955.

W.F.E. "Our Trade with Colombia: It Might Amount to Something If Our Manufacturers Were Businesslike." *New York Times*, 24 February 1895.

Walsh, Robert. "British Colonial and Navigation System." *American Quarterly Review* 2 (1827): 267–306.

Weinstein, Barbara. *The Amazon Rubber Boom, 1850–1920.* Stanford, CA: Stanford University Press, 1983.

White, Randall. *Fur Trade to Free Trade: Putting the Canada-U.S. Trade Agreement in Historical Perspective* Toronto: Dundurn, 1989.

Wilkins, Mira. "Multinational Enterprise in Insurance: An Historical Overview." *Business History* 51, no. 3 (May 2009): 334–63.

Winnipeg Free Press. "$1.55 Wheat: 200,000,000 Bushels Yearly to Britain." 28 January 1946.

– "Trade Commissioner from Colombia Arriving." 25 October 1945.

World Mining Corporation. "Significant Adjacent Mining History." 2005. http://www.wmcus.com/mnrlprop.html.

Young, Patricia T., and Jack S. Levy. "Domestic Politics and the Escalation of Commercial Rivalry: Explaining the War of Jenkins' Ear, 1739–48." *European Journal of International Relations* 17, no. 2 (2011): 209–32.

Zorbas, Jason Gregory. "Diefenbaker, Latin America and the Caribbean: The Pursuit of Canadian Autonomy." PhD diss., University of Saskatchewan, 2009.

Index